RACHEL CARSON

written and illustrated by

WILLIAM ACCORSI

Holiday House/New York

"I can remember no time when I wasn't interested in the out-of-doors and the whole world of nature."

—RACHEL CARSON

For my hometown, Springdale, Pennsylvania,
the birthplace of Rachel Carson,
and
For Betty, Dick, Mickey, and Chuck Grotefend

Library of Congress Cataloging-in-Publication Data
Accorsi, William.
Rachel Carson / by William Accorsi.—1st ed.
p.   cm.
Summary: A biography of the biologist whose writings helped initiate the
environmental movement.
ISBN 0-8234-0994-5
1. Carson, Rachel, 1907–1964—Juvenile literature.   2. Biologists—United States—
Biography—Juvenile literature.
3. Environmentalists—United States—Biography—Juvenile literature.   4. Science writers—
United States—Biography—Juvenile literature.
[1. Carson, Rachel, 1907–1964.   2. Biologists.   3. Environmentalists.
4. Science writers.]   I. Title.
QH31.C33A63   1993   92-43760   CIP   AC
574′.092—dc20
[B]

One morning, walking in the woods, a young girl found some baby robins. She knew the birds could not live outside their nest and took them home. When they were old enough to fly, she set them free. This is the story of a child who loved nature. Her name was Rachel Carson.

Rachel lived with her parents and her older brother and sister on a small farm in Pennsylvania. Because she was much younger, her brother and sister did not play with her very much.

Rachel liked living on the farm. She enjoyed feeding the chickens and hunting for their eggs.

Rachel's mother took her on long walks to study plants and animals. Sometimes they paused as they heard a robin sing. "Is that one of the birds we raised?" Rachel wondered.

Rachel's mother had been a schoolteacher. She read stories to her daughter every evening and helped her with her schoolwork.

Rachel enjoyed listening to her mother read and soon began to write her own stories.

She sent one of them to *St. Nicholas*, a children's magazine. It won the Silver Badge award.

When Rachel got older, she went to college in nearby Pittsburgh. She missed her family and the daily walks in the woods.

At college, Rachel was recognized as a fine writer. She studied the lives and works of famous authors.

She took classes to learn more about plants and animals, and her love of nature grew.

Rachel often came home to be with her parents. She would read to them from her own writings. Once again, she and her mother would walk in the woods.

After college, Rachel went to another school to earn a master's degree. She became very interested in the sea and its many forms of plant and animal life.

This school was in Baltimore, far away from home. The Carsons were always a close family. Her mother and father moved to Baltimore to live with Rachel.

Finally school was over. Rachel started working for the U.S. government in the Bureau of Fisheries. She wrote pamphlets and radio scripts.

In the evenings Rachel wrote late into the night. She sold her
stories to magazines to earn extra money.

When Rachel was thirty years old, she decided to write a book. She called it *Under the Sea-Wind*. It was about the ocean and the creatures that lived there.

When the book was published, few people were interested in reading it. The Second World War had begun, and the war was on everyone's mind. Rachel was very discouraged.

After the war, Rachel wrote another book about the ocean called *The Sea Around Us*. To her surprise, the book became a huge success.

Rachel's writing was so poetic and intelligent, people all over the world sent letters to her.

Many of these letters mentioned that plants and animals were becoming sick and dying before their time.

Music Street,
West Tisbury,
Mass.

Dear Rachel, on my morning
walk, I was saddened to discover
several dead birds. Last week,
our neighbors mentioned they
had found dead birds on
their property. In recent weeks,
other people in our area have
observed the same thing. I
wonder what is going on?
We enjoyed your visit last
winter and look forward to
your being with us in the
fall.

Sincerely,
Mary and John Brewster
AND BECKY
♡ ♡

Rachel knew that farmers used poisons to kill weeds and insects. These poisons were not considered dangerous. Rachel thought there was a connection between the poisons and the plants and the animals that were dying.

She decided to do some research. She discovered all that she loved in nature was threatened by these poisons. She decided she must write a book and share what she had learned with the world.

Her mother and father had since passed away, and now Rachel was ill with cancer. Somehow she would find the energy to write the book.

She called it *Silent Spring*. Rachel believed if we continued to use poisons, then one day there would be no birds to sing or flowers to bloom.

She knew the book would make people angry. The people who made the poisons would be angry. The people who used the poisons would be angry, and the politicians would be angry.

And they were! "What does this woman know?" they said. It seemed the whole country was talking about the book. Rachel went on television. She explained about the poisons, how they worked, and the great harm they could do.

People listened to Rachel. They remembered that she was the woman who wrote the beautiful books about the ocean. Here she was again, speaking quietly and intelligently.

"We think she is right," they said.

The president of the United States, John F. Kennedy, asked important people what they thought about Rachel's book. They studied everything very carefully, then decided, "We think she is right, too. We must find other ways to control insects and grow healthy foods."

After reading Rachel's book *Silent Spring*, people began to think about the health of the environment. Some laws were passed to help protect the earth.

Although *Silent Spring* was published years ago, it is still timely. People are talking about new ways to care for the environment. Men, women, and children of all ages and cultures are working together to make our world healthier.

Author's Note

Rachel Carson never enjoyed robust health. Her activities as a biologist required her to be outdoors in cold and damp weather. Because of her delicate health, these field trips frequently were painful and exhausting.

During her productive years as a scientist and writer, Rachel at times financially and emotionally supported her mother, father, brother, two nieces (Marjie and Ginny), and finally, her great-nephew, Roger. Considering all these responsibilities, it was remarkable that Rachel found time for her work.

With the success of *The Sea Around Us*, Rachel was able to build a house at Southport Island, near Boothbay Harbor, Maine. Here she had a window view of both the sea and the woods she loved so deeply. After her death, the Rachel Carson Wildlife Refuge was established on 4,700 acres of marshland from Kittery to Cape Elizabeth, Maine.

Important Dates

May 27, 1907   Born in Springdale, Pennsylvania.

1917   At age ten, one of her stories was published in *St. Nicholas* magazine and won the Silver Badge award.

1925   Entered Pennsylvania College for Women in Pittsburgh.

1932   Earned master's degree in zoology from Johns Hopkins University.

1936   Started working full-time for the U.S. Bureau of Fisheries in Washington.

1941   *Under the Sea-Wind* was published.

1951   *The Sea Around Us* was published.

1952   Received National Book Award and the John Burroughs Medal for *The Sea Around Us*.

1955   *The Edge of the Sea* was published. Rachel won the Achievement Award of the American Association of University Women for *The Edge of the Sea*, designated "the outstanding book of the year" by the National Council of Women of the United States.

1962   *Silent Spring* was published.

1963   Received "Conservationist of the Year" award of the National Wildlife Federation, the Schweitzer Medal of the Animal Welfare Institute, and an award from the Isaak Walton League of America.

April 4, 1964   Died in Silver Spring, Maryland, at age fifty-six.

more
taste of home
fast FIXES
WITH mixes

taste of home
BOOKS

REIMAN MEDIA GROUP, INC. • GREENDALE, WISCONSIN

taste of home   Reader's Digest

A TASTE OF HOME/READER'S DIGEST BOOK

© 2009 Reiman Media Group, Inc.
5400 S. 60th St., Greendale WI 53129
All rights reserved.

Taste of Home and Reader's Digest are registered
trademarks of The Reader's Digest Association, Inc.

Editor in Chief: Catherine Cassidy
Vice President, Executive Editor/Books:
Heidi Reuter Lloyd
Creative Director: Ardyth Cope
Chief Marketing Officer: Lisa Karpinski
Food Director: Diane Werner RD
Senior Editor/Books: Mark Hagen
Editor: Janet Briggs
Art Director: Edwin Robles, Jr.
Content Production Supervisor: Julie Wagner
Design Layout Artist: Catherine Fletcher
Graphic Design Associate: Heather Miller
Proofreader: Linne Bruskewitz
Recipe Asset System: Coleen Martin, Sue A. Jurack
Premedia Supervisor: Scott Berger
Recipe Testing & Editing: Taste of Home Test Kitchen
Food Photography: Taste of Home Photo Studio
Editorial Assistant: Barb Czysz

The Reader's Digest Associaton, Inc.
President and Chief Executive Officer:
Mary G. Berner
President, U.S. Affinities:
Suzanne M. Grimes
SVP, Chief Marketing Officer: Amy J. Radin

"Timeless Recipes from Trusted Home Cooks"
is a registered trademark of Reiman Media Group, Inc.

For other Taste of Home books and products,
visit **shoptasteofhome.com.**

For more Reader's Digest products and information,
visit **rd.com** (in the United States)
or see **rd.ca** (in Canada).

International Standard Book Number (10): 0-89821-749-0
International Standard Book Number (13): 978-0-89821-749-0
Library of Congress Control Number: 2009925405

Cover Photography
Photographers: Robert Hagen, James Wieland
Food Stylists: Jim Rude, Jennifer Janz
Set Stylists: Grace Natoli Sheldon, Dee Dee Jacq

Pictured on the front cover (clockwise from top center): Apple
Cider Beef Stew (p. 49), Fresh Raspberry Pie (p. 234), Veggie
Spiral Salad (p. 143) and Jamaican Jerk Turkey Wraps (p. 102).

Pictured on the back cover (clockwise from top left):
Sausage Pizza (p. 91), Maple-Mocha Brownie Torte (p. 241),
Banana Cream Cheesecake (p. 244) and Mexican Chicken Soup
(p. 169).

Printed in U.S.A.
5 7 9 10 8 6 4

table of contents

Take a Shortcut
to Flavorful Foods

The **379 recipes** in **More Fast Fixes with Mixes** from *Taste of Home* provide a solution to bring your family back to the dinner table for a home-cooked meal. After all, with everyone's busy schedules some things end up being sacrificed and too often it's the family meal. With the help of packaged mixes, however, you can spend just **30 minutes or less** preparing a dish so you're out of the kitchen in a flash.

From entrees that include Chuck Wagon Burgers (p. 62) and tasty breakfast fare like Blueberry Oatmeal Pancakes (p. 44) to desserts such as Banana Cream Cheesecake (p. 244), you'll find shortcut recipes that appeal to your and your family's taste buds.

Prep and cook times are on every recipe to help you plan your menus. Some dishes are quickly cooked on the stovetop, making them ideal for a no-fuss weeknight meal. Others bake to perfection in the oven, which makes them great for weekend meals. You'll even find items that simmer all day in the slow cooker...a terrific choice when you have errands to run.

Best of all, these recipes were shared by family cooks...just like you! Not only do their families give the easy specialties thumbs-up approval, but each one was prepared and evaluated by the editors and cooking professionals at *Taste of Home,* the world's #1 cooking magazine.

When time is short but you long for home-cooked goodness, turn to **More Fast Fixes with Mixes.** Your family will love the comforting flavor, and you'll appreciate all the time you saved.

snacks

RANCH-SAUSAGE WONTON CUPS

Prep: 20 min. **Bake:** 5 min./batch

To dress up these tasty appetizers, use small cookie cutters to cut shapes out of additional wonton wrappers. Bake until lightly browned and serve with the wonton cups.

Betty Huddleston // Liberty, Indiana

- 32 wonton wrappers
- 1/2 pound bulk Italian sausage
- 1/2 pound ground beef
- 3 cups (12 ounces) shredded Colby-Monterey Jack cheese
- 1 cup mayonnaise
- 1/2 cup sour cream
- 1/2 cup milk
- 2 to 3 teaspoons ranch salad dressing mix
- 1 can (2-1/4 ounces) sliced ripe olives, drained

1 Press wonton wrappers into muffin cups. Bake at 350° for 5 minutes or until lightly browned.

2 Meanwhile, in a large skillet, cook sausage and beef over medium heat until no longer pink; drain. In a large bowl, combine the cheese, mayonnaise, sour cream, milk, salad dressing mix and meat mixture.

3 Spoon 2 tablespoonfuls into each wonton cup; top with olives. Bake for 5-7 minutes or until heated through. Serve warm. Refrigerate leftovers. **YIELD:** 32 appetizers.

These bite-size meatballs are a favorite of mine. You can substitute your favorite cheese for the cheddar or serve the appetizers with Dijon mustard or sweet-and-sour sauce instead of barbecue sauce.

Anna Damon // Bozeman, Montana

SAUSAGE CHEESE BALLS
Prep/Total Time: 30 min.

  1/2 cup shredded cheddar cheese
    3 tablespoons biscuit/baking mix
    1 tablespoon finely chopped onion
    1 tablespoon finely chopped celery
  1/8 teaspoon garlic powder
  1/8 teaspoon pepper
  1/4 pound bulk pork sausage
Sweet-and-sour and barbecue sauce, optional

1 In a small bowl, combine the cheese, biscuit mix, onion, celery, garlic powder and pepper. Crumble sausage over mixture and mix well. Shape into 1-in. balls.

2 Place in a shallow baking pan coated with cooking spray. Bake, uncovered, at 375° for 12-15 minutes or until no longer pink. Drain on paper towels. Serve with sauces if desired. **YIELD:** 1 dozen.

BLACK-EYED PEA SALSA
Prep/Total Time: 15 min.

Whenever there's a family gathering, my sister-in-law brings this zesty bean dip, and it's a big hit. Since it keeps well in the refrigerator, it's great to have on hand for unexpected guests.

Pamela Smith // Flushing, New York

    1 can (15-1/2 ounces) black-eyed peas, rinsed and drained
    1 can (15 ounces) black beans, rinsed and drained
    1 can (11 ounces) shoepeg corn, drained
1-1/3 cups mild salsa
    1 cup medium salsa
  3/4 cup chopped green pepper
  1/2 cup chopped green onions
    1 can (4-1/4 ounces) chopped ripe olives, drained
    1 jalapeno pepper, seeded and chopped
    1 envelope Italian salad dressing mix
    1 teaspoon ground cumin
    1 teaspoon garlic powder
Tortilla chips

1 In a large bowl, combine the first 12 ingredients. Serve with tortilla chips. **YIELD:** 6 cups.

EDITOR'S NOTE: When cutting hot peppers, disposable gloves are recommended. Avoid touching your face.

A crowd usually gathers when I set out my barbecue-flavored taco dip. It's always gone before I know it!

Iola Egle // Bella Vista, Arkansas

TACO APPETIZER PLATTER
Prep/Total Time: 15 min.

1-1/2 pounds ground beef
1/2 cup water
1 envelope taco seasoning
2 packages (8 ounces *each*) cream cheese, softened
1/4 cup milk
1 can (4 ounces) chopped green chilies, drained
2 medium tomatoes, seeded and chopped
1 cup chopped green onions
1-1/2 cups chopped lettuce
1/2 to 3/4 cup honey barbecue sauce
1 to 1-1/2 cups shredded cheddar cheese
Corn chips

1 In a large skillet, cook beef over medium heat until no longer pink; drain. Add water and taco seasoning; simmer for 5 minutes.

2 In a large bowl, combine cream cheese and milk; spread on a 14-in. serving platter or pizza pan. Top with meat mixture. Sprinkle with chilies, tomatoes, onions and lettuce. Drizzle with barbecue sauce. Sprinkle with cheddar cheese. Serve with corn chips. **YIELD:** 8-10 servings.

CHOCOLATE BANANA SMOOTHIES
Prep/Total Time: 5 min.

Instant pudding makes a wonderful creamy chocolate drink when blended with frozen bananas. It's fun, tasty and easy.
Katherine Lipka // Galesburg, Michigan

2 cups cold 2% milk
1 package (1.4 ounces) sugar-free instant chocolate pudding mix
2 tablespoons vanilla extract
2 large ripe frozen bananas, sliced
2 cups coarsely crushed ice cubes

1 In a blender, combine the milk, pudding mix and vanilla; cover and process until blended. Add the bananas and ice; cover and process until smooth. Pour into chilled glasses; serve immediately. **YIELD:** 4 servings.

This rich stylish appetizer adds an elegant touch to any get-together. It takes just minutes to assemble before baking.

Marion Lowery // Medford, Oregon

BRIE IN PUFF PASTRY
Prep/Total Time: 30 min.

    1 frozen puff pastry sheet, thawed
1/4 cup apricot jam
    1 round (13.2 ounces) **Brie** *or* **Camembert cheese**
    1 egg
    1 tablespoon water
Apple slices

1 Roll puff pastry into a 14-in. square. Spread jam into a 4-1/2-in. circle in center of pastry; place cheese over jam. Fold pastry around cheese; trim excess dough. Pinch edges to seal. Place seam side down on ungreased baking sheet. Beat egg and water; brush over pastry.

2 Cut the trimmed pastry pieces into decorative shapes and place on top; brush with egg mixture if desired. Bake at 400° for 20-25 minutes or until puffed and golden brown. Serve warm with apple slices. **YIELD:** 8-10 servings.

SPINACH CHEESE SWIRLS
Prep: 10 min. **Bake:** 25 min.

These super-easy sandwiches are brimming with spinach and onion flavor. Using refrigerated pizza dough shaves minutes off prep time and creates a golden brown crust. You can enjoy them warm or cold.

Mary Nichols // Dover, New Hampshire

    1 tube (13.8 ounces) refrigerated pizza crust
    1 package (10 ounces) frozen chopped spinach, thawed and drained
    2 cups (8 ounces) shredded part-skim mozzarella cheese
    1 cup finely chopped onion
    1 garlic clove, minced

1 On a lightly floured surface, roll pizza dough into a 14-in. x 10-in. rectangle. In a large bowl, combine the spinach, cheese, onion and garlic; spoon over dough to within 1 in. of edges. Roll up jelly-roll style, starting with a long side; tucks ends under and pinch seam to seal.

2 Place seam side down on a baking sheet coated with cooking spray. Bake at 400° for 25-27 minutes or until golden brown. Cut into slices. **YIELD:** 4 servings.

My mother gave me this recipe more than 10 years ago. Since then, I've made these lip-smacking wings for all different occasions.

Tracy Peters // Corinth, Mississippi

SPICY RANCH CHICKEN WINGS

Prep: 20 min. + marinating **Bake:** 40 min.

- 4 pounds whole chicken wings
- 3/4 cup hot pepper sauce
- 1/4 cup butter, melted
- 3 tablespoons cider vinegar
- 1 envelope ranch salad dressing mix
- 1/2 teaspoon paprika

1 Cut the chicken wings into three sections; discard wing tip sections. In a gallon-size resealable plastic bag, combine the hot pepper sauce, butter and vinegar. Add chicken wings; seal bag and toss to coat evenly. Refrigerate for 4-8 hours.

2 Place chicken on racks in two greased 15-in. x 10-in. x 1-in. baking pans. Sprinkle with dressing mix and paprika. Bake, uncovered, at 350° for 40-50 minutes or until juices run clear. **YIELD:** about 4 dozen.

EDITOR'S NOTE: Uncooked chicken wing sections (wingettes) may be substituted for whole chicken wings.

RANCH POPCORN

Prep/Total Time: 20 min.

What's a night at the movies without popcorn to munch? Try a big tub of this buttery showstopping blend. It's easy, Parmesan cheesy and finger-lickin' good!

Taste of Home Test Kitchen

- 3 quarts popped popcorn
- 1/3 cup butter, melted
- 1/4 cup grated Parmesan cheese
- 2 tablespoons ranch salad dressing mix
- 1 teaspoon dried parsley flakes
- 1/4 teaspoon onion powder

1 Place the popcorn in an ungreased 13-in. x 9-in. baking pan. Combine the remaining ingredients; pour over popcorn and toss to coat.

2 Bake, uncovered, at 350° for 10 minutes or until lightly browned. Serve warm. **YIELD:** 8 servings.

Colorful and refreshing, this sweet-tart slush is very popular with my family. I freeze the mix in 2- and 4-cup containers so it can be served in small portions for individuals or the whole family. I also freeze crushed strawberries to make preparation simpler.

Connie Friesen // Atlona, Manitoba

SENSATIONAL SLUSH

Prep: 25 min. + freezing

- 1/2 cup sugar
- 1 package (3 ounces) strawberry gelatin
- 2 cups boiling water
- 1 cup unsweetened pineapple juice
- 2 cups sliced fresh strawberries
- 1 can (12 ounces) frozen lemonade concentrate, thawed
- 1 can (12 ounces) frozen limeade concentrate, thawed
- 2 cups cold water
- 2 liters lemon-lime soda, chilled

1 In a large bowl, dissolve sugar and gelatin in boiling water. In a blender, combine the pineapple juice and strawberries; cover and process until blended. Add to gelatin mixture. Stir in concentrates and cold water. Cover and freeze for 8 hours or overnight.

2 Remove from the freezer 45 minutes before serving. For each serving, combine 1/2 cup slush mixture with 1/2 cup lemon-lime soda; stir well. **YIELD:** 20 servings.

CHEESY MUSHROOM APPETIZERS

Prep: 15 min. **Bake:** 20 min.

My husband loves mushrooms. Sometimes I think he makes up work functions so I make a batch of these savory appetizers...and he can snack on them at his desk!

Kathi Bloomer // Noblesville, Indiana

- 2 tubes (8 ounces *each*) refrigerated crescent rolls
- 2 packages (8 ounces *each*) cream cheese, softened
- 3 cans (4 ounces *each*) mushroom stems and pieces, drained and chopped
- 1-1/4 teaspoons garlic powder
- 1/2 teaspoon Cajun seasoning
- 1 egg
- 1 tablespoon water
- 2 tablespoons grated Parmesan cheese

1 Unroll crescent dough into two long rectangles; seal seams and perforations. In a large bowl, combine the cream cheese, mushrooms, garlic powder and Cajun seasoning. Spread over dough to within 1 in. of edges.

2 Roll up each rectangle jelly-roll style, starting with a long side; seal edges. Place seam side down on a greased baking sheet.

3 Beat egg and water; brush over dough. Sprinkle with cheese. Bake at 375° for 20-25 minutes or until golden brown. Cut into slices. **YIELD:** 16 appetizers.

FESTIVE HAM 'N' CHEESE SPREAD

Prep/Total Time: 15 min.

> 2 packages (8 ounces *each*) cream cheese, softened
> 1/2 cup sour cream
> 2 tablespoons onion soup mix
> 1 cup chopped fully cooked ham
> 1 cup (4 ounces) shredded Swiss *or* cheddar cheese
> 1/4 cup minced fresh parsley

Assorted crackers

1 In a small bowl, beat the cream cheese, sour cream and soup mix until blended. Stir in ham and cheese. Form into a ball and roll in parsley. Or, spoon into a plastic wrap-lined mold, and after refrigerating, unmold and sprinkle with parsley. Refrigerate until serving. Serve with crackers. **YIELD:** about 4 cups.

STUFFED MUSHROOM CAPS

Prep/Total Time: 30 min.

This is a flavorful way to use mushrooms. Not only do they make a tasty appetizer, they also look great along a grilled steak or chicken breast.

Cherie Sechrist // Red Lion, Pennsylvania

> 24 large fresh mushrooms
> 6 tablespoons butter
> 3/4 cup dry bread crumbs
> 1 envelope onion soup mix
> 1/2 cup sliced almonds
> 1/4 cup shredded Parmesan cheese

1 Remove stems from mushrooms and finely chop; set caps aside. In a skillet, saute chopped mushrooms in butter until tender, about 6-8 minutes. Remove from the heat; stir in the bread crumbs, soup mix and almonds. Stuff firmly into mushroom caps.

2 Place in a greased 15-in. x 10-in. x 1-in. baking pan; sprinkle with cheese. Bake, uncovered, at 425° for 12-15 minutes or until tender. **YIELD:** 2 dozen.

TACO MEATBALL RING

Prep: 30 min. **Bake:** 15 min.

While it looks complicated, this attractive meatball-filled ring is really very easy to assemble. My family loves tacos, and we find that the crescent roll dough is a nice change from the usual tortilla shells or chips. There are never any leftovers when I serve this at a meal or as a party appetizer!

Brenda Johnson // Davison, Michigan

  2 cups (8 ounces) shredded cheddar cheese, *divided*
  2 tablespoons water
  2 to 4 tablespoons taco seasoning
1/2 pound ground beef
  2 tubes (8 ounces *each*) refrigerated crescent rolls
1/2 medium head iceberg lettuce, shredded
  1 medium tomato, chopped
  4 green onions, sliced
1/2 cup sliced ripe olives
  2 jalapeno peppers, sliced
Sour cream and salsa, optional

1 In a large bowl, combine 1 cup cheese, water and taco seasoning. Crumble beef over mixture and mix well. Shape into 16 balls.

2 Place meatballs on a greased rack in a shallow baking pan. Bake, uncovered, at 400° for 12 minutes or until meat is no longer pink. Drain meatballs on paper towels. Reduce heat to 375°.

3 Arrange crescent rolls on a greased 15-in. pizza pan, forming a ring with pointed ends facing the outer edge of the pan and wide ends overlapping.

4 Place a meatball on each roll; fold point over meatball and tuck under the wide end of roll (meatball will be visible). Repeat. Bake for 15-20 minutes or until the rolls are golden brown.

5 Transfer to a serving platter. Fill the center of the ring with lettuce, tomato, onions, olives, jalapenos, remaining cheese, and sour cream and salsa if desired. **YIELD:** 16 servings.

EDITOR'S NOTE: When cutting hot peppers, disposable gloves are recommended. Avoid touching your face.

CRISP CARAWAY TWISTS

Prep/Total Time: 30 min.

- 1 egg
- 1 tablespoon water
- 1 teaspoon country-style Dijon mustard
- 3/4 cup shredded Swiss cheese
- 1/4 cup finely chopped onion
- 2 teaspoons minced fresh parsley
- 1-1/2 teaspoons caraway seeds
- 1/4 teaspoon garlic salt
- 1 sheet frozen puff pastry, thawed

1 In a small bowl, beat egg, water and mustard; set aside. In another bowl, combine the cheese, onion, parsley, caraway seeds and garlic salt.

2 Unfold pastry sheet; brush with egg mixture. Sprinkle cheese mixture lengthwise over half of the pastry. Fold pastry over filling; press edges to seal. Brush top with remaining egg mixture. Cut widthwise into 1/2-in. strips; twist each strip several times.

3 Place 1 in. apart on greased baking sheets, pressing ends down. Bake at 350° for 15-20 minutes or until golden brown. Serve warm. **YIELD**: about 1-1/2 dozen.

TROPICAL SMOOTHIES

Prep/Total Time: 10 min.

We like to experiment with different kinds of smoothies, and this refreshing drink is our best creation so far. The thick, creamy blend has fabulous fruit flavors. Serve it as a day-starter or afternoon pick-me-up.

Wendy Thomas // Pickens, South Carolina

- 2 cartons (6 ounces *each*) pina colada *or* pineapple yogurt
- 1 cup milk
- 1 can (11 ounces) mandarin oranges, drained
- 1/2 small ripe banana
- 1/2 cup frozen peach slices
- 2 tablespoons plus 1-1/2 teaspoons instant vanilla pudding mix
- 17 to 20 ice cubes

1 In a blender, combine the yogurt, milk, fruit and pudding mix; cover and process until smooth. While processing, add ice cubes, a few at a time, until mixture achieves desired thickness. Pour into chilled glasses; serve immediately. **YIELD**: 5 servings.

CHICKEN TURNOVERS

Prep/Total Time: 30 min.

My yummy recipe for hot and filling appetizers is a great way to use up leftover chicken. Sometimes, I serve it with fruit salad for a delicious, light meal for up to four people.

Sandra Lee Herr // Stevens, Pennsylvania

- 1 cup diced cooked chicken breast
- 1 cup (4 ounces) shredded reduced-fat cheddar cheese
- 1/4 cup chopped celery
- 1 tablespoon finely chopped onion
- 1/4 teaspoon salt
- 1/4 teaspoon pepper
- 1 tube (8 ounces) refrigerated reduced-fat crescent rolls

1 In a small bowl, combine the chicken, cheese, celery, onion, salt and pepper. Separate crescent dough into eight triangles; top each with chicken mixture. Fold dough over and seal edges.

2 Place on an ungreased baking sheet. Bake at 375° for 13-17 minutes or until golden brown. Serve warm. **YIELD:** 8 servings.

TIP

Turn these Chicken Turnovers into your go-to recipe when you have any type of leftover cooked meat. The combination of cheese, celery and onion would be great with diced roast beef, ham, pork or even a cup of cooked and crumbled sausage.

SWEET 'N' SOUR APPETIZER MEATBALLS

Prep: 30 min. **Cook:** 20 min.

Since a friend shared this recipe with me several years ago, I've fixed it many times. The tangy meatballs also make a great main dish when you serve them with potatoes.

Lucretia Burt // Tallassee, Alabama

  1 egg
1/2 cup quick-cooking oats
  1 envelope onion soup mix
  2 pounds ground beef
  2 cans (5-1/2 ounces *each*) apricot nectar
3/4 cup packed brown sugar
3/4 cup ketchup
1/3 cup cider vinegar
  2 tablespoons prepared mustard
  1 tablespoon prepared horseradish
Minced fresh parsley

1 In a large bowl, combine the egg, oats and soup mix. Crumble beef over mixture and mix well. Shape into 1-in. balls.

2 Place 1 in. apart on a greased rack in a shallow baking pan. Bake at 400° for 18-20 minutes or until no longer pink. Drain on paper towels.

3 In a large skillet, combine the apricot nectar, brown sugar, ketchup, vinegar, mustard and horseradish. Bring to a boil. Reduce heat; simmer, uncovered, for 10 minutes. Add meatballs; simmer 15 minutes longer or until heated through. Sprinkle with parsley. **YIELD:** 4 dozen.

I was born and raised in Australia, but moved to the U.S. when I married my husband. When I long for a taste of home, I bake up a batch of these sausage rolls and share them with neighbors or co-workers.
Melissa Landon // Port Charlotte, Florida

AUSSIE SAUSAGE ROLLS
Prep: 15 min. **Bake:** 20 min.

1-1/4 pounds bulk pork sausage
   1 medium onion, finely chopped
   2 teaspoons snipped chives
   2 teaspoons minced fresh basil *or* 1/2 teaspoon dried basil
   2 garlic cloves, minced
   1 teaspoon paprika, *divided*
1/2 teaspoon salt
1/4 teaspoon pepper
   1 package (17.3 ounces) frozen puff pastry, thawed

1 In a large bowl, combine the sausage, onion, chives, basil, garlic, 3/4 teaspoon paprika, salt and pepper. Unfold pastry onto a lightly floured surface. Roll each pastry sheet into an 11-in. x 10-1/2-in. rectangle. Cut widthwise into 3-1/2-in. strips.

2 Spread 1/2 cup of sausage mixture down the center of each strip. Fold pastry over and press edges together to seal. Cut each roll into six pieces. Place seam side down on a rack in a shallow baking pan. Sprinkle with remaining paprika.

3 Bake at 350° for 20-25 minutes or until golden brown. **YIELD:** 3 dozen.

CHERRY CRANBERRY PUNCH
Prep: 10 min. + chilling

My husband is a pastor, and our church has many functions, which allows me to try out a selection of recipes. This lovely red punch is one of my favorites to serve.
Christine Fletcher // Bronx, New York

   1 package (3 ounces) cherry gelatin
   1 cup boiling water
   4 cups cranberry juice
   3 cups cold water
3/4 cup lemonade concentrate
3-1/2 cups club soda, chilled
Lemon sherbet, optional

1 In a large bowl, dissolve gelatin in boiling water. Stir in the cranberry juice, cold water and lemonade concentrate. Refrigerate until chilled. Just before serving, stir in the soda. Top with scoops of sherbet if desired. **YIELD:** 16 servings (3 quarts).

Give this recipe a try if you're looking for a deliciously different dip to serve with crackers, potato chips or vegetables. Ranch salad dressing adds a little zest.
Kathy Westendorf // Westgate, Iowa

BACON CHEDDAR DIP
Prep: 5 min. + chilling

   2 cups (16 ounces) sour cream
   1 cup (4 ounces) finely shredded cheddar cheese
   1 envelope ranch salad dressing mix
   2 to 4 bacon strips, cooked and crumbled
Crackers *and/or* assorted fresh vegetables

1 In a large bowl, combine the sour cream, cheddar cheese, salad dressing mix and bacon. Cover and refrigerate for at least 1 hour. Serve with crackers and/or vegetables. **YIELD:** 2-1/2 cups.

MARINATED MUSHROOMS
Prep: 15 min. + marinating

This is a nice way to serve mushrooms as an appetizer...and it also makes a great side dish for any type of meat. Sometimes I add these tangy mushrooms to salads for extra flavor, too.
Brenda Swan // Alexandria, Pennsylvania

   2 pounds fresh mushrooms
   1 envelope (.7 ounce) Italian salad dressing mix
   1 cup water
 1/2 cup olive oil
 1/3 cup cider vinegar
   2 tablespoons lemon juice
   1 tablespoon sugar
   1 tablespoon minced fresh parsley
   1 tablespoon soy sauce
   2 teaspoons crushed red pepper flakes
   3 garlic cloves, minced
 1/2 teaspoon salt
 1/8 teaspoon pepper

1 Remove mushroom stems (discard or save for another use). Place caps in a large saucepan and cover with water. Bring to a boil. Reduce heat; cook for 3 minutes, stirring occasionally. Drain and cool.

2 In a bowl, whisk together the salad dressing mix, water, oil, vinegar, lemon juice, sugar and seasonings.

3 Place mushrooms in a large bowl; add dressing and stir to coat. Cover and refrigerate for 8 hours or overnight. **YIELD:** 4 cups.

This colorful pizza is topped with a rainbow of crunchy vegetables. Guests usually don't even guess this delectable pizza is low-fat.
Brooke Wiley // Halifax, Virginia

FRESH VEGGIE PIZZA

Prep: 25 min. + chilling

- 1 tube (8 ounces) reduced-fat crescent rolls
- 1 package (8 ounces) reduced-fat cream cheese
- 1 envelope ranch salad dressing mix
- 2 tablespoons fat-free milk
- 1/2 cup *each* chopped fresh broccoli, cauliflower, carrots, green pepper, sweet red pepper and mushrooms

1 Unroll crescent roll dough into one long rectangle. Press onto the bottom of a 13-in. x 9-in. baking pan coated with cooking spray; seal seams and perforations.

2 Bake at 375° for 11-13 minutes or until golden brown. Cool completely.

3 In a large bowl, beat the cream cheese, salad dressing mix and milk until smooth. Spread over crust. Sprinkle with vegetables. Cover and refrigerate for at least 1 hour before serving. Cut into 16 pieces. **YIELD:** 8 servings.

COCONUT PINEAPPLE POPS

Prep: 10 min. + freezing

There's a taste of the tropics in these shivery sensations that pair pineapple with coconut pudding. With their sunny color and creamy texture, these pops just might be your hottest fresh-from-the-freezer treat!
Taste of Home Test Kitchen

- 1-1/2 cups cold 2% milk
- 1 can (8 ounces) unsweetened crushed pineapple
- 1 can (6 ounces) unsweetened pineapple juice
- 1 teaspoon coconut extract
- 1 package (3.4 ounces) instant vanilla pudding mix
- 14 plastic cups *or* Popsicle molds (3 ounces *each*)
- 14 Popsicle sticks

1 In a blender, combine the milk, pineapple, pineapple juice and extract; cover and process until smooth. Pour into a bowl; whisk in pudding mix for 2 minutes. Pour 1/4 cup into each cup or mold; insert Popsicle sticks. Freeze until firm. **YIELD:** 14 servings.

HOT CHEDDAR-MUSHROOM SPREAD
Prep/Total Time: 25 min.

2 cups mayonnaise
2 cups (8 ounces) shredded cheddar cheese
2/3 cup grated Parmesan cheese
4 cans (4-1/2 ounces each) sliced mushrooms, drained
1 envelope ranch salad dressing mix
Minced fresh parsley
Assorted crackers

1 In a large bowl, combine the mayonnaise, cheeses, mushrooms and dressing mix. Spread into a greased 9-in. pie plate.

2 Bake, uncovered, at 350° for 20-25 minutes or until cheese is melted. Sprinkle with parsley. Serve with crackers. **YIELD:** 3 cups.

EDITOR'S NOTE: Reduced-fat or fat-free mayonnaise is not recommended for this recipe.

SPICED TEA MIX
Prep/Total Time: 5 min.

Perfect for a gift or to keep on hand when friends stop by, this versatile mix can be served hot or cold. The blend of ingredients makes it one of a kind!

Julie Dvornicky // Broadview Heights, Ohio

8 cups sweetened lemonade mix
1 cup orange breakfast drink mix
3/4 cup sugar
1/2 cup unsweetened instant tea
1 teaspoon ground nutmeg
1/2 teaspoon ground cinnamon
1/4 teaspoon ground cloves

1 In a large bowl, combine all ingredients; mix well. Store in an airtight container in a cool dry place for up to 6 months. **YIELD:** about 10 cups total (about 80 servings).

2 **To prepare 1 gallon iced tea:** Dissolve 2 cups of the tea mix in 1 gallon of water; stir well. Serve over ice. **YIELD:** 16 servings.

3 **To prepare 1 cup hot tea:** Dissolve 2 tablespoons of tea mix in 1 cup of boiling water; stir well. **YIELD:** 1 serving.

CHORIZO BEAN DIP

Prep: 25 min. **Bake:** 20 min.

With its zesty Mexican flavors and tempting toppings, this dish is the first to empty on the appetizer table. I serve it with extra-thick tortilla chips for some serious scooping.

Elaine Sweet // Dallas, Texas

1 pound ground sirloin
1/3 pound uncooked chorizo *or* bulk spicy pork sausage
1 medium onion, chopped
1 envelope taco seasoning
2 cans (16 ounces *each*) refried black beans
1 cup (4 ounces) shredded Monterey Jack cheese
1 jar (11 ounces) salsa
2 cans (2-1/4 ounces *each*) sliced ripe olives, drained
2 cups guacamole
6 green onions, thinly sliced
1 cup (8 ounces) sour cream
1/2 cup minced fresh cilantro
3/4 cup jalapeno-stuffed olives, sliced
Tortilla chips

1 In a large skillet, cook the beef, chorizo, onion and taco seasoning over medium heat until meat is no longer pink; drain.

2 Spread the beans into a greased 13-in. x 9-in. baking dish. Layer with the meat mixture, cheese, salsa and ripe olives. Cover and bake at 350° for 20-25 minutes or until heated through.

3 Spread guacamole over the top. Combine the green onions, sour cream and cilantro; spread over guacamole. Sprinkle with stuffed olives. Serve immediately with tortilla chips. Refrigerate leftovers. **YIELD:** 48 servings.

EDITOR'S NOTE: When handling hot peppers, disposable gloves are recommended. Avoid touching your face.

This double feature of dippers and sauce takes only a short time to prepare. The little pretzels are easily shaped using refrigerated breadstick dough. While they bake, mix together the mustard dip.

Taste of Home Test Kitchen

SOFT PRETZELS WITH MUSTARD

Prep/Total Time: 30 min.

 1 tube (11 ounces) refrigerated breadsticks
 1 egg white, lightly beaten
Coarse salt
 1/2 cup Dijon mustard
 1/4 cup maple syrup
 1 tablespoon brown sugar
 1/2 teaspoon dried parsley flakes

1 On an unfloured surface, roll each breadstick into a 20-in. rope; twist into a pretzel shape. Place 2 in. apart on ungreased baking sheets. Brush with egg white and sprinkle with salt.

2 Bake at 375° for 10-13 minutes or until lightly browned. Remove to a wire rack. For mustard dip, combine the remaining ingredients in a small bowl. Serve with pretzels. **YIELD:** 1 dozen.

EDITOR'S NOTE: This recipe was tested with Pillsbury refrigerated breadsticks.

TIP

The classic topping for pretzels is coarse salt, but you can jazz up these pretzels with a number of different toppings. After you brush the pretzels with egg white, sprinkle on one of these toppings: poppy seeds, sesame seeds, sunflower kernels, grated Parmesan or Romano cheese or even cinnamon-sugar.

EFFORTLESS EGGNOG

Prep/Total Time: 5 min.

- 1/2 gallon cold milk, *divided*
- 1 package (3.4 ounces) instant French vanilla pudding mix
- 1/4 cup sugar
- 2 teaspoons vanilla extract
- 1/2 teaspoon ground cinnamon
- 1/2 teaspoon ground nutmeg

1 In a large bowl, whisk 3/4 cup milk and pudding mix until smooth. Whisk in the sugar, vanilla, cinnamon and nutmeg. Stir in the remaining milk. Refrigerate until serving. **YIELD:** 16 servings (2 quarts).

CRACKER SNACK MIX

Prep: 5 min. Bake: 45 min. + cooling

Family and friends will munch this fun mix of crackers, nuts and ranch dressing by the handfuls! Everyone is sure to find something they like. If not, substitute other packaged snack items to vary the flavors.
Sharon Nichols // Brookings, South Dakota

- 12 cups original flavor Bugles
- 6 cups miniature pretzels
- 1 package (11 ounces) miniature butter-flavored crackers
- 1 package (10 ounces) Wheat Thins
- 1 package (9-1/4 ounces) Cheese Nips
- 1 package (7-1/2 ounces) nacho cheese Bugles
- 1 package (6 ounces) miniature Parmesan fish-shaped crackers
- 1 cup mixed nuts *or* peanuts
- 1 bottle (10 *or* 12 ounces) butter-flavored popcorn oil
- 2 envelopes ranch salad dressing mix

1 In a very large bowl, combine the first eight ingredients. In a small bowl, combine oil and salad dressing mix. Pour over cracker mixture; toss to coat evenly.

2 Transfer to four ungreased 15-in. x 10-in. x 1-in. baking pans. Bake at 250° for 45 minutes, stirring every 15 minutes. Cool completely, stirring several times. **YIELD:** about 8 quarts.

CHOCOLATE-CHERRY COFFEE MIX

Prep/Total Time: 20 min.

Cute ice cream cone-shaped packages of this flavored coffee mix are sure to delight friends and family. I wanted something that both coffee and noncoffee drinkers would enjoy, so I added cherry flavoring to a mocha mix. The creamy dessert coffee is a perfect end to a meal.

Jennifer Waters // Lubbock, Texas

- 3 cups sugar
- 2 cups confectioners' sugar
- 1-1/3 cups powdered nondairy creamer
- 1-1/3 cups instant coffee granules
- 1 cup baking cocoa
- 1 envelope (.13 ounce) unsweetened cherry soft drink mix
- 6 cups miniature marshmallows, *divided*
- 6 teaspoons holiday sprinkles, *divided*

ADDITIONAL INGREDIENT (for *each* serving):
- 1 cup hot milk

1 In an airtight container, combine the first six ingredients. Store in a cool dry place for up to 2 months. **YIELD:** 6 cups.

2 To prepare gift: Place 1 cup mix in a 12-in. disposable decorating bag. Fold corners of bag into the center and roll bag down; secure with transparent tape. Place bag in a second disposable decorating bag. Top with 1 cup marshmallows and 1 teaspoon sprinkles. Gather and twist the top of the bag. Attach ribbon and gift tag. Repeat to make five more gift bags. **YIELD:** 6 gift bags (1 cup/8 servings per bag).

3 To prepare coffee: In a mug, dissolve 2 heaping tablespoons mix in hot milk; stir well. Top with marshmallows and sprinkles. **YIELD:** 1 serving.

EDITOR'S NOTE: Disposable decorating bags are available from Wilton Industries. Call 1-800/794-5866 or visit www.wilton.com.

Since receiving this recipe through 4-H, it's been a regular after-school snack. These bite-size pizza treats, made with refrigerated crescent rolls, are especially good served with spaghetti sauce for dipping.
Donna Klettke // Wheatland, Missouri

PIZZA ROLL-UPS
Prep: 20 min. **Bake:** 15 min.

- 1/2 **pound ground beef**
- 1 **can (8 ounces) tomato sauce**
- 1/2 **cup shredded part-skim mozzarella cheese**
- 1/2 **teaspoon dried oregano**
- 2 **tubes (8 ounces *each*) refrigerated crescent rolls**

1 In a large skillet, cook beef over medium heat until no longer pink; drain. Remove from the heat. Add the tomato sauce, mozzarella cheese and oregano.

2 Separate crescent dough into eight rectangles, pinching seams together. Place about 3 tablespoons of meat mixture along one long side of each rectangle. Roll up jelly-roll style, starting with a long side. Cut each roll into three pieces. Place seam side down 2 in. apart on greased baking sheets. Bake at 375° for 15 minutes or until golden brown. **YIELD:** 2 dozen.

HOT BEAN DIP
Prep: 10 min. **Bake:** 25 min.

My hearty dip is extra smooth, thanks to the cream cheese and sour cream I add. It's easy to assemble ahead and then bake before serving. People keep dipping until the dish is empty.
Donna Trout // Las Vegas, Nevada

- 1 **can (16 ounces) refried beans**
- 1 **package (8 ounces) cream cheese, softened**
- 1 **cup (8 ounces) sour cream**
- 3/4 **cup salsa**
- 1 **can (4 ounces) chopped green chilies**
- 3 **tablespoons taco seasoning**
- 6 **green onions, chopped**
Tortilla chips

1 In a large bowl, combine the beans, cream cheese, sour cream, salsa, chilies and taco seaoning. Transfer to a greased shallow 2-qt. baking dish. Sprinkle with onions.

2 Bake, uncovered, at 350° for 25-30 minutes or until heated through. Serve with tortilla chips. **YIELD:** 5 cups.

Mini tart shells are filled with a cream cheese mixture, then topped with seafood sauce and shrimp for a picture-perfect look and delightful taste. This recipe makes a great appetizer, but you can also serve several for a fast, light meal.
Gina Hutchison // Smithville, Missouri

SHRIMP TARTLETS
Prep/Total Time: 15 min.

    1 package (8 ounces) cream cheese, softened
1-1/2 teaspoons Worcestershire sauce
    1 to 2 teaspoons grated onion
    1 teaspoon garlic salt
1/8 teaspoon lemon juice
    2 packages (1.9 ounces *each*) frozen miniature phyllo tart shells

1/2 cup seafood cocktail sauce
30 deveined peeled cooked medium shrimp

1 In a small bowl, combine cream cheese, Worcestershire sauce, onion, garlic salt and lemon juice. Spoon into tart shells. Top with the seafood sauce and shrimp. Refrigerate until serving. **YIELD:** 2-1/2 dozen.

BROCCOLI CHEDDAR SPREAD
Prep: 15 min. Bake: 20 min.

I was able to lighten up the original recipe for this thick, warm spread without losing any of the flavor.
Beth Parker // Graysville, Alabama

    4 cups chopped fresh broccoli
    1 tablespoon water
    2 cups (16 ounces) reduced-fat sour cream
1/2 cup plus 1 tablespoon shredded reduced-fat cheddar cheese, *divided*
    1 envelope vegetable soup mix
Pita chips *or* reduced-fat crackers

1 Place broccoli and water in a 1-1/2-qt. microwave-safe dish. Cover and microwave on high for 4 minutes or until crisp-tender; drain. In a large bowl, combine the sour cream, 1/2 cup cheese and soup mix. Gently stir in the broccoli.

2 Transfer to an ungreased shallow 1-qt. baking dish. Sprinkle with remaining cheese. Bake, uncovered, at 350° for 20-25 minutes or until heated through. Serve with pita chips or crackers. **YIELD:** 3 cups.

EDITOR'S NOTE: This recipe was tested in a 1,100-watt microwave.

Cool off with this yummy ice cream drink that delightfully blends chocolate, coffee and mint flavors.

Edna Hoffman // Hebron, Indiana

MINT MOCHA SHAKES
Prep/Total Time: 5 min.

- 2 cups milk
- 1 teaspoon vanilla extract
- 1/8 teaspoon mint extract
- 1 envelope (.77 ounce) instant cappuccino Irish cream mix
- 2 cups chocolate ice cream, softened

1 In a blender, combine all ingredients; cover and process until blended. Stir if necessary. Pour into chilled glasses; serve immediately. **YIELD:** 4 servings.

TROPICAL FRUIT DIP
Prep: 5 min. + chilling

This fruity dip is easy to prepare and so refreshing for summer get-togethers or brunches. The secret ingredient is the lemon-lime soda. It adds a little extra zing. Crushed pineapple and coconut extract bring a hint of the tropics to the creamy dip. Serve it with strawberries, grapes and bite-size melon pieces.

Linda Venema // Fulton, Illinois

- 3/4 cup cold fat-free milk
- 2 tablespoons diet lemon-lime soda
- 2 drops coconut extract
- 1 can (8 ounces) crushed unsweetened pineapple, undrained
- 1/2 cup reduced-fat sour cream
- 1 package (1 ounce) sugar-free instant vanilla pudding mix

Assorted fruit

1 In a blender, combine the milk, soda, extract, pineapple, sour cream and pudding mix; cover and process for 1 minute or until smooth. Cover and refrigerate for at least 1 hour. Serve with fruit. **YIELD:** 2 cups.

These tasty hors d'oeuvres cut fat as well as cleanup by keeping the deep fryer at bay. The savory bundles are filled with a mixture of turkey sausage, garlic and onion.
Taste of Home Test Kitchen

MINI SAUSAGE BUNDLES
Prep/Total Time: 30 min.

- 1/2 pound turkey Italian sausage links, casings removed
- 1 small onion, finely chopped
- 1/4 cup finely chopped sweet red pepper
- 1 garlic clove, minced
- 1/2 cup shredded cheddar cheese
- 8 sheets phyllo dough (14 inches x 9 inches)
- 12 whole chives, optional

1 Crumble the sausage into a large nonstick skillet; add onion, red pepper and garlic. Cook over medium heat until meat is no longer pink; drain. Stir in cheese; cool slightly.

2 Place one sheet of phyllo dough on a work surface; coat with cooking spray. Cover with a second sheet of phyllo; coat with cooking spray. (Keep remaining phyllo covered with plastic wrap and a damp towel to prevent it from drying out.) Cut widthwise into three 4-in. strips, discarding trimmings. Top each with 2 rounded tablespoons of sausage mixture; fold bottom and side edges over filling and roll up. Repeat with remaining phyllo and filling.

3 Place seam side down on an ungreased baking sheet. Bake at 425° for 5-6 minutes or until lightly browned. Tie a chive around each bundle if desired. Serve warm. **YIELD:** 1 dozen.

RANCH HAM ROLL-UPS
Prep: 15 min. + chilling

These pretty pinwheel appetizers are easy to make and fun to nibble, with a yummy cream cheese filling that's layered with ham.
Charlie Clutts // New Tazewell, Tennessee

- 2 packages (8 ounces *each*) cream cheese, softened
- 1 envelope ranch salad dressing mix
- 3 green onions, chopped
- 11 flour tortillas (8 inches)
- 22 thin slices deli ham

1 In a small bowl, beat cream cheese and salad dressing mix until smooth. Stir in onions. Spread about 3 tablespoons over each tortilla; top each with two ham slices.

2 Roll up tightly and wrap in plastic wrap. Refrigerate until firm. Unwrap and cut into 3/4-in. slices. **YIELD:** about 7-1/2 dozen.

CHICKEN FAJITA PIZZA

Prep: 20 min. **Bake:** 20 min.

Pizza takes a southwest turn in this version. My wife made this recipe on our first date—an evening of cooking at her apartment.

Gary Longo // Spencer, Massachusetts

- 1 tube (13.8 ounces) refrigerated pizza crust
- 1/2 pound boneless skinless chicken breasts, cut into strips
- 2 tablespoons olive oil
- 1/2 cup sliced onion
- 1/2 cup julienned green pepper
- 3 garlic cloves, minced
- 1 teaspoon chili powder
- 1/4 teaspoon salt
- 1/8 teaspoon pepper
- 1 cup salsa
- 2 cups (8 ounces) shredded Mexican cheese blend

1 Unroll crust into a greased 15-in. x 10-in. x 1-in. baking pan; flatten dough and build up edges slightly. Bake at 400° for 8-10 minutes or until lightly browned.

2 Meanwhile, in a large skillet, saute chicken in oil until lightly browned. Add the onion, green pepper, garlic, chili powder, salt and pepper. Cook and stir until vegetables are tender and chicken is no longer pink.

3 Spread salsa over crust. Top with 1 cup cheese, chicken mixture and remaining cheese. Bake at 400° for 10-15 minutes or until cheese is bubbly and golden brown. **YIELD:** 12 slices.

My husband, Cory, farms, so supper can sometimes be quite late. A hearty appetizer like these meaty, mini quiches is a perfect way to start the meal. They taste super made with ground beef, but I sometimes substitute bacon, ham, ground pork or sausage.

Stacy Atkinson // Rugby, North Dakota

GROUND BEEF SNACK QUICHES

Prep: 15 min. **Bake:** 20 min.

- 1/4 **pound ground beef**
- 1/8 **to 1/4 teaspoon garlic powder**
- 1/8 **teaspoon pepper**
- 1 **cup biscuit/baking mix**
- 1/4 **cup cornmeal**
- 1/4 **cup cold butter**
- 2 **to 3 tablespoons boiling water**
- 1 **egg**
- 1/2 **cup half-and-half cream**
- 1 **tablespoon chopped green onion**
- 1 **tablespoon chopped sweet red pepper**
- 1/8 **to 1/4 teaspoon salt**
- 1/8 **to 1/4 teaspoon cayenne pepper**
- 1/2 **cup finely shredded cheddar cheese**

1 In a large saucepan over medium heat, cook the beef, garlic powder and pepper until meat is no longer pink; drain and set aside.

2 Meanwhile, in a small bowl, combine biscuit mix and cornmeal; cut in butter. Add enough water to form a soft dough.

3 Press onto the bottom and up the sides of greased miniature muffin cups. Place teaspoonfuls of beef mixture into each shell.

4 In a small bowl, combine the egg, cream, onion, red pepper, salt and cayenne; pour over beef mixture. Sprinkle with cheese.

5 Bake at 375° for 20 minutes or until a knife inserted near the center comes out clean. **YIELD:** 1-1/2 dozen.

TIP

Would you like to save some of these mini quiches for later? Arrange in a single layer on a waxed paper-lined baking sheet and cover. Place in the freezer until frozen, then transfer to a resealable freezer bag. They may be frozen up to 1 month. Reheat in the microwave.

breakfast

SUNRISE MINI PIZZAS

Prep/Total Time: 30 min.

    8 to 10 eggs
    3 tablespoons milk
Salt and pepper to taste
    1 tablespoon butter
   10 frozen white dinner rolls, thawed
   10 bacon strips, cooked and crumbled
    2 cups (8 ounces) shredded cheddar cheese

1 In a bowl, beat the eggs. Add milk, salt and pepper. Melt butter in a skillet; add the egg mixture. Cook and stir over medium heat until the eggs are set. Remove from the heat and set aside.

2 Roll each dinner roll into a 5-in. circle. Place on greased baking sheets. Spoon egg mixture evenly over crusts. Sprinkle with bacon and cheese. Bake at 350° for 15 minutes or until the cheese is melted. **YIELD:** 10 pizzas.

CORN 'N' HAM FRITTERS

Prep/Total Time: 30 min.

Nothing beats the down-home taste of golden-brown fritters. This version offers diced ham and kernels of corn, and it uses a biscuit mix for fast assembly.

Nancy Foust // Stoneboro, Pennsylvania

    1 cup biscuit/baking mix
  1/2 teaspoon sugar
    1 egg
  1/2 cup milk
    1 cup frozen corn, thawed
  1/2 cup finely diced fully cooked ham

Oil for deep-fat frying
Maple syrup, optional

1 In a small bowl, combine the biscuit mix and sugar. In another bowl, whisk the egg and milk; stir into dry ingredients just until moistened. Fold in corn and ham.

2 In an electric skillet, heat 1-1/2 in. of oil to 375°. Drop batter by rounded tablespoonfuls, a few at a time, into hot oil. Fry until golden brown, about 1 minute on each side. Drain on paper towels. Serve warm with syrup if desired. **YIELD:** 16 fritters.

LIGHT MONTEREY QUICHE

Prep: 25 min. **Bake:** 45 min. + standing

With its creamy goodness and Southwestern flair, the original version of this savory specialty was a hit with my family. The lighter version below replicates the mouthwatering taste with fewer calories. It's perfect for special brunches or lunches with fresh fruit on the side.

Pam Pressly // Beachwood, Ohio

1/2 cup chopped onion
 1 tablespoon butter
 2 garlic cloves, minced
 8 egg whites, *divided*
 4 eggs
 2 cups (16 ounces) 1% small-curd cottage cheese
 2 cups (8 ounces) shredded reduced-fat Mexican cheese blend *or* Monterey Jack cheese, *divided*
 2 cans (4 ounces *each*) chopped green chilies
1/3 cup all-purpose flour
3/4 teaspoon baking powder
1/4 teaspoon salt
 2 unbaked deep-dish pastry shells (9 inches)

1 In a small nonstick skillet, cook onion in butter over medium-low heat until tender, stirring occasionally. Add garlic; cook 2 minutes longer.

2 In a large bowl, combine 6 egg whites, eggs, cottage cheese, 1-1/2 cups shredded cheese, chilies, flour, baking powder, salt and onion mixture. In a large bowl, beat remaining egg whites until stiff peaks form. Fold into cheese mixture. Pour into pastry shells.

3 Bake at 400° for 10 minutes. Reduce heat to 350°; bake for 30 minutes. Sprinkle with remaining cheese; bake 5 minutes longer or until a knife inserted near the center comes out clean and cheese is melted. Let stand for 10 minutes before cutting. **YIELD:** 2 quiches (6 servings each).

This is a different way to use up leftover mashed potatoes. It was an instant hit with our teenagers.
Brad Eichelberger // York, Pennsylvania

HAM POTATO PUFFS
Prep: 20 min. **Bake:** 20 min.

    1 tube (12 ounces) refrigerated buttermilk biscuits
    1 cup cubed fully cooked ham
    1 cup leftover mashed potatoes
    1 cup (4 ounces) shredded cheddar cheese, *divided*
1/2 teaspoon dried parsley flakes
1/4 teaspoon garlic powder

1 Press each biscuit onto the bottom and up the sides of a greased muffin cup. In a large bowl, combine the ham, potatoes, 1/2 cup cheese, parsley and garlic powder.

2 Spoon 1/4 cup into each prepared cup. Sprinkle with remaining cheese. Bake at 350° for 20-25 minutes or until lightly browned. Serve warm. Refrigerate leftovers. **YIELD:** 10 puffs.

BAKED APPLE PANCAKE
Prep: 20 min. **Bake:** 15 min.

This recipe originated when we changed the focus of our restaurant from breakfast/lunch/dinner to featuring breakfast all day. This popular item became one of 25 pancake and waffle varieties on our menu.
Debbie and Don Smith // Gatlinburg, Tennessee

    1 cup pancake mix
2/3 cup milk
    2 tablespoons canola oil
    1 egg, lightly beaten
1/4 cup butter, cubed
1/3 cup packed brown sugar
    1 medium Golden Delicious apple, peeled and sliced
Maple syrup

1 In a large bowl, combine the pancake mix, milk, oil and egg. In an 8-in. ovenproof skillet, melt butter. Stir in brown sugar and apple slices; saute until sugar is dissolved. Pour batter over apple mixture.

2 Cook, uncovered, over medium heat until bubbles form on top of pancake. Bake, uncovered, at 350° for 12-17 minutes or until golden brown. Invert onto a serving platter. Serve with syrup. **YIELD:** 1-2 servings.

Guaranteed to impress, these sensational crepes come together easily on the stovetop—without any hard-to-find ingredients. In fact, no one will ever suspect that the delicate crepes start with a biscuit/baking mix.

Taste of Home Test Kitchen

STRAWBERRY CREAM CREPES

Prep/Total Time: 30 min.

- 1/2 cup biscuit/baking mix
- 1 egg
- 1/2 cup milk
- 1/4 teaspoon vanilla extract
- 2 packages (3 ounces *each*) cream cheese, softened
- 1/4 cup sour cream
- 2 tablespoons sugar
- 1/4 teaspoon ground cinnamon
- 1 package (10 ounces) frozen sweetened sliced strawberries, thawed and drained
- 1/2 cup strawberry glaze

1 In a large bowl, combine the biscuit mix, egg, milk and vanilla. Cover and refrigerate for 1 hour.

2 Heat a lightly greased 8-in. nonstick skillet over medium heat; pour 2 tablespoons batter into the center of skillet. Lift and tilt pan to coat bottom evenly. Cook until top appears dry; turn and cook 15-20 seconds longer. Remove to a wire rack. Repeat with remaining batter, greasing skillet as needed. When cool, stack crepes with waxed paper or paper towels in between.

3 In a small bowl, beat the cream cheese, sour cream, sugar and cinnamon until blended. Spoon 2 rounded tablespoonfuls down the center of each crepe; roll up.

4 In a microwave-safe bowl, combine the strawberries and glaze. Cover and microwave on high for 1-2 minutes or until heated through. Serve with the crepes. **YIELD:** 4 servings.

COCONUT PECAN ROLLS

Prep: 20 min. **Bake:** 25 min.

Your family will enjoy the old-fashioned appeal of these nutty rolls. Convenient refrigerated breadsticks are dressed up with a coconut coating that's oh-so-good.

Theresa Gingry // Blue Springs, Nebraska

- 1 tablespoon sugar
- 1/2 teaspoon ground cinnamon
- 1 tube (11 ounces) refrigerated breadsticks
- 2/3 cup coconut pecan frosting
- 1/3 cup chopped pecans

1 In a small bowl, combine sugar and cinnamon. Remove breadstick dough from tube (do not unroll); cut into eight slices with a serrated knife. Dip both sides of each slice in cinnamon-sugar.

2 Place in a greased 9-in. round baking pan. Spread with frosting; sprinkle with pecans. Bake at 350° for 25-30 minutes or until rolls are golden brown. Serve warm. **YIELD:** 8 rolls.

EDITOR'S NOTE: This recipe was tested with Pillsbury refrigerated breadsticks.

SAUSAGE BREAKFAST LOAF

Prep: 20 min. **Bake:** 25 min.

- 1 pound smoked kielbasa *or* Polish sausage, julienned
- 1-1/2 cups (6 ounces) shredded part-skim mozzarella cheese
- 2 eggs
- 1-1/2 teaspoons minced fresh parsley
- 1/2 teaspoon onion salt
- 1/2 teaspoon garlic salt
- 1 tube (10 ounces) refrigerated pizza dough

1 In a large skillet, saute the sausage; cool. In a large bowl, combine the sausage, cheese, one egg, parsley, onion salt and garlic salt.

2 Unroll pizza dough; roll into a 12-in. x 8-in. rectangle. Spread sausage mixture down the center of dough. Bring dough over filling; pinch seams to seal.

3 Place seam side down on a greased baking sheet; tuck ends under. Beat remaining egg; brush over top. Bake at 350° for 25-30 minutes or until golden brown. Let stand for 5 minutes before slicing. **YIELD:** 6 servings.

BISCUIT EGG BAKE

Prep: 20 min. **Bake:** 40 min.

Determined to come up with a brunch dish that didn't keep me in the kitchen all morning, I created this casserole made with everyone's favorite ingredients. Preparation is minimal, and then it goes right into the oven, so you can spend more time with the ones you love. Simply serve with a fruit salad for a hearty weekend breakfast.

Jenny Flake // Gilbert, Arizona

- 1 tube (16.3 ounces) large refrigerated buttermilk biscuits
- 12 eggs
- 1 cup milk
- 1 cup chopped fresh tomatoes
- 1/2 cup chopped green onions
- 1 can (4 ounces) chopped green chilies
- 1 teaspoon salt
- 1/2 teaspoon pepper
- 1/2 teaspoon salt-free garlic seasoning blend
- 1 package (2.1 ounces) ready-to-serve fully cooked bacon, diced
- 2 cups (8 ounces) shredded cheddar cheese

1 Separate biscuits. Cut each biscuit into fourths; arrange in a greased 13-in. x 9-in. baking dish. In a large bowl, whisk the eggs, milk, tomatoes, onions, chilies, salt, pepper and seasoning blend. Pour over biscuits. Sprinkle with bacon and cheese.

2 Bake, uncovered, at 350° for 40-45 minutes or until a thermometer reads 160°. **YIELD:** 10-12 servings.

This delicious quiche features chicken, spinach and cheddar cheese, but you can use Swiss cheese if you'd like.

Barbara McCalley
Allison Park, Pennsylvania

CHICKEN SPINACH QUICHE

Prep: 10 min. **Bake:** 40 min. + standing

- 1 cup (4 ounces) shredded cheddar cheese, *divided*
- 1 unbaked pastry shell (9 inches)
- 1 cup diced cooked chicken
- 1 package (10 ounces) frozen chopped spinach, thawed and squeezed dry
- 1/4 cup finely chopped onion
- 2 eggs
- 3/4 cup milk
- 3/4 cup mayonnaise
- 1/4 teaspoon salt
- 1/8 teaspoon pepper

1 Sprinkle 1/4 cup cheese into the pastry shell. In a bowl, combine the chicken, 1/2 cup spinach, onion and remaining cheese (save remaining spinach for another use). Spoon into pastry shell. In a bowl, whisk the eggs, milk, mayonnaise, salt and pepper; pour over the chicken mixture.

2 Bake at 350° for 40-45 minutes or until a knife inserted near the center comes out clean. Let stand for 15 minutes before cutting. **YIELD:** 6-8 servings.

EDITOR'S NOTE: Reduced-fat or fat-free mayonnaise is not recommended for this recipe.

EGG 'N' PEPPERONI BUNDLES

Prep: 20 min. **Bake:** 15 min.

My family calls these "one more gift to open" because it's the last present they unwrap on Christmas morning. Everyone's mouth waters when they bite into these tasty bundles loaded with great ingredients.

Helen Meadows // Trout Creek, Montana

- 7 sheets phyllo dough (14 inches x 9 inches)
- 1/2 cup butter, melted
- 8 teaspoons dry bread crumbs
- 2 ounces cream cheese, cut into 8 cubes
- 4 eggs
- 24 slices pepperoni, quartered or 1-1/2 ounces

Canadian bacon, diced
- 1/3 cup provolone cheese
- 2 teaspoons minced chives

1 Place one sheet of phyllo dough on a work surface; brush with butter. Top with another sheet of phyllo; brush with butter. Repeat five times. Cut phyllo in half widthwise, then cut in half lengthwise. Carefully place one stack in each of four greased jumbo muffin cups. Brush edges of dough with butter. Sprinkle 2 teaspoons of bread crumbs onto the bottom of each cup. Top each with two cubes of cream cheese.

2 Break each egg separately into a custard cup; gently pour egg over cream cheese. Sprinkle with pepperoni, provolone cheese and chives. Pinch corners of phyllo together to seal. Bake at 400° for 13-17 minutes or until golden brown. Serve warm. **YIELD:** 4 servings.

CHICKEN CLUB BRUNCH RING

Prep: 20 min. **Bake:** 20 min.

A few tubes of crescent rolls make this impressive recipe a snap. I fill the ring with chicken salad and serve warm slices with mustard-flavored mayonnaise.

Rebecca Clark // Warrior, Alabama

- 1/2 cup mayonnaise
- 1 tablespoon minced fresh parsley
- 2 teaspoons Dijon mustard
- 1-1/2 teaspoons finely chopped onion
- 1-3/4 cups cubed cooked chicken breast (1/2-inch cubes)
- 2 bacon strips, cooked and crumbled
- 1 cup (4 ounces) shredded Swiss cheese, *divided*
- 2 tubes (8 ounces *each*) refrigerated crescent rolls
- 2 plum tomatoes
- 2 cups shredded lettuce

1 In a large bowl, combine the mayonnaise, parsley, mustard and onion. Stir in the chicken, bacon and 3/4 cup cheese.

2 Unroll crescent dough; separate into 16 triangles. Arrange on an ungreased 12-in. round pizza pan, forming a ring with pointed ends facing outer edge of pan and wide ends overlapping.

3 Spoon chicken mixture over wide ends; fold points over filling and tuck under wide ends (filling will be visible). Chop half of a tomato; set aside. Slice remaining tomatoes; place over filling and tuck into dough.

4 Bake at 375° for 20-25 minutes or until golden brown. Sprinkle with remaining cheese. Let stand for 5 minutes. Place lettuce in center of ring; sprinkle with chopped tomato. **YIELD:** 16 servings.

Fresh asparagus and other spring garden vegetables crop up in this light and flavorful egg dish. The biscuit mix in this "impossible" pie settles to the bottom during baking to create a cheesy crust.

Barbara Gigliotti // Ocala, Florida

IMPOSSIBLE GARDEN PIE
Prep: 15 min. **Bake:** 30 min.

   2 cups cut fresh asparagus (1-inch pieces)
1-1/2 cups chopped fresh tomatoes
   1 medium onion, chopped
   1 garlic clove, minced
1/4 teaspoon dried basil
1/4 teaspoon salt
1/4 teaspoon pepper
   1 cup (4 ounces) shredded part-skim mozzarella cheese
1/2 cup grated Parmesan cheese
3/4 cup reduced-fat biscuit/baking mix
   3 eggs
1-1/2 cups fat-free milk

1 In a large bowl, combine the vegetables, garlic and seasonings. Transfer to an 8-in. square baking dish coated with cooking spray. Sprinkle with cheeses.

2 In another large bowl, whisk the biscuit mix, eggs and milk until smooth; pour over the cheeses. Bake, uncovered, at 400° for 30-35 minutes or until set and a thermometer inserted near the center reads 160°. Let stand for 5 minutes before cutting. **YIELD:** 6 servings.

BERRY-FILLED DOUGHNUTS
Prep/Total Time: 25 min.

Just four ingredients and 25 minutes are all you'll need for this sure-to-be-popular treat. Friends and family will never guess that refrigerated buttermilk biscuits are the base for these golden, jelly-filled doughnuts.

Ginny Watson // Broken Arrow, Oklahoma

   4 cups canola oil
   1 tube (7-1/2 ounces) refrigerated buttermilk biscuits, separated into 10 biscuits
3/4 cup seedless strawberry jam
   1 cup confectioners' sugar

1 In an electric skillet or deep-fat fryer, heat oil to 375°. Fry biscuits, a few at a time, for 1-2 minutes on each side or until golden brown. Drain on paper towels.

2 Cut a small hole in the corner of a pastry or plastic bag; insert a very small tip. Fill bag with jam. Push the tip through the side of each doughnut to fill with jam. Dust with the confectioners' sugar while warm. Serve immediately. **YIELD:** 10 servings.

An envelope of hollandaise sauce mix turns asparagus, deli turkey and English muffins into a special-occasion entree. The open-faced sandwiches easily impress.

Glenda Campbell // Kodak, Tennessee

TURKEY EGGS BENEDICT

Prep/Total Time: 20 min.

- 1/2 envelope hollandaise sauce mix
- 2 tablespoons butter
- 1/2 cup water
- 1 teaspoon white vinegar
- 2 eggs
- 2 slices deli turkey
- 1 English muffin, split and toasted
- 4 bacon strips, cooked
- 4 asparagus spears, cooked and drained

1 Prepare the hollandaise sauce with butter and water according to package directions.

2 Place 2-3 in. of water in a large skillet, saucepan, or omelet pan with high sides; add vinegar. Bring to a boil; reduce heat and simmer gently. Break cold eggs, one at a time, into a custard cup or saucer; holding the cup close to the surface of the water, slip each egg into water. Cook, uncovered, until whites are completely set and yolks begin to thicken (but are not hard), about 4 minutes.

3 Place a slice of turkey on each muffin half. With a slotted spoon, lift each egg out of the water; place over turkey. Top with bacon, asparagus and hollandaise sauce. **YIELD:** 2 servings.

EDITOR'S NOTE: This recipe was tested with McCormick's Hollandaise Sauce Blend (1.25-ounce envelope).

BRUNCH POCKETS

Prep: 25 min. **Bake:** 25 min.

These hefty handfuls promise everyone a good hot breakfast with little fuss. Everyone loves the toasty grab-and-go pockets stuffed with pineapple, ham, turkey and cheese.

Jean Kimm // Coeur d'Alene, Idaho

- 1 package (15 ounces) refrigerated pie crust
- 2 pineapple slices, cut in half
- 4 thin slices deli ham
- 4 thin slices deli turkey
- 4 slices Swiss cheese
- 1 egg, lightly beaten

1 Cut each pastry sheet into four wedges. Pat pineapple slices dry with paper towels. Top four pastry wedges with one slice each of ham, turkey, cheese and pineapple, folding meat and cheese to fit if necessary. Top each with a pastry wedge; seal and crimp edges with a fork. Cut slits in pastry.

2 Place on an ungreased baking sheet. Brush lightly with egg. Bake at 350° for 25-30 minutes or until golden brown. Serve warm. **YIELD:** 4 servings.

PECAN CHOCOLATE WAFFLES

Prep/Total Time: 25 min.

If you like waffles and chocolate, this recipe is for you. These tender but crunchy waffles are great for breakfast or as an after-dinner dessert. Instead of chocolate topping, top with berries and whipped cream or simply sprinkle with powdered sugar.

Agnes Golian // Garfield Heights, Ohio

- 1 cup pancake mix
- 1 egg
- 3/4 cup 2% milk
- 1/4 cup chocolate syrup
- 2 tablespoons canola oil
- 1/3 cup chopped pecans

CHOCOLATE BUTTER:
- 1/4 cup butter, softened
- 1/4 cup confectioners' sugar
- 1 tablespoon baking cocoa

1 Place pancake mix in a bowl. In another bowl, whisk the egg, milk, chocolate syrup and oil. Stir into pancake mix just until combined. Stir in pecans.

2 Bake in a preheated waffle iron according to the manufacturer's directions until waffles are golden brown. Meanwhile, in a small bowl, beat the chocolate butter ingredients until smooth. Serve with the waffles. **YIELD:** 8 waffles.

TIP

Serve leftover waffles for a quick breakfast on another day. Arrange in a single layer on a wire rack to cool completely. Place in a resealable food storage bag and store in the refrigerator for a few days. To reheat, remove from the bag, and heat for a few seconds in the microwave.

CRESCENT SAUSAGE ROLLS
Prep/Total Time: 30 min.

Loaded with pork sausage and cheese, these fun, golden brown sausage rolls are perfect for brunch or lunch.

Cherie Durbin // Hickory, North Carolina

1/3 **pound bulk pork sausage, cooked and drained**
1 **teaspoon garlic powder**
1 **teaspoon minced fresh parsley**
1/2 **teaspoon grated Parmesan cheese**
1/4 **teaspoon dried basil**
1 **egg, lightly beaten,** *divided*
1 **tube (4 ounces) refrigerated crescent rolls**
1/2 **cup shredded cheddar cheese**

1 In a small bowl, combine the sausage, garlic powder, parsley, Parmesan cheese, basil and 2 tablespoons beaten egg. Unroll crescent dough and separate into two rectangles. Place on an ungreased baking sheet; seal perforations.

2 Spoon sausage mixture into the center of each rectangle. Sprinkle with cheddar cheese. Roll up from a long side; pinch seam to seal. Brush with remaining egg.

3 Bake at 350° for 15-20 minutes or until golden. Cut into slices; serve warm. **YIELD:** 2 servings.

Whether you serve it for your morning meal or for supper, this flavorful "pie" will fill you up without all the cholesterol. You can make it even healthier by substituting turkey bacon for the traditional variety.

Jessica Salman // Dublin, Ohio

BRUNCH PIZZA
Prep: 20 min. **Bake:** 25 min.

- 2/3 cup reduced-fat biscuit/baking mix
- 2 tablespoons plus 1 teaspoon water
- 2 cups fresh baby spinach, chopped
- 1/2 cup egg substitute
- 1/3 cup sour cream
- 1/3 cup shredded reduced-fat cheddar cheese
- 2 green onions, chopped
- 1/2 teaspoon garlic powder
- 2 bacon strips, cooked and crumbled

1 In a small bowl, combine biscuit mix and water to form a soft dough. Press onto the bottom and up the sides of a 7-in. pie plate coated with cooking spray.

2 Bake at 450° for 5 minutes or until golden brown. Remove from the oven. Reduce heat to 375°.

3 In a small bowl, combine the spinach, egg substitute, sour cream, cheese, onions and garlic powder. Pour into crust. Sprinkle with bacon. Bake for 25-30 minutes or until golden brown. **YIELD:** 2 servings.

LEMON POPPY SEED WAFFLES
Prep/Total Time: 20 min.

When spring arrives to your area, serve these lemony waffles for a refreshing rise-and-shine breakfast.

Taste of Home Test Kitchen

- 2 cups biscuit/baking mix
- 2 eggs, lightly beaten
- 1/2 cup canola oil
- 1 cup club soda
- 1 tablespoon lemon juice
- 1 teaspoon vanilla extract
- 2 teaspoons poppy seeds

1 In a large bowl, combine the biscuit mix, eggs and oil. In a small bowl, combine the club soda, lemon juice and vanilla; gradually stir into biscuit mixture until smooth. Gently fold in poppy seeds.

2 Bake in a preheated waffle iron according to manufacturer's directions until golden brown. **YIELD:** 12 waffles.

Wonderful blueberry flavor abounds in these thick and moist pancakes. My kids love them, and they are easy and inexpensive!

Amy Spainhoward
Bowling Green, Kentucky

BLUEBERRY OATMEAL PANCAKES

Prep: 20 min. **Cook:** 5 min./batch

- 2 cups all-purpose flour
- 2 packets (1.51 ounces *each*) instant maple and brown sugar oatmeal mix
- 2 tablespoons sugar
- 2 teaspoons baking powder
- 1/8 teaspoon salt
- 2 egg whites
- 1 egg
- 1-1/2 cups fat-free milk
- 1/2 cup reduced-fat sour cream
- 2 cups fresh *or* frozen blueberries

BLUEBERRY SYRUP:
- 1-1/2 cups fresh *or* frozen blueberries
- 1/2 cup sugar

1 In a large bowl, combine the flour, oatmeal mix, sugar, baking powder and salt. In another bowl, whisk the egg whites, egg, milk and sour cream. Stir into dry ingredients just until moistened. Fold in blueberries.

2 Spoon batter by 1/4 cupfuls onto a hot griddle coated with cooking spray. Turn when bubbles form on top of pancake; cook until the second side is golden brown.

3 In a microwave-safe bowl, combine syrup ingredients. Microwave, uncovered, on high for 1 minute; stir. Microwave 1-2 minutes longer or until syrup is hot and bubbly. Serve warm with the pancakes. **YIELD:** 14 pancakes (1-1/4 cups syrup).

VERY VANILLA FRENCH TOAST

Prep/Total Time: 10 min.

These French toast slices have a creamy vanilla flavor from convenient pudding mix, plus a hint of cinnamon. We like to top them with syrup or powdered sugar and fresh berries.

Linda Bernhagen // Plainfield, Illinois

- 1 cup milk
- 1 package (3 ounces) cook-and-serve vanilla pudding mix
- 1 egg
- 1/2 teaspoon ground cinnamon
- 8 slices Texas toast
- 2 teaspoons butter

1 In a large bowl, whisk the milk, pudding mix, egg and cinnamon for 2 minutes or until well blended. Dip toast in pudding mixture, coating both sides.

2 In a large skillet, melt butter over medium heat. Cook the bread on both sides until golden brown. **YIELD:** 4 servings.

My husband's a busy farmer and sometimes eats his breakfast on the run. He's able to take these omelet biscuit cups with him in his truck or tractor cab.
Leila Zimmer // York, South Carolina

OMELET BISCUIT CUPS
Prep/Total Time: 30 min.

- 1 tube (12 ounces) large refrigerated buttermilk biscuits
- 4 eggs
- 1/4 cup milk
- 1/8 teaspoon salt
- 1/8 teaspoon pepper
- 1 cup diced fully cooked ham
- 3/4 cup shredded cheddar cheese, *divided*
- 1/3 cup chopped canned mushrooms
- 1 tablespoon butter

1 Press biscuits onto the bottom and up the sides of greased muffin cups; set aside. In a large bowl, beat the eggs, milk, salt and pepper. Stir in the ham, 1/4 cup cheese and mushrooms.

2 In a skillet, melt butter; add the egg mixture. Cook and stir until eggs are nearly set. Spoon into biscuit cups.

3 Bake at 375° for 10-15 minutes or until biscuits are golden brown. Sprinkle with remaining cheese. Bake 2 minutes longer or until cheese is melted. **YIELD:** 5 servings.

HAM 'N' SWISS ROLLS
Prep/Total Time: 20 min.

I depend on no-fuss recipes in planning breakfast for husband, Joseph, and me. Our grown children are big fans of ham and cheese. These rolls are perfect for families on the go.
Marjorie Carey // Freeport, Florida

- 1 tube (8 ounces) refrigerated crescent rolls
- 1 cup diced fully cooked ham
- 3/4 cup finely shredded Swiss cheese
- 1-1/2 teaspoons prepared mustard
- 1 teaspoon finely chopped onion

1 Separate crescent rolls into eight triangles. In a bowl, combine the ham, cheese, mustard and onion; place 2 tablespoons mixture in the center of each triangle.

2 Fold points toward center and pinch edges to seal. Place on a lightly greased baking sheet. Bake at 375° for 11-13 minutes or until the rolls are lightly browned. **YIELD:** 4 servings (2 rolls each).

This attractive bread is brimming with eggs, ham and cheese, making it a real meal-in-one. By using refrigerated crescent rolls, it's a snap to prepare.
Julie Deal // China Grove, North Carolina

SCRAMBLED EGG BRUNCH BREAD

Prep: 25 min. **Bake:** 25 min.

    2 tubes (8 ounces *each*) refrigerated crescent rolls
    4 ounces thinly sliced deli ham, julienned
    4 ounces cream cheese, softened
  1/2 cup milk
    8 eggs
  1/4 teaspoon salt
Dash pepper
  1/4 cup chopped sweet red pepper
    2 tablespoons chopped green onion
    1 teaspoon butter
  1/2 cup shredded cheddar cheese

1 Unroll each tube of crescent dough (do not separate rectangles). Place side by side on a greased baking sheet with long sides touching; seal seams and perforations. Arrange ham lengthwise down center third of rectangle.

2 In a large bowl, beat cream cheese and milk until smooth. Separate one egg; set egg white aside. Add the egg yolk, salt, pepper and remaining eggs to cream cheese mixture; beat until blended. Stir in red pepper and onion.

3 In a large skillet, melt butter; add egg mixture. Cook and stir over medium heat just until set. Remove from the heat. Spoon scrambled eggs over the ham. Sprinkle with the cheese.

4 On each long side of dough, cut 1-in.-wide strips to the center to within 1/2 in. of filling. Starting at one end, fold alternating strips at an angle across the filling. Pinch ends to seal and tuck under.

5 Beat reserved egg white; brush over dough. Bake at 375° for 25-28 minutes or until the bread is golden brown.
YIELD: 6 servings.

TIP

This brunch bread will be sure to impress family and company. To make an elegant spread, serve it with mixed fruits, such as berries and melons. And for a beverage, mix a glass of orange juice with a squirt of lime juice and about a 1/4 cup of club soda.

beef

GRILLED FAJITAS

Prep: 20 min. + marinating **Grill:** 10 min.

  1 envelope onion soup mix
1/4 cup canola oil
1/4 cup lime juice
1/4 cup water
  2 garlic cloves, minced
  1 teaspoon grated lime peel
  1 teaspoon ground cumin
1/2 teaspoon dried oregano
1/4 teaspoon pepper
  1 beef flank steak (about 1 pound)
  1 medium onion, thinly sliced
Green, sweet red *and/or* yellow peppers, julienned

  1 tablespoon canola oil
  8 flour tortillas (8 inches), warmed

1 In a large resealable plastic bag, combine the soup mix, oil, lime juice, water and seasonings; add steak. Seal bag; turn to coat. Cover and refrigerate 4 hours or overnight.

2 Drain and discard marinade. Grill, covered, over medium-high heat for 4 to 7 minutes on each side until meat reaches desired doneness (for medium-rare, a meat thermometer should read 145°; medium, 160°; well-done, 170°).

3 Meanwhile, in a small skillet, saute onion and peppers if desired in oil for 3-4 minutes or until crisp-tender. Slice meat into thin strips across the grain; place on tortillas. Top with vegetables; roll up. **YIELD:** 4 servings.

CHILI-GHETTI

Prep/Total Time: 30 min.

I came up with this recipe when unexpected guests stopped by and I didn't have enough chili. The spur-of-the-moment main dish is now a favorite.

Cindy Cuykendall // Skaneateles, New York

  1 package (7 ounces) spaghetti
  1 pound ground beef
  1 small onion, chopped
  1 can (16 ounces) kidney beans, rinsed and drained
  1 can (14-1/2 ounces) diced tomatoes, undrained
  1 can (4 ounces) mushroom stems and pieces, drained

1/3 cup water
  1 envelope chili seasoning
  2 tablespoons grated Parmesan cheese
1/4 cup shredded part-skim mozzarella cheese

1 Cook spaghetti according to package directions. Meanwhile, in a large skillet, cook beef and onion over medium heat until meat is no longer pink; drain.

2 Drain spaghetti; add to beef mixture. Stir in the beans, tomatoes, mushrooms, water, chili seasoning and Parmesan cheese. Cover and simmer for 10 minutes. Sprinkle with mozzarella cheese. **YIELD:** 8 servings.

APPLE CIDER BEEF STEW

Prep: 20 min. **Cook:** 6-1/4 hours

I created this slow cooker recipe using convenience products to save time chopping vegetables and browning beef. Apple cider and cinnamon are the unique additions that give a down-home flavor to this oh-so-easy and economical stew.

Margaret Wilson // Sun City, California

- 4 cups frozen vegetables for stew (about 24 ounces), thawed
- 1 can (8 ounces) sliced water chestnuts, drained
- 1 jar (4-1/2 ounces) sliced mushrooms, drained
- 1 tablespoon dried minced onion
- 2 envelopes brown gravy mix
- 2 tablespoons onion soup mix
- 2 teaspoons steak seasoning
- 1/8 teaspoon ground cinnamon
- 2 pounds beef stew meat, cut into 1-inch cubes
- 1 can (14-1/2 ounces) beef broth
- 1-1/4 cups apple cider *or* unsweetened apple juice
- 1 can (8 ounces) tomato sauce
- 1 bay leaf
- 3 tablespoons cornstarch
- 1/3 cup cold water

1 Place the vegetables, water chestnuts, mushrooms and onion in a 5-qt. slow cooker. In a large resealable plastic bag, combine the gravy mix, soup mix, steak seasoning and cinnamon; add beef, a few pieces at a time, and shake to coat. Add to slow cooker.

2 Combine the broth, cider and tomato sauce; pour over beef. Add bay leaf. Cover and cook on low for 6-7 hours or until meat is tender.

3 Combine cornstarch and water until smooth; stir into stew. Cover and cook on high for 15 minutes or until thickened. Discard bay leaf. **YIELD:** 12 servings.

EDITOR'S NOTE: This recipe was tested with McCormick's Montreal Steak Seasoning. Look for it in the spice aisle.

Great for tailgating and other events, this party sandwich is so quick to make. You can also slice it thin and serve as an appetizer. Or, I like to "Reubenize" them by using corned beef, sauerkraut, caraway seeds and Thousand Island dressing.

Clarissa Jo Seeger // Columbiana, Ohio

ROAST BEEF ROLL-UPS
Prep/Total Time: 15 min.

- 1 package (16 ounces) coleslaw mix
- 3/4 cup coleslaw salad dressing
- 1/2 cup mayonnaise
- 1/4 cup Dijon mustard
- 2 tablespoons cider vinegar
- 2 teaspoons sugar
- 1/2 teaspoon celery seed
- 1 pound thinly sliced deli roast beef
- 4 Italian herb flatbread wraps
- 1/2 pound Swiss cheese, thinly sliced

1 In a small bowl, combine the first seven ingredients. Divide roast beef among flatbread wraps. Top with the cheese and coleslaw mixture; roll up tightly. **YIELD:** 4 servings.

SWEET 'N' TANGY POT ROAST
Prep: 10 min. Cook: 9-1/2 hours

I fixed this roast the first time I cooked for my husband-to-be more than 20 years ago. For dessert, I made chocolate pudding spooned over marshmallows. He thought he'd died and gone to heaven!

Carol Mulligan // Honeoye Falls, New York

- 1 boneless beef chuck roast (3 pounds)
- 1/2 teaspoon salt
- 1/2 teaspoon pepper
- 1 cup water
- 1 cup ketchup
- 1/4 cup red wine *or* beef broth
- 1 envelope brown gravy mix
- 2 teaspoons Dijon mustard
- 1 teaspoon Worcestershire sauce
- 1/8 teaspoon garlic powder
- 3 tablespoons cornstarch
- 1/4 cup cold water

1 Cut meat in half and place in a 5-qt. slow cooker. Sprinkle with the salt and pepper. In a small bowl, combine the water, ketchup, wine, gravy mix, mustard, Worcestershire sauce and garlic powder; pour over meat. Cover and cook on low for 9-10 hours or until meat is tender.

2 Combine cornstarch and cold water until smooth. Stir into slow cooker. Cover and cook on high for 30 minutes or until gravy is thickened. Remove meat from slow cooker. Slice and serve with gravy. **YIELD:** 8 servings.

Barbecue sauce and dry onion soup mix give plenty of flavor to these moist meat loaves. This recipe is also handy during the summer when I don't want to turn on the oven.
Nicole Russman // Lincoln, Nebraska

BARBECUED ONION MEAT LOAVES
Prep/Total Time: 25 min.

1 egg, lightly beaten
1/3 cup milk
2 tablespoons plus 1/4 cup barbecue sauce, *divided*
1/2 cup crushed seasoned stuffing
1 tablespoon onion soup mix
1-1/4 pounds lean ground beef

1 In a bowl, combine the egg, milk, 2 tablespoons barbecue sauce, stuffing and onion soup mix. Crumble beef over mixture and mix well. Shape into five loaves; arrange around the edge of a microwave-safe dish.

2 Microwave, uncovered, on high for 4-1/2 to 5-1/2 minutes or until no pink remains and a meat thermometer reads 160°. Cover and let stand for 5-10 minutes. Top with the remaining barbecue sauce. **YIELD:** 5 servings.

EDITOR'S NOTE: This recipe was tested in a 1,100-watt microwave.

VEGETABLE BEEF CASSEROLE
Prep/Total Time: 30 min.

My sister made this flavorful entree often as a newlywed, and shared the recipe with me when I got married. The biscuit-topped dish has a comforting flavor and is speedy to assemble.
Andrea Hickerson // Trenton, Tennessee

1-1/2 pounds ground beef
2 cups frozen cut green beans, thawed
1 can (15-1/4 ounces) whole kernel corn, drained
1 can (10-3/4 ounces) condensed tomato soup, undiluted
3/4 cup water
1 teaspoon Worcestershire sauce
1 tube (12 ounces) refrigerated buttermilk biscuits
1 cup (4 ounces) shredded cheddar cheese

1 In a large skillet, cook beef over medium heat until no longer pink; drain. Stir in the beans, corn, soup, water and Worcestershire sauce. Bring to a boil; cook and stir for 2-3 minutes or until heated through. Keep warm.

2 Separate biscuits and cut into quarters; place on an ungreased baking sheet. Bake at 400° for 5 minutes.

3 Transfer beef mixture to a greased 13-in. x 9-in. baking dish. Top with biscuits and cheese. Bake for 8-10 minutes or until biscuits are golden brown. **YIELD:** 6 servings.

ITALIAN ROAST WITH ALFREDO POTATOES

Prep: 10 min. **Cook:** 7 hours 20 min.

This hearty meal is a great way to start the week. And since most of the work is done by the slow cooker, you'll have very little to do. Just boil the potatoes and smash them with Alfredo sauce, butter and pepper. They go great with the roast and gravy.

Taste of Home Test Kitchen

- 1 boneless beef chuck roast (4 pounds), trimmed
- 1 envelope brown gravy mix
- 1 envelope Italian salad dressing mix
- 1/2 cup water
- 1 medium sweet red pepper, cut into 1-inch pieces
- 1 cup chopped green pepper
- 2/3 cup chopped onion
- 8 medium red potatoes, quartered
- 2 tablespoons cornstarch
- 1/4 cup cold water
- 3/4 cup refrigerated Alfredo sauce
- 2 tablespoons butter
- 1/4 teaspoon pepper
- 1 tablespoon minced chives

1 Cut roast in half; place in a 5-qt. slow cooker. In a small bowl, combine the gravy mix, dressing mix and water; pour over roast. Top with peppers and onion. Cover and cook on low for 7-8 hours or until meat is tender.

2 Place potatoes in a large saucepan; cover with water. Bring to a boil. Reduce heat; cover and simmer for 15-20 minutes or until tender. Meanwhile, remove roast and cut a portion of the meat into cubes, measuring 3 cups; cover and save for another use. Slice the remaining beef and keep warm.

3 Skim fat from cooking juices if necessary; pour into a large saucepan. Combine cornstarch and cold water until smooth; stir into cooking juices. Bring to a boil; cook and stir for 2 minutes or until thickened.

4 Drain potatoes; mash with Alfredo sauce, butter and pepper. Sprinkle with chives. Serve with sliced beef and gravy. **YIELD:** 4 servings plus leftovers.

Anyone who likes the distinctive taste of reuben sandwiches is sure to love these. Using coleslaw mix speeds up the preparation.
Mary Ann Dell // Phoenixville, Pennsylvania

OPEN-FACED REUBENS
Prep/Total Time: 20 min.

2-1/2 cups coleslaw mix
   8 green onions, sliced
  1/2 cup mayonnaise, *divided*
   2 tablespoons cider vinegar
  1/2 teaspoon salt
  1/2 teaspoon pepper
  1/4 cup Dijon mustard
   8 slices rye bread, lightly toasted
 16 slices Swiss cheese
   1 pound thinly sliced deli corned beef

1 In a large bowl, combine the coleslaw mix, onions, 1/4 cup mayonnaise, vinegar, salt and pepper. Cover and refrigerate until chilled.

2 Meanwhile, combine the mustard and remaining mayonnaise. Spread over one side of each slice of toast; top with a cheese slice, corned beef and another cheese slice. Place on foil-lined baking sheets. Bake at 450° for 5-6 minutes or until cheese is melted. Top each with 1/4 cup coleslaw. **YIELD:** 8 servings.

MUSHROOM RIB EYES
Prep/Total Time: 30 min.

Who can resist a juicy rib eye steak topped with mushrooms and onions in a rich gravy? Simply add a green salad and an impressive dinner is served.
Kathleen Hendrick // Alexandria, Kentucky

   2 boneless rib eye steaks (8 ounces *each*)
  1/4 teaspoon seasoned salt
  1/8 teaspoon pepper
   2 teaspoons canola oil
   1 small onion, thinly sliced
   1 cup sliced fresh mushrooms
   1 envelope brown gravy mix
  1/3 cup sour cream

1 Sprinkle steaks with seasoned salt and pepper. In a large skillet, brown steaks on both sides in oil. Transfer to an 11-in. x 7-in. baking dish.

2 In the same skillet, saute onion and mushrooms until tender. Spoon over steaks. Prepare gravy mix according to the package directions; stir in sour cream. Pour over steaks.

3 Cover and bake at 350° for 10-15 minutes or until meat reaches desired doneness (for medium-rare, a meat thermometer should read 145°; medium, 160°; well-done, 170°). **YIELD:** 2 servings.

My cousin is of Mexican heritage, and I've watched her make these crunchy burritos for years. The very first time I made them for my own family, they became an instant favorite meal. They're even better warmed up the next day in the microwave as a great snack. I like to serve them with Spanish rice or just chips and salsa.

Debi Lane // Chattanooga, Tennessee

TASTY BURRITOS
Prep/Total Time: 30 min.

- 1 pound ground beef
- 1 envelope taco seasoning
- 1 can (16 ounces) refried beans
- 6 flour tortillas (12 inches), warmed
- 1 cup (4 ounces) shredded Colby-Monterey Jack cheese
- 4 teaspoons canola oil

Sour cream and salsa

1 In a large skillet, cook beef over medium heat until no longer pink; drain. Stir in taco seasoning. In a small saucepan, cook refried beans over medium-low heat for 2-3 minutes or until heated through.

2 Spoon about 1/3 cup of beans off-center on each tortilla; top with about 2 rounded tablespoons of beef mixture. Sprinkle with cheese. Fold sides and ends of tortilla over filling and roll up. In a large skillet over medium-high heat, brown burritos in oil on all sides. Serve with sour cream and salsa. **YIELD:** 6 servings.

SLOPPY JOE PASTA
Prep: 20 min. Bake: 30 min.

Since I found this recipe a few years ago, it's become a regular part of my menu plans. Everyone loves the combination of sloppy joe ingredients, shell pasta and cheddar cheese.

Lynne Leih // Idyllwild, California

- 1 pound ground beef
- 1 envelope sloppy joe mix
- 1 cup water
- 1 can (8 ounces) tomato sauce
- 1 can (6 ounces) tomato paste
- 1 package (7 ounces) small shell pasta, cooked and drained
- 1 cup (8 ounces) 4% cottage cheese
- 1/2 cup shredded cheddar cheese

1 In a large saucepan, cook beef over medium heat until no longer pink; drain. Stir in the sloppy joe mix, water, tomato sauce and paste. Bring to a boil. Reduce heat; simmer, uncovered, for 5-8 minutes or until heated through. Remove from the heat; stir in pasta.

2 Spoon half into a greased 2-1/2-qt. baking dish. Top with cottage cheese and remaining pasta mixture. Sprinkle with cheddar cheese.

3 Bake, uncovered, at 350° for 30-35 minutes or until bubbly and cheese is melted. **YIELD:** 4-6 servings.

For St. Patrick's Day, I usually prepare this dish instead of the traditional corned beef dinner. This takes less time because it makes good use of the microwave...and it's just as tasty.

Brooke Staley // Mary Esther, Florida

CORNED BEEF POTATO DINNER
Prep/Total Time: 30 min.

   1 pound red potatoes, cut into small wedges
1-1/2 cups water
   1 large onion, thinly sliced and separated into rings
   4 cups coleslaw mix
   8 ounces thinly sliced deli corned beef, cut into 1/4-inch strips
   1 tablespoon canola oil
1/3 cup red wine vinegar
   4 teaspoons spicy brown mustard
   1 teaspoon sugar
   1 teaspoon caraway seeds
1/2 teaspoon garlic powder
1/2 teaspoon salt
1/2 teaspoon pepper

1 Place potatoes and water in a 3-qt. microwave-safe bowl. Cover; microwave on high for 4-5 minutes or until potatoes are crisp-tender. Add the onion; cover and cook for 1-2 minutes or until onions are tender. Stir in the coleslaw mix. Cover and cook for 2-3 minutes longer or until potatoes are tender; drain.

2 In a large skillet, saute corned beef in oil for 3-4 minutes; drain. Stir in the remaining ingredients. Cook and stir for 1 minute or until heated through. Add to the potato mixture; toss to combine. Cover and microwave for 1-2 minutes or until heated through. **YIELD:** 4 servings.

EDITOR'S NOTE: This recipe was tested in a 1,100-watt microwave.

RED-EYE BEEF ROAST
Prep: 25 min. **Bake:** 2 hours + standing

The addition of hot sauce zips up this cut of meat. It takes me back to spicy dinners I enjoyed as a child in the Southwest. I like to use the leftovers in different dishes, including barbecued beef sandwiches, quesadillas and burritos.

Carol Stevens // Basye, Virginia

   1 boneless beef eye of round roast (about 3 pounds)
   1 tablespoon canola oil
2-1/2 cups water, *divided*
   1 envelope onion soup mix
   3 tablespoons cider vinegar
   2 tablespoons Louisiana hot sauce
   2 tablespoons all-purpose flour

1 In a Dutch oven over medium-high heat, brown roast on all sides in oil; drain. Combine 3/4 cup water, soup mix, vinegar and hot sauce; pour over roast.

2 Cover and bake at 325° for 2-3 hours or until tender. Transfer to a serving platter and keep warm. Let stand for 10-15 minutes before slicing.

3 For gravy, combine flour and remaining water until smooth; stir into meat juices. Bring to a boil; cook and stir for 2 minutes or until thickened. Serve with meat. **YIELD:** 10-12 servings.

CHEESE-TOPPED BEEF BAKE

Prep: 20 min. **Bake:** 25 min.

- 1 package (16 ounces) medium pasta shells
- 1 pound ground beef
- 1 jar (26 ounces) spaghetti sauce
- 1 envelope taco seasoning
- 1 carton (8 ounces) spreadable chive and onion cream cheese
- 1 cup (8 ounces) sour cream
- 1 cup (4 ounces) shredded cheddar cheese

1 Cook the pasta according to package directions. Meanwhile, in a large skillet, cook beef over medium heat until no longer pink; drain. Stir in the spaghetti sauce and taco seasoning. In a small bowl, combine cream cheese and sour cream; set aside.

2 Drain the pasta; stir into beef mixture. Transfer to a greased 13-in. x 9-in. baking dish. Spread with cream cheese mixture; sprinkle with cheddar cheese. Bake, uncovered, at 350° for 25-30 minutes or until cheese is melted. **YIELD:** 8-10 servings.

ITALIAN BEEF SANDWICHES

Prep: 10 min. **Cook:** 7-1/2 hours

My mother-in-law often served these flavorful sandwiches after church when we'd visit. Because there's little prep work, I make them on busy weeknights alongside french fries and raw veggies. Our children get excited when they smell the beef simmering in the slow cooker.
Jan Kent // Knoxville, Tennessee

- 1 beef tip sirloin roast (4-1/2 pounds), cut in half
- 1 can (14-1/2 ounces) beef broth
- 1 can (12 ounces) beer *or* additional beef broth
- 1 cup water
- 1/4 cup cider vinegar
- 1 envelope onion soup mix
- 1 envelope Italian salad dressing mix
- 1 garlic clove, minced
- 1-1/2 teaspoons dried oregano
- 1 teaspoon dried basil
- 10 Italian sandwich rolls (6 inches), split

1 Place roast in a 5-qt. slow cooker. Combine the broth, beer, water, vinegar, soup mix, salad dressing mix, garlic, oregano and basil; pour over roast. Cover and cook on low for 7-8 hours or until meat is tender.

2 Remove roast. When cool enough to handle, shred meat, using two forks. Return to slow cooker and heat through. Using a slotted spoon, spoon shredded meat onto each roll. Serve juices as a dipping sauce. **YIELD:** 10 servings.

LOADED PIZZA

Prep: 30 min. **Bake:** 10 min.

This is a lightened-up version of my favorite homemade pizza. It's smothered with toppings, which makes it hearty and extra special.
Louie Rossignolo // Athens, Alabama

- 1-1/2 cups sliced fresh mushrooms
- 1/4 cup *each* chopped green pepper, sweet red pepper, white onion and red onion
- 1 tablespoon canola oil
- 2 garlic cloves, minced
- 1/4 pound lean ground beef
- 1 turkey Italian sausage link (4 ounces), casing removed
- 2 teaspoons cornmeal
- 1 loaf (1 pound) frozen bread dough, thawed
- 1 can (8 ounces) tomato sauce
- 2 tablespoons minced fresh parsley
- 2 teaspoons Italian seasoning
- 1/4 teaspoon garlic powder
- 1/8 teaspoon pepper
- 15 turkey pepperoni slices (1 ounce)
- 2 tablespoons sliced ripe olives
- 1-1/4 cups shredded part-skim mozzarella cheese
- 1/4 cup shredded reduced-fat cheddar cheese

1 In a nonstick skillet, saute the mushrooms, peppers and onions in oil until almost tender. Add garlic and saute 1 minute longer; remove and set aside. In the same skillet, cook beef and sausage over medium heat until no longer pink; drain.

2 Coat a 14-in. pizza pan with cooking spray and sprinkle with cornmeal. On a lightly floured surface, roll dough into a 15-in. circle. Transfer to prepared pan. Build up edges slightly; prick dough thoroughly with a fork. Bake at 400° for 8-10 minutes or until lightly browned.

3 In a large bowl, combine the tomato sauce, parsley, Italian seasoning, garlic powder and pepper; spread over crust. Top with the vegetables, meat mixture, pepperoni and olives. Sprinkle with cheeses. Bake for 8-10 minutes or until crust is golden and cheese is melted. **YIELD:** 8 servings.

MEXICAN LASAGNA

Prep: 25 min. **Bake:** 40 min. + standing

Tortillas replace lasagna noodles in this beefy casserole with a south-of-the-border twist. With salsa, enchilada sauce, chilies, cheese and refried beans, it's a fiesta of flavors.

Tina Newhauser // Peterborough, New Hampshire

1-1/4 pounds ground beef
    1 medium onion, chopped
    4 garlic cloves, minced
    2 cups salsa
    1 can (16 ounces) refried beans
    1 can (15 ounces) black beans, rinsed and drained
    1 can (10 ounces) enchilada sauce
    1 can (4 ounces) chopped green chilies
    1 envelope taco seasoning
 1/4 teaspoon pepper
    6 flour tortillas (10 inches)
    3 cups (12 ounces) shredded Mexican cheese blend, *divided*
    2 cups crushed tortilla chips
Sliced ripe olives, guacamole, chopped tomatoes and sour cream, optional

1 In a large skillet, cook the beef, onion and garlic over medium heat until meat is no longer pink; drain. Stir in the salsa, beans, enchilada sauce, chilies, taco seasoning and pepper; heat through.

2 Spread 1 cup sauce in a greased 13-in. x 9-in. baking dish. Layer with two tortillas, a third of the meat mixture and 1 cup cheese. Repeat layers. Top with remaining tortillas and meat mixture.

3 Cover and bake at 375° for 30 minutes. Uncover; sprinkle with remaining cheese and top with tortilla chips.

4 Bake 10-15 minutes longer or until cheese is melted. Let stand for 10 minutes before serving. Garnish with the olives, guacamole, tomatoes and sour cream if desired. **YIELD:** 12 servings.

When I prepare my favorite meat loaf, I usually end up with an extra half pound of ground beef. I created this Cajun-flavored dish as a way to use it up.

June Ellis // Erie, Illinois

CAJUN MACARONI

Prep: 15 min. **Cook:** 20 min.

- 1/2 **pound ground beef**
- 1/3 **cup chopped onion**
- 1/3 **cup chopped green pepper**
- 1/3 **cup chopped celery**
- 1 **can (14-1/2 ounces) diced tomatoes, undrained**
- 1-1/2 **teaspoons Cajun seasoning**
- 1 **package (7-1/4 ounces) macaroni and cheese dinner mix**
- 2 **tablespoons milk**
- 1 **tablespoon butter**

1 In a large saucepan, cook the beef, onion, green pepper and celery over medium heat until meat is no longer pink; drain. Add tomatoes and Cajun seasoning. Cook, uncovered, for 15-20 minutes, stirring occasionally.

2 Meanwhile, prepare macaroni and cheese mix, using 2 tablespoons milk and 1 tablespoon butter. Stir in beef mixture; cook for 2-3 minutes or until heated through. **YIELD:** 4 servings.

SLOW 'N' EASY CHILI

Prep: 10 min. **Cook:** 6 hours

What's nice about this recipe is that you can add any extras (like chopped bell peppers or sliced fresh mushrooms) to make your own specialty. I get the best reviews when I serve this chili.

Ginny Puckett // Lutz, Florida

- 1/2 **pound ground beef, cooked and drained**
- 1/2 **pound bulk pork sausage, cooked and drained**
- 1 **can (28 ounces) crushed tomatoes**
- 1 **can (15 ounces) chili beans, undrained**
- 1 **can (10-3/4 ounces) condensed tomato soup, undiluted**
- 1 **large onion, chopped**
- 2 **envelopes chili seasoning**
- **Shredded cheddar cheese, optional**

1 In a 3-qt. slow cooker, combine the meat, tomatoes, beans, soup, onion and seasoning. Cover and cook on low for 6-8 hours or until thickened and heated through, stirring occasionally. Garnish with cheese if desired. **YIELD:** 6-8 servings.

A favorite traditional dinner turns into a fuss-free meal when you use a slow cooker. Tender sirloin steak in tasty gravy is served over noodles for a home-style meal your whole family will request time and again.
Lisa VanEgmond // Annapolis, Illinois

BEEF STROGANOFF
Prep: 25 min. **Cook:** 7 hours

3 to 4 pounds boneless beef sirloin steak, cubed
2 cans (14-1/2 ounces *each*) chicken broth
1 pound sliced fresh mushrooms
1 can (12 ounces) regular cola
1/2 cup chopped onion
1 envelope onion soup mix
1 to 2 teaspoons garlic powder
2 teaspoons dried parsley flakes
1/2 teaspoon pepper
2 envelopes country gravy mix
2 cups (16 ounces) sour cream
Hot cooked noodles

1 In a 5-qt. slow cooker, combine the first nine ingredients. Cover and cook on low for 7-8 hours or until beef is tender.

2 With a slotted spoon, remove beef and mushrooms. Place gravy mix in a large saucepan; gradually whisk in cooking liquid. Bring to a boil; cook and stir for 2 minutes or until thickened. Remove from the heat; stir in sour cream. Add beef and mushrooms to the gravy. Serve with noodles. **YIELD:** 12-16 servings.

SIRLOIN SANDWICHES
Prep: 10 min. + marinating **Grill:** 1 hour + chilling

Mom is always happy to share her cooking, and these delicious beef sandwiches are a real crowd-pleaser. A simple three-ingredient marinade flavors the grilled beef wonderfully.
Judi Messina // Coeur d'Alene, Idaho

1 cup soy sauce
1/2 cup canola oil
1/2 cup cranberry *or* apple juice
1 boneless beef sirloin tip roast (3 to 4 pounds)
1 envelope beef au jus gravy mix
1 dozen French rolls, split

1 In a large resealable plastic bag, combine the soy sauce, oil and juice. Remove 1/2 cup for basting. Add the roast to remaining marinade; seal bag and turn to coat. Refrigerate roast for 8 hours or overnight, turning occasionally. Cover and refrigerate reserved marinade.

2 Drain and discard marinade from roast. Grill roast, covered, over indirect heat, for 1 hour, turning every 15 minutes or until meat reaches desired doneness (for medium-rare, a meat thermometer should read 145°; medium, 160°; well-done, 170°), basting frequently with reserved marinate. Remove from the grill; let stand for 1 hour. Cover and refrigerate overnight.

3 Just before serving, prepare gravy mix according to package directions. Thinly slice roast; add to the gravy and heat through. Serve on rolls. **YIELD:** 12 servings.

This flavorful meal-in-one dish is all you need to serve for a satisfying and quick weeknight dinner.

Taste of Home Test Kitchen

CRESCENT BEEF CASSEROLE

Prep/Total Time: 30 min.

    1 pound lean ground beef
    1 cup diced zucchini
 1/4 cup chopped onion
 1/4 cup chopped green pepper
    2 teaspoons olive oil
    1 cup tomato puree
    1 teaspoon dried oregano
 1/4 teaspoon salt
 1/8 teaspoon pepper
1-1/2 cups mashed potatoes
    1 cup (4 ounces) crumbled feta cheese
    1 tube (8 ounces) refrigerated crescent rolls

1 In a large skillet, cook beef over medium heat until no longer pink; drain and set aside. In the same skillet, saute the zucchini, onion and green pepper in oil until crisp-tender. Stir in the beef, tomato puree, oregano, salt and pepper; heat through.

2 Spread mashed potatoes in an 11-in. x 7-in. baking dish coated with cooking spray. Top with beef mixture; sprinkle with feta cheese.

3 Unroll crescent dough. Separate into four rectangles; arrange three rectangles over the casserole. Bake at 375° for 12-15 minutes or until top is browned. Roll remaining dough into two crescent rolls; bake for another use. **YIELD:** 6 servings.

FESTIVE FILLETS

Prep/Total Time: 20 min.

When the weather's not right for outdoor cooking and you want an outstanding steak, this recipe is the answer. We like the zippy gravy so much we don't wait for inclement evenings to fix this.

Donna Cline // Pensacola, Florida

    1 envelope brown gravy mix
    1 jar (4-1/2 ounces) sliced mushrooms, drained
    2 teaspoons prepared horseradish
    4 beef tenderloin steaks (5 ounces *each*)
 1/8 teaspoon pepper

1 Prepare gravy according to package directions; add mushrooms and horseradish. Set aside and keep warm.

2 In a nonstick skillet, cook steaks over medium-high heat until meat reaches desired doneness. Season with pepper. Serve with gravy. **YIELD:** 4 servings.

EDITOR'S NOTE: Steaks can be baked. First brown in a skillet for 1 minute on each side, then transfer to an 8-in. square baking dish. Bake, uncovered, at 350° for 10-12 minutes or until meat reaches desired doneness.

This tender brisket is served with a savory cranberry gravy that's made right in the bag. You'll want to serve the slices with mashed potatoes just so you can drizzle the gravy over them.

Peggy Stigers // Fort Worth, Texas

BRISKET IN A BAG
Prep: 15 min. **Bake:** 2-1/2 hours

- 3 tablespoons all-purpose flour, *divided*
- 1 large oven roasting bag
- 1 fresh beef brisket (5 pounds), trimmed
- 1 can (16 ounces) whole-berry cranberry sauce
- 1 can (10-3/4 ounces) condensed cream of mushroom soup, undiluted
- 1 can (8 ounces) tomato sauce
- 1 envelope onion soup mix

1 Place 1 tablespoon flour in oven bag; shake to coat. Place bag in an ungreased 13-in. x 9-in. baking pan; place brisket in bag.

2 Combine the cranberry sauce, soup, tomato sauce, soup mix and remaining flour; pour over beef. Seal bag. Cut slits in top of bag according to package directions.

3 Bake at 325° for 2-1/2 to 3 hours or until meat is tender. Let stand for 5 minutes. Carefully remove brisket from bag. Thinly slice meat across the grain; serve with gravy. **YIELD:** 12 servings.

EDITOR'S NOTE: This is a fresh beef brisket, not corned beef.

CHUCK WAGON BURGERS
Prep/Total Time: 25 min.

Howdy, pardner! When our son requested a cowboy theme for his birthday party, I planned a Western-style meal including these savory burgers. In the spirit of true chuck wagon fare, I served them on large biscuits rather than buns.

Sharon Thompson // Oskaloosa, Iowa

- 1 envelope onion soup mix
- 1/2 cup water
- 2 pounds ground beef
- 1 tube (16.3 ounces) large refrigerated biscuits
- 1/8 teaspoon seasoned salt

1 In a large bowl, combine soup mix and water; crumble beef over mixture and mix well. Shape into eight 3/4-in.-thick patties.

2 Grill, uncovered, or broil 4 in. from the heat for 5-6 minutes on each side or until a meat thermometer reads 160° and juices run clear.

3 Meanwhile, place biscuits on ungreased baking sheets; sprinkle with seasoned salt. Bake at 375° for 12-14 minutes or until golden brown. Split; top each biscuit with a hamburger. **YIELD:** 8 servings.

TACO TWISTS

Prep: 15 min. **Bake:** 25 min.

Why just serve tacos in ordinary flour or corn tortillas? For a mouthwatering change of pace, bake the taco beef in flaky, golden crescent rolls. My family enjoys these for a hearty lunch or light dinner.

Carla Kreider // Quarryville, Pennsylvania

- 1 pound ground beef
- 1 large onion, chopped
- 2 cups (8 ounces) shredded cheddar cheese
- 1 jar (8 ounces) salsa
- 1 can (4 ounces) chopped green chilies
- 1 teaspoon garlic powder
- 1/2 teaspoon hot pepper sauce
- 1/4 teaspoon salt
- 1/4 teaspoon ground cumin
- 3 tubes (8 ounces *each*) refrigerated crescent rolls

1 In a skillet, cook beef and onion over medium heat until the meat is no longer pink; drain. Add the cheese, salsa, chilies, garlic powder, hot pepper sauce, salt and cumin; mix well.

2 Unroll crescent roll dough and separate into 12 rectangles. Place on ungreased baking sheets; press perforations to seal. Place 1/2 cup meat mixture in the center of each rectangle. Bring four corners to the center and twist; pinch to seal. Bake at 350° for 25-30 minutes or until golden brown. **YIELD:** 12 servings.

TIP

If you're counting your calories, you can lighten up these tasty Taco Twists by using either lean ground beef or ground turkey breast for the ground beef. Also use the reduced-fat versions of the cheddar cheese and the refrigerated crescent rolls.

I have good memories of eating this meal-in-one often while growing up. We all loved the flavor and seldom had leftovers. Instead of sprinkling it with cheddar, I sometimes create a cheese sauce using American cheese and milk. It makes it so cheesy!

Andrea Brandt // Newton, Kansas

HAMBURGER SUPPER
Prep/Total Time: 30 min.

- 1 **pound ground beef**
- 1-1/2 **cups water**
- 1/2 **teaspoon poultry seasoning**
- 1/4 **teaspoon pepper**
- 1 **envelope brown gravy mix**
- 1 **medium onion, sliced and separated into rings**
- 1 **medium carrot, sliced**
- 2 **medium potatoes, sliced**
- 1 **cup (4 ounces) shredded cheddar cheese**

1 In a large skillet, cook beef over medium heat until no longer pink; drain. Stir in the water, poultry seasoning and pepper. Bring to a boil. Stir in gravy mix. Cook and stir for 2 minutes or until slightly thickened.

2 Arrange the onion, carrot and potatoes over beef. Reduce heat; cover and simmer for 10-15 minutes or until vegetables are tender. Sprinkle with cheese. Cover and cook 3-5 minutes longer or until cheese is melted. **YIELD:** 4 servings.

TANGY ROUND STEAK STRIPS
Prep: 15 min. **Cook:** 1 hour

I like to fix this dish for a party or a buffet dinner. It adapts easily for any number and makes a delicious entree served over hot egg noodles.

Kathleen Roberts // St. Augustine, Florida

- 2 **pounds boneless beef round steak, cut into 2-1/2-inch strips**
- 1 **medium onion, chopped**
- 1/2 **cup French salad dressing**
- 1 **envelope Stroganoff sauce mix**

- 1-1/2 **cups water**
- 1 **jar (4-1/2 ounces) sliced mushrooms, drained**
- 1 **celery rib, chopped**
- 1 **teaspoon Worcestershire sauce**
Hot cooked noodles

1 In a large skillet, saute beef and onion in salad dressing until meat is no longer pink. Combine sauce mix and water until blended; stir into beef mixture. Stir in the mushrooms; celery and Worcestershire sauce. Bring to a boil. Reduce heat; cover and simmer for 60-70 minutes or until meat is tender. Serve with noodles. **YIELD:** 6-8 servings.

What do you get when you combine macaroni and cheese with pizza fixings? This hearty, family-pleasing casserole. It's easy and tasty, and my grandchildren really like it.
Nancy Porterfield // Gap Mills, West Virginia

PIZZA MACARONI BAKE

Prep: 30 min. **Bake:** 20 min.

- 1 package (7-1/4 ounces) macaroni and cheese dinner mix
- 6 cups water
- 1 pound ground beef
- 1 medium onion, chopped
- 1 small green pepper, chopped
- 1 cup (4 ounces) shredded cheddar cheese
- 1 jar (14 ounces) pizza sauce
- 1 package (3-1/2 ounces) sliced pepperoni
- 1 cup (4 ounces) shredded part-skim mozzarella cheese

1 Set aside the cheese packet from dinner mix. In a saucepan, bring water to a boil. Add macaroni; cook for 8-10 minutes or until tender.

2 Meanwhile, in a large skillet, cook the beef, onion and green pepper over medium heat until meat is no longer pink; drain. Drain macaroni; stir in the contents of cheese packet.

3 Transfer to a greased 13-in. x 9-in. baking dish. Sprinkle with cheddar cheese. Top with the beef mixture, pizza sauce, pepperoni and mozzarella cheese. Bake, uncovered, at 350° for 20-25 minutes or until heated through. **YIELD:** 6-8 servings.

SPICY FRENCH DIP

Prep: 5 min. **Cook:** 8 hours

If I'm cooking for a party or family get-together, I can put this beef in the slow cooker in the morning and then concentrate on other preparations. It's a great time-saver and never fails to get rave reviews.

Ginny Koeppen // Winnfield, Louisiana

- 1 boneless beef sirloin tip roast (about 3 pounds), cut in half
- 1/2 cup water
- 1 can (4 ounces) diced jalapeno peppers, drained
- 1 envelope Italian salad dressing mix
- 12 crusty rolls (5 inches)

1 Place beef in a 5-qt. slow cooker. In a small bowl, combine the water, jalapenos and dressing mix; pour over beef. Cover and cook on low for 8-10 hours or until meat is tender. Remove beef and shred using two forks. Skim fat from cooking juices. Serve beef on buns with juice. **YIELD:** 12 servings.

ONION-BEEF MUFFIN CUPS

Prep: 25 min. **Bake:** 15 min.

A tube of refrigerated biscuits makes these delicious bites so quick and easy! They're one of my tried-and-true, great lunch recipes and always bring raves. In fact, I usually double the recipe just to be sure I have leftovers.

Barbara Carlucci // Orange Park, Florida

- 3 medium onions, thinly sliced
- 1/4 cup butter, cubed
- 1 boneless beef top sirloin steak (1 inch thick and 6 ounces), cut into 1/8-inch slices
- 1 teaspoon all-purpose flour
- 1 teaspoon brown sugar
- 1/4 teaspoon salt
- 1/2 cup beef broth
- 1 tube (16.3 ounces) large refrigerated flaky biscuits
- 3/4 cup shredded part-skim mozzarella cheese
- 1/3 cup grated Parmesan cheese, *divided*

1 In a large skillet, cook onions in butter over medium heat for 10-12 minutes or until very tender. Remove and keep warm. In the same skillet, cook steak for 2-3 minutes or until no longer pink.

2 Return onions to pan. Stir in the flour, brown sugar and salt until blended; gradually add broth. Bring to a boil; cook and stir for 4-6 minutes or until thickened.

3 Separate biscuits; split each horizontally into three portions. Press onto the bottom and up the sides of eight ungreased muffin cups, overlapping the sides and tops. Fill each with about 2 tablespoons beef mixture.

4 Combine mozzarella cheese and 1/4 cup Parmesan cheese; sprinkle over filling. Fold dough over completely to enclose filling. Sprinkle with remaining Parmesan cheese.

5 Bake at 375° for 12-15 minutes or until golden brown. Let stand for 2 minutes before removing from pan. Serve warm. **YIELD:** 4 servings.

Simmering browned beef patties in bean and bacon soup and diced tomatoes makes a moist and tasty burger—no bun needed.

Taste of Home Test Kitchen

SOUTHWESTERN SKILLET BURGERS

Prep/Total Time: 30 min.

   2 **pounds ground beef**
1/2 **cup dry bread crumbs**
   1 **envelope taco seasoning**
   1 **can (14-1/2 ounces) diced tomatoes with onions, undrained**
   1 **can (11-1/2 ounces) condensed bean with bacon soup, undiluted**
1/2 **cup shredded cheddar cheese**

1 In a large bowl, combine the beef, bread crumbs and taco seasoning and mix well. Shape mixture into six 3/4-in.-thick patties.

2 In a large skillet over medium heat, cook patties for 3 minutes on each side or until browned. Remove patties; drain skillet.

3 Add tomatoes and soup to the skillet; return patties to the pan. Bring to a boil. Reduce heat; cover and simmer for 10 minutes or until a meat thermometer reads 160° and juices run clear. Sprinkle with cheese; cover and heat until cheese is melted. **YIELD:** 6 servings.

BEEF 'N' GRAVY ON POTATOES

Prep/Total Time: 30 min.

My husband was raised on meat and potatoes, and this quick dish is one of his favorites. Round out this dinner in a jiffy by zapping frozen vegetables in the microwave or tossing together a green salad.

Michelle Hallock // Warwick, Rhode Island

   3 **medium potatoes, peeled and cut into 1-inch cubes**
1/3 **cup water**
   1 **pound ground beef**
   1 **teaspoon garlic powder**
   1 **teaspoon onion powder**
   1 **envelope brown gravy mix**
1/4 **cup milk**

   3 **tablespoons butter, softened**
1/8 **teaspoon salt**
1/8 **teaspoon pepper**

1 Place potatoes and water in a microwave-safe dish. Cover and microwave on high for 8-10 minutes or until potatoes are tender. Meanwhile, in a large skillet, cook beef over medium heat until no longer pink; drain. Stir in garlic powder and onion powder.

2 Prepare gravy according to package directions. Place the potatoes in a large bowl; add the milk, butter, salt and pepper. Beat on medium speed until smooth. Serve beef and gravy over mashed potatoes. **YIELD:** 4 servings.

EDITOR'S NOTE: This recipe was tested in a 1,100-watt microwave.

BAKED VEGETABLE BEEF STEW

Prep: 20 min. **Bake:** 2 hours

1-1/2 pounds boneless beef sirloin tip roast, cut into 1-inch cubes
3 cups cubed peeled potatoes
3 celery ribs, cut into 1-inch pieces
1-1/2 cups cubed peeled sweet potatoes
3 large carrots, cut into 1-inch pieces
1 large onion, cut into 12 wedges
1 cup cubed peeled rutabaga
1 envelope reduced-sodium onion soup mix
2 teaspoons dried basil
1/2 teaspoon salt
1/4 teaspoon pepper
1/2 cup water
1 can (14-1/2 ounces) stewed tomatoes

1 In a large resealable plastic bag, combine the beef, vegetables, soup mix and seasonings. Seal bag; shake to coat evenly.

2 Transfer to a Dutch oven or 13-in. x 9-in. baking dish coated with cooking spray (pan will be very full). Pour water over beef mixture.

3 Cover and bake at 325° for 1-1/2 hours. Stir in tomatoes. Bake, uncovered, for 30-40 minutes or until beef and vegetables are tender, stirring after 25 minutes. **YIELD:** 6 servings.

SPINACH-MUSHROOM BEEF PATTIES

Prep/Total Time: 25 min.

Whether grilled or broiled, these juicy, flavorful burgers flecked with spinach and cheese were always a yummy summertime favorite. With or without a bun, they're sure to bring raves!
Jan Komarek // Friendswood, Texas

1 package (10 ounces) frozen chopped spinach, thawed and squeezed dry
1 cup (4 ounces) shredded part-skim mozzarella cheese
1 cup chopped fresh mushrooms
1 envelope onion mushroom soup mix
2 pounds ground beef

1 In a large bowl, combine spinach, cheese, mushrooms and soup mix. Crumble beef over mixture and mix well.

2 Shape into eight patties. Grill, covered, over medium-hot heat for 5-7 minutes on each side or until a meat thermometer reads 160° and meat juices run clear. **YIELD:** 8 servings.

Kids will really enjoy this cheesy pasta dish souped up with corn and beef; it's perfect for a chilly spring night.

Taste of Home Test Kitchen

WAGON WHEEL SUPPER

Prep/Total Time: 25 min.

  1/2 **pound uncooked wagon wheel pasta**
  1 **pound ground beef**
  1/2 **cup chopped onion**
1-3/4 **cups water**
  1 **can (10-3/4 ounces) condensed tomato soup, undiluted**
  1 **can (8-3/4 ounces) whole kernel corn, drained**
  1 **envelope spaghetti sauce mix**
  1/8 **teaspoon pepper**
  4 **ounces sliced Colby cheese, cut into strips**

1 Cook the pasta according to package directions. Meanwhile, in a large skillet, cook beef and onion over medium heat until meat is no longer pink; drain.

2 Stir in water, soup, corn, spaghetti sauce mix and pepper. Bring to a boil. Reduce heat; simmer, uncovered, for 2-3 minutes or until heated through.

3 Drain the pasta; stir into the beef mixture. Top with cheese; cook and stir for 2 minutes or until cheese is melted. **YIELD:** 4 servings.

CHILI CHEESE TURNOVERS

Prep/Total Time: 30 min.

I serve these stuffed pockets with a creamy dipping sauce. They're a great grab-and-go lunch or even a hearty late-night snack. Using tubes of refrigerated dough keeps the preparation quick.
Margaret Wilson // Hemet, California

  2 **tubes (13.8 ounces each) refrigerated pizza crust**
  2 **cups (8 ounces) shredded Mexican cheese blend**
  1 **can (15 ounces) chili without beans**
  1 **can (15 ounces) ranch-style beans or chili beans, drained**
  1 **can (10 ounces) diced tomatoes and green chilies, drained**
  1 **cup (8 ounces) sour cream**

1 On a lightly floured surface, press pizza dough into two 12-inch squares. Cut each into four 6-inch squares. In a large bowl, combine the cheese, chili and beans. Spoon 1/2 cup in the center of each square. Fold dough diagonally over filling; press edges to seal.

2 Place in two greased 15-in. x 10-in. x 1-in. baking pans. Bake at 425° for 13-18 minutes or until golden brown. Cool for 5 minutes.

3 Meanwhile, in a small bowl, combine tomatoes and sour cream. Serve with turnovers. **YIELD:** 8 servings.

Filled with a scrumptious, packaged rice mixture and seasoned with teriyaki sauce, these steaks are a favorite. Just four ingredients are required for the delightful entree, so it comes together in a snap.

Ardith Baker // Beaverton, Oregon

WILD RICE-STUFFED STEAKS
Prep/Total Time: 30 min.

> 1 package (6.2 ounces) fast-cooking long grain and wild rice mix
> 1/4 cup chopped green onions
> 6 New York strip steaks (about 12 ounces *each*)
> 1/2 cup teriyaki sauce, *divided*

1 Cook the rice according to package directions for microwave; cool. Stir in onions. Cut a pocket in each steak by slicing to within 1/2 in. of opposite side. Stuff each with 1/4 cup rice mixture; secure with toothpicks. Brush steaks with 2 tablespoons teriyaki sauce.

2 Place on a broiler pan. Broil 4-6 in. from the heat for 4-6 minutes. Turn steaks; brush with 2 tablespoons teriyaki sauce. Broil 6-8 minutes longer or until meat reaches desired doneness (for medium-rare, a meat thermometer should read 145°; medium, 160°; well-done, 170°), basting frequently with remaining sauce. Discard toothpicks. **YIELD:** 6 servings.

SUPER CALZONES
Prep: 30 min. **Bake:** 20 min.

A friend gave this recipe to me at my wedding shower. I realized then and there that I'd better learn how to cook! My husband loves these handheld pizzas.

Laronda Warrick // Parker, Kansas

> 1/2 pound ground beef
> 2 tablespoons finely chopped onion
> 2 tablespoons finely chopped green pepper
> 1 garlic clove, minced
> 1 can (15 ounces) tomato sauce
> 1 teaspoon Italian seasoning
> 1 tube (13.8 ounces) refrigerated pizza crust
> 1 package (3 ounces) cream cheese, softened
> 1 cup (4 ounces) shredded part-skim mozzarella cheese
> 1 can (4 ounces) mushroom stems and pieces, drained
> 1 can (2-1/4 ounces) sliced ripe olives, drained

1 In a large skillet, cook the beef, onion, green pepper and garlic over medium heat until meat is no longer pink; drain and set aside.

2 In a small saucepan, bring tomato sauce and Italian seasoning to a boil. Reduce heat; cover and simmer for 5 minutes. Stir 1/2 cup into the meat mixture; keep remaining sauce warm.

3 Unroll pizza crust onto a floured surface. Roll into a 12-in. square; cut into four squares. Spread cream cheese over each to within 1/2 in. of edges. Top with meat mixture. Sprinkle with mozzarella cheese, mushrooms and olives. Fold dough over filling, forming a triangle; press edges with a fork to seal.

4 Place on a greased baking sheet. Bake at 400° for 20-25 minutes or until golden brown. Serve with the remaining sauce. **YIELD:** 4 servings.

HEARTY NEW ENGLAND DINNER

Prep: 20 min. **Cook:** 7-1/2 hours

This favorite slow cooker recipe came from a friend. At first, my husband was a bit skeptical about a roast that wasn't fixed in the oven, but he loves the old-fashioned goodness of this version. The horseradish in the gravy adds zip.

Claire McCombs // San Diego, California

2 medium carrots, sliced
1 medium onion, sliced
1 celery rib, sliced
1 boneless beef chuck roast (about 3 pounds)
1 teaspoon salt, *divided*
1/4 teaspoon pepper
1 envelope onion soup mix
2 cups water
1 tablespoon white vinegar
1 bay leaf
1/2 small head cabbage, cut into wedges

3 tablespoons butter
2 tablespoons all-purpose flour
1 tablespoon dried minced onion
2 tablespoons prepared horseradish

1 Place carrots, onion and celery in a 5-qt. slow cooker. Cut roast in half. Place roast over vegetables; sprinkle with 1/2 teaspoon salt and pepper. Add the soup mix, water, vinegar and bay leaf. Cover and cook on low for 7-9 hours or until beef is tender.

2 Remove beef and keep warm; discard bay leaf. Add cabbage. Cover and cook on high for 30-40 minutes or until cabbage is tender.

3 Meanwhile, melt butter in a small saucepan; stir in flour and onion. Skim fat from cooking liquid in slow cooker. Add 1-1/2 cups cooking liquid to the saucepan. Stir in horseradish and remaining salt; bring to a boil. Cook and stir for 2 minutes or until thickened and bubbly. Serve with roast and vegetables. **YIELD:** 6-8 servings.

My mom used to make this wonderful dish, and it's always been one that I love. I especially like how the thick gravy drapes both the meat and the potatoes.
Deanne Stephens // McMinnville, Oregon

ROUND STEAK ITALIANO
Prep: 15 min. **Cook:** 7-1/4 hours

- 2 pounds boneless beef top round steak
- 1 can (8 ounces) tomato sauce
- 2 tablespoons onion soup mix
- 2 tablespoons canola oil
- 2 tablespoons red wine vinegar
- 1 teaspoon ground oregano
- 1/2 teaspoon garlic powder
- 1/4 teaspoon pepper
- 8 medium potatoes (7 to 8 ounces *each*)
- 1 tablespoon cornstarch
- 1 tablespoon cold water

1 Cut steak into serving-size pieces; place in a 5-qt. slow cooker. In a large bowl, combine the tomato sauce, soup mix, oil, vinegar, oregano, garlic powder and pepper; pour over meat.

2 Scrub and pierce potatoes; place over meat. Cover and cook on low for 7 to 7-1/2 hours or until meat and potatoes are tender.

3 Remove meat and potatoes; keep warm. For gravy, pour cooking juices into a small saucepan; skim fat. Combine cornstarch and water until smooth; gradually stir into juices. Bring to a boil; cook and stir for 2 minutes or until thickened. Serve with meat and potatoes. **YIELD:** 8 servings.

FLAVORFUL BEEF IN GRAVY
Prep: 15 min. **Cook:** 7 hours

Served over noodles, this fantastic supper showcases tender chunks of savory beef stew meat. Canned soups combined with onion soup mix to make a mouthwatering gravy. With a green salad and crusty bread, dinner is complete.
Cheryl Sindergard // Plover, Iowa

- 1/3 cup all-purpose flour
- 3 pounds beef stew meat, cut into 1-inch cubes
- 3 tablespoons canola oil
- 2 cans (10-3/4 ounces *each*) condensed cream of mushroom soup, undiluted
- 1 can (10-3/4 ounces) condensed golden mushroom soup, undiluted
- 1 can (10-3/4 ounces) condensed cream of celery soup, undiluted
- 1-1/3 cups milk
- 1 envelope onion soup mix
- **Hot cooked noodles *or* mashed potatoes**

1 Place flour in a large resealable plastic bag; add beef and toss to coat. In a skillet, brown beef in oil.

2 Transfer beef to a 5-qt. slow cooker. Stir in the soups, milk and soup mix. Cover and cook on low for 7-8 hours or until the meat is tender. Serve with noodles or potatoes. **YIELD:** 10-12 servings.

I came up with this dish after combining several different recipes. I wrap up each beef tenderloin, topped with a tasty mushroom mixture, in a sheet of puff pastry. It sounds like a lot of work, but it really isn't.

Julie Mahoney // St. Edward, Nebraska

TENDERLOIN IN PUFF PASTRY

Prep: 20 min. + chilling **Bake:** 20 min.

- 4 **beef tenderloin steaks (1-3/4 inches thick and about 5 ounces** *each***)**
- 1 **tablespoon canola oil**
- 1/2 **pound sliced fresh mushrooms**
- 4 **green onions, chopped**
- 1/4 **cup butter**
- 1/2 **teaspoon salt**
- 1/4 **teaspoon pepper**
- 1 **frozen puff pastry sheet, thawed**
- 1 **egg**
- 1 **tablespoon water**

1 In a large skillet, brown steaks in oil on both sides. Place a wire rack on a baking sheet. Transfer steaks to wire rack; refrigerate for 1 hour. In the same skillet, saute mushrooms and onions in butter until tender; drain. Stir in the salt and pepper.

2 On a lightly floured surface, roll pastry into a 13-in. square. Cut into four squares. Place one steak in the center of each square; top with mushroom mixture. Combine egg and water; brush over pastry.

3 Bring up corners to center and tuck in edges; press to seal. Place on a parchment paper-lined baking sheet. Cover and refrigerate for 1 hour or overnight.

4 Bake, uncovered, at 400° for 20-25 minutes or until pastry is golden brown and the meat reaches desired doneness (for medium-rare, a meat thermometer should read 145°; medium, 160°; well-done, 170°). **YIELD:** 4 servings.

SUPER SLOPPY JOES

Prep/Total Time: 30 min.

Five ingredients are all you need for these hearty sandwiches. They're great for family gatherings. Onion soup mix and sweet pickle relish add tangy flavor without much effort.

Marge Napalo // Brunswick, Ohio

- 3 **pounds ground beef**
- 3 **cups ketchup**
- 2/3 **cup sweet pickle relish**
- 1 **envelope onion soup mix**
- 14 **hamburger buns, split**

1 In a Dutch oven, cook beef over medium heat until no longer pink; drain. Stir in the ketchup, relish and soup mix; heat through. Spoon about 1/2 cup onto each bun. Or, cool and freeze in freezer containers for up to 3 months.

2 **To use frozen sloppy joes:** Thaw in the refrigerator; place in a saucepan and heat through. Serve on buns. **YIELD:** 14 servings.

A packaged rice mix speeds up preparation of this meal-in-one entree. Cayenne pepper gives the beef a little kick, and an assortment of veggies add color and crunch.

Janelle Christensen // Big Lake, Minnesota

BEEF AND WILD RICE MEDLEY
Prep: 5 min. **Cook:** 40 min.

- 1/2 teaspoon garlic powder
- 1/2 teaspoon dried thyme
- 1/8 teaspoon cayenne pepper
- 1 pound boneless beef sirloin steak, cut into 3/4-inch cubes
- 1 tablespoon canola oil
- 1/4 cup sliced celery
- 1/4 cup julienned green pepper
- 2-1/4 cups water
- 1 package (6 ounces) long grain and wild rice mix
- 1 small tomato, chopped
- 2 tablespoons chopped green onion

1 In a small bowl, combine the garlic powder, thyme and cayenne. Sprinkle over beef.

2 In a large saucepan coated with cooking spray, cook beef in oil until no longer pink; drain. Stir in celery and green pepper; cook 2 minutes longer or until vegetables are crisp-tender. Stir in the water and rice mix with contents of seasoning packet.

3 Bring to a boil. Reduce heat; cover and simmer for 23-28 minutes or until rice is tender. Stir in tomato; heat through. Sprinkle with onion. **YIELD:** 4 servings.

TIP

If you'd like to bulk up this dish with even more veggies, cook julienned red pepper, broccoli florets and cauliflowerets with the celery and green pepper. If those aren't your family's favorite vegetables, just stir in cooked sliced carrots or cooked green beans with the tomato.

pork

RANCH-STYLE PORK BURGERS

Prep/Total Time: 30 min.

1/2 pound ground pork
1 tablespoon ranch salad dressing mix
1 teaspoon dried minced onion
1/4 teaspoon pepper
2 slices Swiss cheese
2 hamburger buns, split
Lettuce leaves and tomato slices, optional

1 In a small bowl, combine the pork, dressing mix, onion and pepper. Shape into two patties. Grill, uncovered, over medium heat for 7-8 minutes on each side or until a meat thermometer reads 160°.

2 Top each patty with a cheese slice; cover and grill just until cheese begins to melt. Serve on buns with lettuce and tomato if desired. **YIELD:** 2 servings.

TANGY MEATBALLS

Prep: 30 min. **Bake:** 1-3/4 hours

These tasty meatballs floating in a thick, tangy sauce are a hearty main dish you can make ahead. They are sure to please.
Inez Orsburn // De Motte, Indiana

2 cups cubed rye bread
2 cups milk
3 eggs, lightly beaten
1 envelope onion soup mix
2 teaspoons salt
1-1/2 teaspoons dried thyme
1/2 teaspoon pepper
1/4 teaspoon ground nutmeg
5 pounds ground beef
2 pounds bulk pork sausage
1 bottle (40 ounces) ketchup
2 cups crab apple *or* apple jelly, melted
4 teaspoons browning sauce, optional

1 Combine the bread cubes and milk; let stand for 5 minutes. Add the eggs, soup mix and seasonings; mix well. Crumble meat into bread mixture; stir just until blended. Form into 1-1/2-in. balls.

2 Place meatballs on four greased racks in four shallow baking pans. Bake, uncovered, at 350° for 45 minutes; drain pans.

3 Meanwhile, combine ketchup, jelly and browning sauce if desired; spoon over meatballs. Reduce heat to 300°; cover and bake for 1 hour. **YIELD:** 7 to 7-1/2 dozen.

GRILLED STUFFED PORK TENDERLOIN

Prep: 20 min. + marinating **Grill:** 25 min.

We serve this stuffed tenderloin with a salad and a glass of wine. It's very good and so easy you won't believe it.

Bobbie Carr // Lake Oswego, Oregon

2 pork tenderloins (3/4 pound *each*)
3/4 cup dry red wine *or* reduced-sodium beef broth
1/3 cup packed brown sugar
1/4 cup ketchup
2 tablespoons reduced-sodium soy sauce
2 garlic cloves, minced
1 teaspoon curry powder
1/2 teaspoon minced fresh gingerroot
1/4 teaspoon pepper
1-1/4 cups water
2 tablespoons butter
1 package (6 ounces) stuffing mix

1 Cut a lengthwise slit down the center of each tenderloin to within 1/2 in. of bottom. In a large resealable plastic bag, combine the wine, brown sugar, ketchup, soy sauce, garlic, curry, ginger and pepper; add pork. Seal bag and turn to coat; refrigerate for 2-3 hours.

2 In a small saucepan, bring water and butter to a boil. Stir in stuffing mix. Remove from the heat; cover and let stand for 5 minutes. Cool.

3 Drain and discard marinade. Open tenderloins so they lie flat; spread stuffing down the center of each. Close tenderloins; tie at 1-1/2-in. intervals with kitchen string.

4 Coat grill rack with cooking spray before starting the grill. Prepare grill for indirect heat. Grill pork, covered, over indirect medium-hot heat for 25-40 minutes or until a meat thermometer reads 160°. Let stand for 5 minutes before slicing. **YIELD:** 6 servings.

BEANS AND FRANKS BAKE

Prep: 20 min. **Bake:** 40 min.

I have made this casserole several times, and it's always a hit. The kid-pleasing combo has a sweet flavor from the baked beans and the corn bread topping.

Roxanne VanGelder // Rochester, New Hampshire

- 2 packages (8-1/2 ounces *each*) corn bread/muffin mix
- 1 can (28 ounces) baked beans
- 4 hot dogs, halved lengthwise and sliced
- 1/2 pound sliced bacon, cooked and crumbled
- 1 cup ketchup
- 1/2 cup packed brown sugar
- 1/2 cup chopped onion
- 2 cups (8 ounces) shredded part-skim mozzarella cheese

1 Prepare corn bread batter according to package directions; set aside. In a large bowl, combine the beans, hot dogs, bacon, ketchup, brown sugar and onion. Transfer to two greased 8-in. square baking dishes. Sprinkle with cheese; top with corn bread batter.

2 Cover and freeze one casserole for up to 3 months. Bake the second casserole, uncovered, at 350° for 40-45 minutes or until a toothpick inserted near the center comes out clean.

3 **To use frozen casserole:** Remove from the freezer 30 minutes before baking. Cover and bake at 350° for 40 minutes. Uncover; bake 15-20 minutes longer or until heated through. **YIELD:** 2 casseroles (4 servings each).

It's a snap to make this dish using baking mix. I got the idea from a similar recipe with hamburger and cheddar cheese. That version was too bland for my family, but I made a few changes, and this is a hit!

Bonnie Marlow // Ottoville, Ohio

MONTEREY SAUSAGE PIE

Prep: 15 min. **Bake:** 25 min. + standing

- 1 pound bulk pork sausage
- 1 cup chopped onion
- 1 cup chopped sweet red pepper
- 1/2 cup chopped fresh mushrooms
- 3 teaspoons minced garlic
- 2-1/2 cups (10 ounces) shredded Monterey Jack cheese, *divided*
- 1-1/3 cups milk
- 3 eggs
- 3/4 cup biscuit/baking mix
- 3/4 teaspoon rubbed sage
- 1/4 teaspoon pepper

1 In a large skillet, cook the sausage, onion, red pepper, mushrooms and garlic over medium heat until meat is no longer pink; drain. Stir in 2 cups cheese. Transfer to a greased 9-in. deep-dish pie plate.

2 In a small bowl, combine the milk, eggs, biscuit mix, sage and pepper. Pour over sausage mixture.

3 Bake at 400° for 20-25 minutes or until a knife inserted near the center comes out clean. Sprinkle with the remaining cheese; bake 1-2 minutes longer or until cheese is melted. Let stand for 10 minutes before cutting. **YIELD:** 8 servings.

SEASONED PORK SANDWICHES

Prep: 20 min. **Cook:** 5 hours

This is one of those meals that my husband never seems to get tired of. The bonus for me is that it's quick, easy to make and even easier to clean up!

Jacque Thompson // Houston, Texas

- 1 boneless whole pork loin roast (2 to 3 pounds)
- 1 tablespoon fajita seasoning mix
- 1/4 teaspoon garlic powder
- 1/2 cup Italian salad dressing
- 1/4 cup Worcestershire sauce
- 8 sandwich rolls, split

1 Cut roast in half; place in a 5-qt. slow cooker. Sprinkle with fajita seasoning and garlic powder. Pour salad dressing and Worcestershire sauce over meat. Cover and cook on low for 5-6 hours or until tender.

2 Remove roast; shred meat with two forks. Return to cooking juices; heat through. Using a slotted spoon, serve pork on rolls. **YIELD:** 8 servings.

SOUTH-OF-THE-BORDER SUBMARINE

Prep: 20 min. **Bake:** 20 min.

- **2 pounds ground pork**
- **1/2 cup chopped onion**
- **1 envelope taco seasoning**
- **1 teaspoon salt**
- **1 can (8 ounces) tomato sauce**
- **1-1/2 cups (6 ounces) shredded sharp cheddar cheese, *divided***
- **1/2 cup chopped pimiento-stuffed olives**
- **1 unsliced loaf French *or* Italian breadbread (1 pound)**

1 In a large skillet, cook pork and onion until meat is no longer pink; drain. Add taco seasoning and salt. Stir in tomato sauce, 1/2 cup cheese and olives; cook over medium heat for 5-10 minutes, stirring occasionally.

2 Cut bread in half lengthwise. Remove center from each half to form a 1-in. shell. Crumble removed bread to make 1 cup crumbs; stir into meat mixture. Place bread shells on a baking sheet; toast lightly under broiler. Fill with meat mixture and top with remaining cheese. Tent loosely with foil.

3 Bake at 350° for 20 minutes or until cheese is melted and filling is heated through. Cut into slices. **YIELD:** 6-8 servings.

HAM AND SWISS CASSEROLE

Prep: 15 min. **Bake:** 30 min.

Here's a delightfully rich and creamy, all-in-one meal. My family just loves the easy-to-fix sauce, and it's a great way to use up leftover ham. For a delectable, creamy and comforting side dish, simply eliminate the ham.

Julie Jackman // Bountiful, Utah

- **8 ounces uncooked penne pasta**
- **2 envelopes country gravy mix**
- **1 package (10 ounces) frozen chopped spinach, thawed and squeezed dry**
- **2 cups (8 ounces) shredded Swiss cheese**
- **2 cups cubed fully cooked ham**
- **4-1/2 teaspoons ground mustard**

1 Cook pasta according to package directions. Meanwhile, in a large saucepan, cook gravy mix according to package directions. Stir in the spinach, cheese, ham and mustard. Drain the pasta; stir into ham mixture.

2 Transfer to a greased 13-in. x 9-in. baking dish. Cover and bake at 350° for 20 minutes. Uncover; bake 10-15 minutes longer or until heated through. **YIELD:** 8 servings.

Mandarin oranges add a splash of color and citrus flavor to this tasty entree. With just a few minutes of prep, it's a complete dinner.
Melanie Gable // Roseville, Michigan

MANDARIN PORK AND WILD RICE

Prep/Total Time: 25 min.

> 4 boneless pork loin chops (3/4 inch thick and 5 ounces *each*), cut into strips
> 1/4 teaspoon pepper
> 1/8 teaspoon salt
> 1 tablespoon canola oil
> 1 can (11 ounces) mandarin oranges
> 1-1/2 cups water

> 1 package (6.2 ounces) fast-cooking long grain and wild rice mix
> 1/4 cup thinly sliced green onions

1 Sprinkle pork with pepper and salt. In a large skillet, brown pork in oil. Meanwhile, drain oranges, reserving juice; set oranges aside.

2 Add the water, rice mix with contents of seasoning packet, onions and reserved juice to the skillet. Bring to a boil. Reduce heat; cover and simmer for 10-12 minutes or until meat is no longer pink and liquid is absorbed. Stir in oranges; heat through. **YIELD:** 4 servings.

CITY KABOBS

Prep: 20 min. **Cook:** 1 hour

This old-fashioned mock chicken dish, actually made of tender perfectly seasoned pork, is one that my mom relied on often. The delicious gravy is so good over mashed potatoes.
Barbara Hyatt // Folsom, California

> 2 pounds boneless pork, cut into cubes
> 1/2 cup all-purpose flour
> 1/2 teaspoon garlic salt
> 1/4 teaspoon pepper
> 1/4 cup butter, cubed
> 3 tablespoons canola oil
> 1 envelope onion soup mix
> 1 can (14-1/2 ounces) chicken broth
> 1 cup water
> Hot mashed potatoes

1 Thread pork on small wooden skewers. Combine the flour, garlic salt and pepper on a plate; roll kabobs in flour mixture until coated.

2 In a large skillet, heat butter and oil over medium heat. Brown kabobs, turning frequently; drain. Sprinkle with soup mix. Add broth and water. Reduce heat; cover and simmer for 1 hour or until tender.

3 Remove kabobs and keep warm. If desired, thicken the pan juices and serve with mashed potatoes and kabobs. **YIELD:** 4-6 servings.

We first had Aunt Dolly's potpie at a family get-together. We loved it and were so happy she shared the recipe. Now, we make it almost every time we bake a ham.

Mary Zinsmeister // Slinger, Wisconsin

AU GRATIN HAM POTPIE

Prep: 15 min. **Bake:** 40 min.

  1 package (4.9 ounces) au gratin potatoes
1-1/2 cups boiling water
  2 cups frozen peas and carrots
1-1/2 cups cubed fully cooked ham
  1 can (10-3/4 ounces) condensed cream of chicken soup, undiluted
  1 can (4 ounces) mushroom stems and pieces, drained
1/2 cup milk
1/2 cup sour cream
  1 jar (2 ounces) diced pimientos, drained
  1 sheet refrigerated pie pastry

1 In a large bowl, combine the potatoes, contents of sauce mix and water. Stir in the peas and carrots, ham, soup, mushrooms, milk, sour cream and pimientos. Transfer to an ungreased 2-qt. round baking dish.

2 Roll out pastry to fit top of dish; place over potato mixture. Flute edges; cut slits in pastry. Bake at 400° for 40-45 minutes or until golden brown. Let stand for 5 minutes before serving. **YIELD:** 4-6 servings.

SAVORY SAUSAGE AND PEPPERS

Prep/Total Time: 30 min.

My mother gave me the recipe for this tasty kielbasa meal that's loaded with colorful pepper chunks. I like to use a soup mix that adds a hint of garlic, but you can substitute other varieties to suit your family's tastes.

Rickey Madden // Americus, Georgia

1/2 pound smoked kielbasa *or* Polish sausage, cut into 1/2-inch slices
  3 tablespoons olive oil
  1 *each* medium sweet red pepper, sweet yellow pepper and green pepper, cut into 1-inch chunks
  1 medium onion, cut into small wedges
  1 cup water
  1 package (1.2 ounces) herb and garlic soup mix
1/8 teaspoon hot pepper sauce
Hot cooked rice

1 In a large skillet, brown sausage in oil over medium-high heat. Remove with a slotted spoon and keep warm. In drippings, saute peppers and onion until crisp-tender.

2 In a large bowl, combine the water and contents of one soup mix envelope (save the second envelope for another use). Add soup mixture, hot pepper sauce and sausage to the vegetables. Reduce heat; cover and simmer for 5 minutes or until thickened. Serve with rice. **YIELD:** 2-3 servings.

MOO SHU PORK

Prep/Total Time: 20 min.

Stir-fried vegetables make a nice accompaniment to this great dish. Since it takes only 20 minutes to make, it's perfect for a weeknight dinner.

Taste of Home Test Kitchen

- 1 tablespoon cornstarch
- 1/4 cup cold water
- 2 tablespoons reduced-sodium soy sauce
- 2 teaspoons minced fresh gingerroot
- 5 boneless pork loin chops (4 ounces *each*), cut into thin strips
- 2 teaspoons sesame oil
- 1 teaspoon minced garlic
- 1/4 cup hoisin sauce
- 3 cups coleslaw mix with carrots
- 8 flour tortillas (8 inches), warmed

1 In a small bowl, combine the cornstarch, water, soy sauce and ginger until blended; set aside. In a large skillet, saute pork in oil for 3 minutes. Add garlic and saute for 1-2 minutes longer or until meat is no longer pink.

2 Stir cornstarch mixture and add to the skillet. Bring to a boil; cook and stir for 1-2 minutes or until thickened. Stir in hoisin sauce. Add coleslaw mix; stir to coat. Spoon about 1/2 cup pork mixture into the center of each tortilla; roll up tightly. **YIELD:** 4 servings.

TIP

As a side for this pork dish, you can stir-fry a variety of veggies, such as the snow peas and baby carrots shown here, or broccoli florets, cauli-flowerets, red or green pepper strips, water chestnuts and onion slices. After cooking, drizzle a little dark sesame oil over the vegetables.

This meal-in-one grills to perfection in heavy-duty foil packets and is ideal for camping. Loaded with chunks of bratwurst, red potatoes, mushrooms and carrots, it's easy to season with onion soup mix and a little soy sauce.

Janice Meyer // Medford, Wisconsin

BRATWURST SUPPER

Prep: 10 min. **Grill:** 45 min.

3 pounds uncooked bratwurst links
3 pounds small red potatoes, cut into wedges
1 pound baby carrots
1 large red onion, sliced and separated into rings
2 jars (4-1/2 ounces *each*) whole mushrooms, drained
1/4 cup butter, cubed
1 envelope onion soup mix
2 tablespoons soy sauce
1/2 teaspoon pepper

1 For each of two foil packets, arrange a double thickness of heavy-duty foil (about 17 in. x 15 in.) on a flat surface.

2 Cut brats into thirds. Divide the brats, potatoes, carrots, onion and mushrooms evenly between the two double-layer foil pieces. Dot with butter. Sprinkle with soup mix, soy sauce and pepper. Bring edges of foil together; crimp to seal, forming two large packets. Seal tightly; turn to coat.

3 Grill, covered, over medium heat for 23-28 minutes on each side or until vegetables are tender and sausage is no longer pink. **YIELD:** 12 servings.

APPLE PORK CHOP CASSEROLE

Prep: 30 min. **Bake:** 30 min.

I've loved this recipe since the first time I tried it. The apple and raisins give a nice homey flavor to the stuffing.

Beverly Baxter // Kansas City, Kansas

2 boneless pork loin chops (3/4 inch and 8 ounces *each*)
2 teaspoons canola oil
3/4 cup water
1 tablespoon butter
1 small tart green apple, chopped
2 tablespoons raisins

1-1/2 cups crushed chicken stuffing mix
2/3 cup condensed cream of mushroom soup, undiluted

1 In a large skillet, brown meat in oil for about 5 minutes on each side. Meanwhile, in a large saucepan, combine the water, butter, apple and raisins; bring to a boil. Stir in stuffing mix. Remove from the heat; cover and let stand for 5 minutes. Fluff with a fork.

2 Transfer to a greased shallow 1-qt. baking dish. Top with meat. Spoon soup over meat and stuffing.

3 Cover and bake at 350° for 30-35 minutes or until a meat thermometer inserted into pork chops reads 160°. **YIELD:** 2 servings.

This is a dish Mom used to make when I was still living at home. The sweetness of the apple mixture makes such a nice complement to the savory stuffing and chops.

Simone Greene // Winchester, Virginia

SMOTHERED PORK CHOPS
Prep/Total Time: 30 min.

- 1 package (6 ounces) chicken stuffing mix
- 4 boneless pork loin chops (6 ounces *each*)
- 1 tablespoon butter
- 4 medium apples, peeled and cut into wedges
- 1/2 cup packed brown sugar
- 1/4 cup water
- 1/4 teaspoon salt
- 1/4 teaspoon ground cinnamon

1 Prepare stuffing mix according to package directions. Meanwhile, in a large skillet, cook pork chops in butter over medium heat for 2-3 minutes on each side or until lightly browned. Stir in the apples, brown sugar, water and salt. Bring to a boil. Reduce heat; cover and simmer for 8-10 minutes or until apples are tender.

2 Top with stuffing; sprinkle with cinnamon. Cook, uncovered, over medium heat for 10-12 minutes or until a meat thermometer reads 160°. **YIELD:** 4 servings.

ROAST PORK AND POTATOES
Prep: 20 min. **Bake:** 2-1/2 hours + standing

We used to raise our own hogs. This recipe was given to me by a fellow farmer who also had pork on the dinner table a couple of times a week.

Denise Collins // Chillicothe, Ohio

- 1 envelope onion soup mix
- 2 garlic cloves, minced
- 1 tablespoon dried rosemary, crushed
- 1/2 teaspoon salt
- 1/2 teaspoon pepper
- 1/4 teaspoon ground cloves
- 3 cups water, *divided*
- 1 bone-in pork loin roast (4 to 5 pounds)
- 24 small red potatoes, halved (2 to 3 pounds)
- 1-1/2 cups sliced onions

1 In a large bowl, combine the soup mix, garlic, rosemary, salt, pepper and cloves. Stir in 1/2 cup water; let stand for 3 minutes.

2 Place roast fat side up on a greased rack in a roasting pan. Pour remaining water into the pan. Combine potatoes and onions; spoon around the roast. Brush vegetables and roast with seasoning mixture.

3 Bake, uncovered, at 325° for 2-1/2 to 3 hours or until a meat thermometer reads 160° and potatoes are tender. Baste and stir potatoes occasionally. Tent with foil if browning too fast. Thicken juices for gravy if desired. Let stand for 10 minutes before slicing. **YIELD:** 8-10 servings.

APPLE HAM BAKE

Prep: 20 min. **Bake:** 35 min.

*A great use for leftover ham, this dish has been served at
countless church suppers. A puffy topping covers a mixture of
sweet potatoes, ham and apples.*

Amanda Denton // Barre, Vermont

- 3 medium tart apples, peeled and sliced
- 2 medium sweet potatoes, peeled and thinly sliced
- 3 cups cubed fully cooked ham
- 3 tablespoons brown sugar
- 1/2 teaspoon salt
- 1/4 teaspoon pepper
- 1/4 teaspoon curry powder
- 2 tablespoons cornstarch
- 1/3 cup apple juice
- 1 cup pancake mix
- 1 cup milk
- 2 tablespoons butter, melted
- 1/2 teaspoon ground mustard

1 In a large skillet, combine the apples, sweet potatoes, ham, brown sugar, salt, pepper and curry. Cook over medium heat until apples are crisp-tender; drain. Combine cornstarch and apple juice until smooth; stir into apple mixture. Bring to a boil; cook and stir for 1-2 minutes or until mixture is thickened.

2 Transfer to a greased 2-qt. baking dish. Cover and bake at 375° for 10 minutes or until sweet potatoes are tender. Meanwhile, in a large bowl, whisk together the pancake mix, milk, butter and mustard; pour over ham mixture.

3 Bake, uncovered, for 25-30 minutes or until puffed and golden brown. **YIELD:** 8 servings.

Tart apple adds a delicious hint of autumn to the moist stuffing that fills these savory chops. The elegant entree looks like you fussed but comes together in just an hour or less.
Taste of Home Test Kitchen

STUFFED PORK CHOPS
Prep: 20 min. **Cook:** 25 min. + cooling

- 1 bacon strip, diced
- 1/4 cup chopped onion
- 1/2 cup corn bread stuffing mix
- 1/2 cup chopped peeled tart apple
- 2 tablespoons chopped pecans
- 2 tablespoons raisins
- 2 tablespoons plus 1 cup chicken broth, *divided*
- 1/4 teaspoon rubbed sage
- Dash ground allspice
- 2 bone-in pork loin chops (1 inch thick and 7 ounces *each*)
- 1 tablespoon butter

1 In a 6-qt. pressure cooker, cook the bacon and onion over medium heat until the bacon is crisp. In a small bowl, combine the bacon mixture, stuffing mix, apple, pecans, raisins, 2 tablespoons broth, sage and allspice. Cut a pocket in each pork chop by slicing almost to the bone; fill with stuffing.

2 In pressure cooker, brown chops in butter on both sides; add remaining broth. Close cover securely; place pressure regulator on vent pipe. Bring cooker to full pressure over high heat. Reduce heat to medium-high and cook for 15 minutes. (Pressure regulator should maintain a slow steady rocking motion; adjust heat if needed.)

3 Remove from the heat; immediately cool according to manufacturer's directions until pressure is completely reduced. **YIELD:** 2 servings.

CRANBERRY PORK CHOPS
Prep/Total Time: 20 min.

Family and guests will really enjoy the tender chops with the sweet-tart sauce. The sauce is equally good on chicken.
Tina Lust // Nevada, Ohio

- 4 boneless pork loin chops (6 ounces *each*)
- 1 tablespoon canola oil
- 1 can (16 ounces) whole-berry cranberry sauce
- 1 cup French salad dressing
- 4 teaspoons onion soup mix

1 In a large skillet, cook pork chops in oil for 12-15 minutes on each side or a meat thermometer reads 160°.

2 Meanwhile, in a microwave-safe bowl, combine the cranberry sauce, salad dressing and soup mix. Cover and microwave on high 1-1/2 to 2 minutes or until heated through. Serve with pork chops. **YIELD:** 4 servings.

EDITOR'S NOTE: This recipe was tested in a 1,100-watt microwave.

My husband and I first sampled this delicious open-faced sandwich at a restaurant. It seemed so easy, I duplicated it at home. It's also tasty with cheese sauce in place of hollandaise sauce or asparagus instead of broccoli.

Phyllis Smith // Mariposa, California

OPEN-FACED SANDWICH SUPREME
Prep/Total Time: 20 min.

    3 cups small fresh broccoli florets
    1 package (.9 ounces) hollandaise sauce mix
    8 ounces sliced deli turkey
    8 ounces sliced deli ham
    4 slices sourdough bread, toasted

1 In a large saucepan, bring 1 in. of water and broccoli to a boil. Reduce heat; cover and simmer for 5-8 minutes or until crisp-tender; drain.

2 Prepare the hollandaise sauce according to package directions. Warm turkey and ham if desired; layer over toast. Top with broccoli and sauce. **YIELD:** 4 servings.

BARBECUE SAUSAGE SKILLET
Prep/Total Time: 25 min.

I came up with this when I had to bring a dish for a church supper. I got a lot of compliments on it—even our teenage boys requested I make it again. I usually serve it over a mixture of white and wild rice.

Janis Plourde // Smooth Rock Falls, Ontario

    1 pound Italian sausage links
    2 cups fresh broccoli florets
    1 cup chopped onion
    1/2 cup chopped celery
    1/4 cup chopped sweet red pepper
    1 tablespoon canola oil
    1/2 cup water
    1/2 to 2/3 cup barbecue sauce
    1 envelope onion soup mix
    1/2 teaspoon dried thyme
    1/4 teaspoon salt
    1/4 teaspoon pepper
Hot cooked noodles *or* rice

1 In a large skillet, cook sausage over medium heat until no longer pink. Meanwhile, in another skillet, stir-fry the broccoli, onion, celery and red pepper in oil until onion is tender. Stir in the water, barbecue sauce, soup mix, thyme, salt and pepper.

2 Cut sausage into 1/2-in. slices; add to vegetable mixture. Reduce heat; cook uncovered, for 5-8 minutes, stirring occasionally. Serve over noodles or rice. **YIELD:** 4-6 servings.

My husband and I both work the midnight shift, so I'm always on the lookout for slow cooker recipes. This one couldn't be simpler.

Michelle McKay // Garden City, Michigan

SAUSAGE SPANISH RICE

Prep: 5 min. **Cook:** 5 hours

- 1 pound smoked kielbasa *or* Polish sausage, cut into 1/4-inch slices
- 2 cans (14-1/2 ounces *each*) diced tomatoes, undrained
- 2 cups water
- 1-1/2 cups uncooked converted rice
- 1 cup salsa
- 1 medium onion
- 1/2 cup chopped green pepper
- 1/2 cup chopped sweet red pepper
- 1 can (4 ounces) chopped green chilies
- 1 envelope taco seasoning

1 In a 3-qt. slow cooker, combine all the ingredients. Cover and cook on low for 5-6 hours or until rice is tender. **YIELD:** 9 servings.

PORK TENDERLOIN WITH GRAVY

Prep/Total Time: 25 min.

I recently began experimenting with pork and came up with this easy dish, which turned out to be a keeper. I like to vary it occasionally by using lemon-pepper or garlic-seasoned tenderloin for added flavor.

Marilyn McGee // Tulsa, Oklahoma

- 1 envelope brown gravy mix
- 1/2 cup water
- 3 tablespoons soy sauce
- 2 tablespoons balsamic vinegar
- 1 garlic clove, minced
- 1 pork tenderloin (about 3/4 pound), cut into 1/2-inch slices
- 1/4 cup olive oil
- 1/2 pound fresh mushrooms, sliced
- 1 medium onion, sliced and separated into rings

Hot cooked rice

1 In a small bowl, combine the gravy mix, water, soy sauce, vinegar and garlic; set aside. In a large skillet, brown pork in oil on all sides.

2 Stir in the gravy mixture, mushrooms and onion. Bring to a boil. Reduce heat; cover and simmer for 10-15 minutes or until meat juices run clear and vegetables are tender. Serve over rice. **YIELD:** 2 servings.

Not only is it easy to use my slow cooker, but the results are fabulous. Meat cooked this way is always so tender and juicy. These pork chops in a thick tomato sauce turn out great.
Bonnie Marlow // Ottoville, Ohio

TENDER PORK CHOPS

Prep: 15 min. **Cook:** 5-1/2 hours

- 6 boneless pork loin chops (1/2 inch thick and 6 ounces *each*)
- 1 tablespoon canola oil
- 1 medium green pepper, diced
- 1 can (6 ounces) tomato paste
- 1 jar (4-1/2 ounces) sliced mushrooms, drained
- 1/2 cup water
- 1 envelope spaghetti sauce mix
- 1/2 to 1 teaspoon hot pepper sauce

1 In a large skillet, brown pork chops in oil over medium heat for 3-4 minutes on each side; drain. In a 5-qt. slow cooker, combine the remaining ingredients. Top with pork chops. Cover and cook on low for 5-1/2 to 6 hours or until a meat thermometer reads 160°. **YIELD:** 6 servings.

MARMALADE-GLAZED HAM LOAF

Prep: 15 min. **Bake:** 70 min.

Ham loaf is an old-fashioned dish with great flavor. Both my family and my guests enjoy this delicious entree.
Janet Fisher // Butler, Pennsylvania

- 2 eggs
- 2 cups milk
- 1-1/2 cups crushed herb stuffing mix
- 1 medium onion, chopped
- 1/4 teaspoon salt
- 1-1/2 pounds ground pork
- 1-1/2 pounds ground fully cooked ham
- 1 jar (12 ounces) orange marmalade
- 2 tablespoons cider vinegar
- 1 teaspoon ground mustard
- 1/4 teaspoon ground cinnamon
- 1/8 to 1/4 teaspoon ground cloves

1 In a large bowl, combine eggs, milk and stuffing mix; let stand for 5 minutes. Add onion and salt. Crumble pork and ham over mixture and mix well. Pat into a greased 9-in. square baking dish (pan will be full). Bake, uncovered, at 350° for 30 minutes; drain. Bake 30 minutes longer; drain.

2 Combine the marmalade, vinegar, mustard, cinnamon and cloves; spread over ham loaf. Bake 10-15 minutes longer or until a meat thermometer reads 160°. Let stand for 5-10 minutes before cutting. **YIELD:** 9 servings.

SAUSAGE PIZZA

Prep: 20 min. **Bake:** 15 min.

Spicy sausage, onions, mushrooms and plenty of cheese make this pizza a real keeper. It beats the delivery variety every time—and there's no wait! Bake up two or more and keep one on hand for busy nights.

Taste of Home Test Kitchen

- 1 loaf (1 pound) frozen bread dough, thawed
- 3/4 pound bulk hot Italian sausage
- 1/2 cup sliced onion
- 1/2 cup sliced fresh mushrooms
- 1/2 cup chopped green pepper
- 1/2 cup pizza sauce
- 2 cups (8 ounces) shredded part-skim mozzarella cheese

1 With greased fingers, pat dough onto an ungreased 12-in. pizza pan. Prick dough thoroughly with a fork. Bake at 400° for 10-12 minutes or until lightly browned. Meanwhile, in a large skillet, cook the sausage, onion, mushrooms and green pepper over medium heat until sausage is no longer pink; drain.

2 Spread pizza sauce over crust. Top with sausage mixture; sprinkle with cheese. Bake at 400° for 12-15 minutes or until golden brown. **YIELD:** 8 slices.

TIP

This pizza is so easy to make and can be modified to suit most folks' tastes. For example, you can substitute less spicy sausage, chicken, ham or ground beef for the sausage. And top the pizza with a variety of veggies, olives, anchovies and even pineapple!

PORK LO MEIN

Prep/Total Time: 30 min.

This colorful main dish with crispy snow peas and baby carrots is one of my favorites. It's fast, healthy and the variety is endless. I sometimes use chicken, mushrooms, bean sprouts and cashews! You can also serve this over rice or spaghetti.

Denise DuBois // Coral Springs, Florida

2-1/4 teaspoons brown gravy mix
1-1/2 teaspoons cornstarch
   3 cups water, *divided*
   1 tablespoon reduced-sodium soy sauce
 3/4 pound pork tenderloin, sliced
 1/2 to 3/4 teaspoon minced fresh gingerroot
 1/8 teaspoon pepper
   3 teaspoons olive oil, *divided*
   2 garlic cloves, minced
   1 cup baby carrots
   1 cup fresh snow peas
   1 package (3 ounces) ramen noodles

1 In a small bowl, combine the gravy mix, cornstarch, 1 cup water and soy sauce until smooth; set aside.

2 In a large skillet or wok, stir-fry the pork, ginger and pepper in 1-1/2 teaspoons oil for 4 minutes. Add the garlic and stir-fry for 1 minute longer or until meat is no longer pink. Remove and keep warm. In the same pan, stir-fry carrots in remaining oil for 5 minutes. Add peas; stir-fry 4 minutes longer or until vegetables are crisp-tender.

3 Stir cornstarch mixture and add to the vegetable mixture. Bring to a boil; cook and stir for 2 minutes or until thickened and bubbly. Return pork to the pan; heat through.

4 Meanwhile, in a large saucepan, bring remaining water to a boil; add ramen noodles (discard seasoning packet or save for another use). Cook for 3 minutes, stirring occasionally; drain. Serve with pork mixture. **YIELD:** 2 servings.

People compare this comforting casserole to their grandmother's macaroni and cheese, not realizing this version starts with a box mix. Ham and broccoli add flavor and color.

Janet Twigg // Campbellford, Ontario

FANCY MAC 'N' CHEESE

Prep/Total Time: 30 min.

    2 packages (7-1/4 ounces *each*) macaroni and white
       cheddar *or* cheddar cheese dinner mix
    6 cups water
    2 cups fresh broccoli florets
1/2 cup chopped onion
    2 garlic cloves, minced
1/2 cup plus 1 tablespoon butter, *divided*
1/2 cup milk
    2 cups cubed fully cooked ham
    1 tablespoon Dijon mustard
Salt and pepper to taste
    1 cup soft bread crumbs
1/4 cup grated Parmesan cheese

1 Set cheese sauce packet from dinner mix aside. Bring water to a boil. Add macaroni; cook for 4 minutes. Add the broccoli, onion and garlic. Cook 3-6 minutes longer or until macaroni is tender; drain.

2 In a large saucepan, melt 1/2 cup butter. Stir in cheese sauce mix and milk. Add the ham, mustard, salt and pepper. Stir in macaroni mixture.

3 Transfer to a greased broiler-proof 2-1/2-qt. baking dish. Melt remaining butter; toss with bread crumbs and cheese. Sprinkle over top. Broil 4-6 in. from the heat for 4-5 minutes or until top is golden brown. **YIELD:** 8 servings.

SAUSAGE 'N' BLACK BEAN PASTA

Prep/Total Time: 20 min.

For a hot and hearty meal, try this super-quick, super-easy pasta dish you can fix in a flash. Serve it up with a tossed salad and bread for a fast, wholesome meal.

Taste of Home Test Kitchen

    1 package (4.4 ounces) jalapeno jack pasta mix
1/2 pound smoked sausage, chopped
    1 cup canned black beans, rinsed and drained

1 Prepare the pasta mix according to package directions. Stir in sausage and black beans; heat through. **YIELD:** 3 servings.

I love homemade ham and pineapple pizza, but I don't care to make the pizza crust. So I came up with this sub sandwich that has the same flavors but is a snap to put together.

Julie Valdez // Walnut Hill, Florida

HOT HAM AND PINEAPPLE SUB

Prep: 30 min. **Bake:** 35 min.

- 1 tube (11 ounces) refrigerated crusty French loaf
- 2 tablespoons canola oil
- 1 teaspoon Italian seasoning
- 1/4 teaspoon garlic salt
- 1 can (8 ounces) pizza sauce, *divided*
- 1/3 pound sliced deli ham
- 1 can (8 ounces) crushed pineapple, drained
- 1 cup (4 ounces) shredded part-skim mozzarella cheese

1 Place the French loaf dough seam side down on a lightly greased baking sheet. With a sharp knife, cut six slashes, about 1/2 in. deep, on top of dough. Bake at 350° for 25-30 minutes or until golden brown.

2 In a small bowl, combine the oil, Italian seasoning and garlic salt; brush over hot bread. Cool on a wire rack for 8 minutes.

3 Split bread in half lengthwise. Hollow out bottom half, leaving a 1/4-in. shell (discard removed bread or save for another use).

4 Spread 2-3 tablespoons of pizza sauce over shell; top with the ham, pineapple and cheese. Replace bread top. Bake for 6-8 minutes or until cheese is melted. Heat the remaining pizza sauce; serve with sandwich. **YIELD:** 4-6 servings.

SESAME PORK

Prep/Total Time: 20 min.

This recipe is a cinch to make on a night when my opera-singing husband has to be out the door for an evening rehearsal. It's really tasty and reheats well, so I always make extra for lunches later in the week.

Stephanie Gillett // Ann Arbor, Michigan

- 2 teaspoons cornstarch
- 3/4 cup chicken broth
- 4 teaspoons soy sauce
- 2 tablespoons canola oil
- 1 pork tenderloin (3/4 pound), cut into 1-inch cubes
- 1 garlic clove, minced
- 3 cups broccoli coleslaw mix
- 1-1/2 teaspoons sesame seeds, toasted
- Hot cooked rice, optional

1 In a small bowl, combine the cornstarch, broth and soy sauce until smooth; set aside. In a large skillet or wok, heat oil; stir-fry the pork and garlic for 5 minutes. Add broccoli coleslaw mix; stir-fry 3-4 minutes longer or until meat is no longer pink and broccoli is crisp-tender.

2 Stir cornstarch mixture and gradually add to the pan. Bring to a boil; cook and stir for 1 minute or until thickened. Sprinkle with sesame seeds. Serve with rice if desired. **YIELD:** 2 servings.

When brushed with butter and baked over custard cups, these spinach tortillas make crunchy bowls for lettuce salads topped with seasonal pork and peppers.
Katie Koziolek // Hartland, Minnesota

FAJITA TORTILLA BOWLS
Prep/Total Time: 30 min.

        6 **spinach tortillas**
        2 **tablespoons butter, melted**
        1 **tablespoon canola oil**
        1 **pound boneless pork loin chops, cut into thin strips**
        1 **envelope fajita seasoning mix**
        1 **medium onion, thinly sliced**
        1 **sweet red pepper, thinly sliced**
        1 **green pepper, thinly sliced**
  4-1/2 **cups shredded lettuce**
        1 **medium tomato, chopped**

1 Place six 10-oz. custard cups upside down in a shallow baking pan; set aside. Brush both sides of tortillas with butter; place in a single layer on ungreased baking sheets.

2 Bake, uncovered, at 425° for 1 minute. Place a tortilla over each custard cup, pinching sides to form a bowl shape. Bake for 7-8 minutes longer or until crisp. Remove tortilla from cups to cool on wire racks.

3 In a large skillet, combine pork and seasoning mix. Cook and stir in oil over medium-high heat until meat juices run clear. Remove pork with a slotted spoon.

4 In the drippings, saute onion and peppers until crisp-tender. Place lettuce in tortilla bowls; top with the pork, pepper mixture and tomato. **YIELD:** 6 servings.

GLAZED HOLIDAY PORK ROAST
Prep: 10 min. **Bake:** 2-1/2 hours + standing

With its sweet and tangy fruit glaze, this pretty pork roast is perfect for a holiday meal. But don't save it for special occasions! My husband and son love this warm and satisfying supper whenever I serve it.
Sherry Kreiger // York, Pennsylvania

      1 **pork rib roast (4 to 4-1/2 pounds)**
      1 **cup dried fruit bits,** *divided*
   2/3 **cup water**
   2/3 **cup honey**
      1 **envelope onion soup mix**
   1/4 **cup ketchup**
      2 **tablespoons lemon juice**
      2 **teaspoons grated lemon peel**

1 Make 15-20 slits, about 1 to 1-1/2 in. deep, in the roast; place some fruit in each slit. In a small bowl, combine the water, honey, soup mix, ketchup, lemon juice, peel and remaining fruit.

2 Place roast fat side up in a roasting pan. Pour fruit mixture over the top. Cover and bake at 325° for 2-1/2 to 3 hours or until a meat thermometer reads 160°. Let stand for 10-15 minutes before carving. **YIELD:** 6-8 servings.

COUNTRY PIZZA PIE

Prep: 25 min. **Bake:** 35 min. + standing

This hearty sausage dish has been a family favorite for over 20 years. My four children were raised on it.

Joyce Leigh // Grand Junction, Colorado

- 1 unbaked pastry shell (9 inches)
- 1 pound bulk Italian sausage
- 1 small onion, chopped
- 4 eggs, lightly beaten
- 1 cup (4 ounces) shredded cheddar cheese
- 1/2 cup milk
- 1/2 teaspoon dried oregano
- 1/8 teaspoon pepper
- 1 can (8 ounces) pizza sauce
- 6 slices part-skim mozzarella cheese

1 Line unpricked pastry shell with a double thickness of heavy-duty foil. Bake at 450° for 8 minutes. Remove foil; bake 5 minutes longer. Cool on a wire rack. Reduce heat to 350°.

2 In a large skillet, cook sausage and onion over medium heat until meat is no longer pink; drain. Transfer to a large bowl. Stir in the eggs, cheddar cheese, milk, oregano and pepper. Pour into crust.

3 Bake for 30-35 minutes or until a knife inserted near the center comes out clean. Spread pizza sauce over sausage mixture; top with mozzarella cheese. Bake 5-8 minutes longer or until cheese is melted. Let stand for 10 minutes before cutting. **YIELD:** 6 servings.

poultry

CHICKEN TOSTADAS WITH MANGO SALSA

Prep: 30 min. + marinating **Cook:** 20 min.

The ginger adds a pleasant zing to this twist on a traditional tostada. It's so easy to eat healthful foods when good fresh salsa is around.

Erin Renouf Mylroie // Santa Clara, Utah

- 1/3 cup orange juice
- 5 tablespoons lime juice, *divided*
- 1 teaspoon garlic powder
- 1 teaspoon ground cumin
- 1 pound boneless skinless chicken breast halves
- 2 medium mangoes, peeled and diced
- 1 small red onion, chopped
- 1/2 cup minced fresh cilantro
- 1 serrano pepper, seeded and minced
- 2 tablespoons finely chopped candied ginger
- 1 tablespoon brown sugar
- 1/4 teaspoon salt
- 6 corn tortillas (6 inches)
- 3 cups coleslaw mix
- 6 tablespoons fat-free sour cream

1 In a large resealable plastic bag, combine the orange juice, 3 tablespoons lime juice, garlic powder and cumin; add chicken. Seal bag and turn to coat; refrigerate for at least 20 minutes.

2 For salsa, in a small bowl, combine the mangoes, onion, cilantro, serrano pepper, ginger, brown sugar, salt and remaining lime juice. Cover and chill until serving.

3 Drain and discard marinade. Place chicken on a broiler pan coated with cooking spray. Broil 4-6 in. from the heat for 5-7 minutes on each side or until a meat thermometer reads 170°. Cut into thin strips.

4 In a nonstick skillet, cook tortillas over medium heat for 1-2 minutes on each side or until lightly browned. Top each with coleslaw mix, chicken, mango salsa and sour cream. **YIELD:** 6 servings.

EDITOR'S NOTE: When cutting hot peppers, disposable gloves are recommended. Avoid touching your face.

All it takes is four ingredients and 20 minutes to have this hearty dish ready to eat. Chicken, snap peas and pasta star in this dish, and the garlicky sauce ties it all together nicely.

Anne Nock // Avon Lake, Ohio

GARLIC CHICKEN PENNE

Prep/Total Time: 20 min.

   8 ounces uncooked penne pasta
1-1/2 cups frozen sugar snap peas
   1 package (1.6 ounces) garlic-herb pasta sauce mix
   1 package (6 ounces) sliced cooked chicken

1 In a large saucepan, cook pasta in boiling water for 6 minutes. Add peas; return to a boil. Cook for 4-5 minutes or until pasta is tender. Meanwhile, prepare sauce mix according to package directions.

2 Drain pasta mixture; add chicken. Drizzle with sauce and toss to coat. **YIELD:** 4 servings.

ROASTED TURKEY DRUMSTICKS

Prep: 30 min. **Bake:** 1 hour

Of all the turkey recipes I've tried, I like this one best. The tender drumsticks have just a bit of zip.

H. Ross Njaa // Salinas, California

1/4 cup all-purpose flour
1/8 teaspoon white pepper
   2 turkey drumsticks, skin removed
     (about 3/4 pound *each*)
   2 tablespoons canola oil
   1 can (8 ounces) tomato sauce
3/4 cup chicken broth
3/4 cup red wine *or* additional chicken broth
   5 teaspoons onion soup mix
1-1/2 teaspoons paprika
1-1/2 teaspoons Worcestershire sauce
   2 garlic cloves, minced
3/4 teaspoon sugar
1/4 teaspoon salt
   1 bay leaf

1 In a large resealable plastic bag, combine flour and white pepper. Add drumsticks, one at a time, and shake to coat. In a skillet, brown drumsticks on all sides in oil. Transfer to a greased 11-in. x 7-in. baking dish; set aside.

2 In a large saucepan, combine the tomato sauce, broth, wine, soup mix, paprika, Worcestershire sauce, garlic, sugar and salt. Bring to a boil. Reduce heat; simmer, uncovered, for 3 minutes or until flavors are blended. Add bay leaf. Pour sauce over the drumsticks.

3 Cover and bake at 350° for 30 minutes. Turn drumsticks over; cover and bake 30-40 minutes longer or until juices run clear and thermometer reads 180°. Discard bay leaf. **YIELD:** 2 servings.

Flavored with taco seasoning and cilantro and topped with salsa and sour cream, these Southwestern turkey burgers are so good. I round out the menu with roasted corn on the cob and deep-fried pita pieces topped with a little cinnamon.

Nancy Bourget // Round Rock, Texas

TEX-MEX TURKEY BURGERS
Prep/Total Time: 25 min.

1-1/4 pounds ground turkey
   1 envelope reduced-sodium taco seasoning
   1 tablespoon dried cilantro flakes
   1 cup (4 ounces) shredded Mexican cheese blend
1/2 cup sour cream
1/2 cup salsa
   4 hamburger buns, split
   4 lettuce leaves

1 In a large bowl, combine the turkey, taco seasoning and cilantro; shape into four patties. Grill, covered, over medium heat or broil 4-6 in. from the heat for 5 minutes on each side.

2 Sprinkle cheese over burgers; grill 2-3 minutes longer or until a meat thermometer reads 165° and juices run clear. Combine sour cream and salsa. Serve burgers on buns with sour cream mixture and lettuce. **YIELD:** 4 servings.

BUFFALO CHICKEN CALZONES
Prep: 30 min. **Bake:** 10 min.

I'm always looking for creative ways to jazz up pizza. I came up with this "pizza turnover," to incorporate my love of buffalo chicken wings.

Ruth Ann Riendeau // Twin Mountain, New Hampshire

   1 can (8 ounces) pizza sauce
   2 teaspoons plus 1/2 cup hot pepper sauce, *divided*
1-1/4 pounds boneless skinless chicken breasts, cubed
   3 celery ribs, chopped
   3 tablespoons butter
Dash Cajun seasoning
   2 tubes (13.8 ounces *each*) refrigerated pizza crust
1-1/2 cups (6 ounces) shredded Monterey Jack cheese
   1 cup (4 ounces) crumbled blue cheese
Cornmeal

1 In a small bowl, combine pizza sauce and 2 teaspoons hot pepper sauce; set aside. In a large skillet, cook chicken and celery over medium heat in butter for 3-5 minutes or until chicken is no longer pink; drain if necessary. Stir in Cajun seasoning and remaining hot pepper sauce; cover and simmer for 10-15 minutes or until heated through.

2 Unroll pizza dough; divide each portion in half. On a floured surface, roll each into an 8-in. circle. Spread pizza sauce mixture over half of each circle to within 1 in. of edges. Top with chicken mixture and cheeses. Fold dough over filling; pinch edges to seal.

3 Sprinkle greased baking sheets with cornmeal. Place calzones over cornmeal. Bake at 400° for 10-12 minutes or until golden brown. **YIELD:** 4 calzones.

Stuffing mix gives these moist chicken breasts a fast coating you'll enjoy.
Rosemary Dibble // Sandy, Utah

STUFFING-COATED CHICKEN
Prep: 10 min. **Bake:** 25 min.

    1 envelope cream of chicken soup mix
    1/3 cup hot water
    3/4 cup stuffing mix
    2 boneless skinless chicken breast halves (4 ounces *each*)
    1 tablespoon butter, melted

1 In a shallow bowl, combine soup mix and water. Place stuffing mix in another shallow bowl. Dip chicken in soup mixture, then coat with stuffing.

2 Place in an 8-in. square baking dish coated with cooking spray. Drizzle with butter. Bake, uncovered, at 375° for 25-30 minutes or until juices run clear. **YIELD:** 2 servings.

PUFF PASTRY CHICKEN BUNDLES
Prep: 30 min. **Bake:** 25 min.

Inside these golden puff pastry packages, chicken breasts rolled with spinach, herbed cream cheese and walnuts are a savory surprise. I like to serve this elegant entree when we have guests or are celebrating a holiday or special occasion.
Brad Moritz // Limerick, Pennsylvania

    8 boneless skinless chicken breast halves (about
      6 ounces *each*)
    1 teaspoon salt
    1/2 teaspoon pepper
    40 large spinach leaves
    2 cartons (8 ounces *each*) spreadable chive and onion
      cream cheese
    1/2 cup chopped walnuts, toasted
    2 sheets frozen puff pastry, thawed
    1 egg
    1/2 teaspoon cold water

1 Cut a lengthwise slit in each chicken breast to within 1/2 in. of the other side; open meat so it lies flat. Cover with plastic wrap; pound to flatten to 1/8-in. thickness. Remove plastic wrap. Sprinkle salt and pepper over chicken.

2 In a small saucepan, bring 1 in. of water to a boil; add spinach. Cover and cook for 1-2 minutes or until wilted; drain. Place five spinach leaves on each chicken breast. Spoon 2 tablespoons of cream cheese down the center of each chicken breast; sprinkle with walnuts. Roll up chicken and tuck in ends.

3 Unroll puff pastry; cut into eight portions. Roll each into an 8-in. x 7-in. rectangle. Combine egg and cold water; brush over edges of pastry. Place chicken at one short end; roll up tightly, tucking in ends.

4 Place on a greased 15-in. x 10-in. x 1-in. baking sheet. Bake at 350° for 25-30 minutes or until golden brown. **YIELD:** 8 servings.

JAMAICAN JERK TURKEY WRAPS

Prep: 20 min. **Grill:** 20 min.

I received this recipe after tasting the spicy wraps at a neighborhood party. The grilled turkey tenderloin and light jalapeno dressing make them tops with my gang.

Mary Ann Dell // Phoenixville, Pennsylvania

- 2 cups broccoli coleslaw mix
- 1 medium tomato, seeded and chopped
- 3 tablespoons reduced-fat coleslaw dressing
- 1 jalapeno pepper, seeded and chopped
- 1 tablespoon prepared mustard
- 1-1/2 teaspoons Caribbean jerk seasoning
- 2 turkey breast tenderloins (8 ounces *each*)
- 4 fat-free flour tortillas (8 inches)

1 In a large bowl, toss the coleslaw mix, tomato, coleslaw dressing, jalapeno and mustard; set aside. Rub the seasoning over turkey tenderloins.

2 Coat grill rack with cooking spray before starting the grill. Grill tenderloins, covered, over medium heat for 8-10 minutes on each side or until a meat thermometer reads 170°. Let stand for 5 minutes.

3 Grill tortillas, uncovered, over medium heat for 45-55 seconds on each side or until warmed. Thinly slice turkey; place down the center of tortillas. Top with coleslaw mixture and roll up. **YIELD:** 4 servings.

EDITOR'S NOTE: When cutting hot peppers, disposable gloves are recommended. Avoid touching your face.

This recipe is definitely a must-try! Convenient crescent roll dough is wrapped around a creamy turkey filling to form cute golden bundles. My family loves them.
Lydia Garrod // Tacoma, Washington

TURKEY BUNDLES

Prep/Total Time: 30 min.

- 4 ounces cream cheese, softened
- 2 tablespoons milk
- 1/2 teaspoon dill weed
- 1/4 teaspoon celery salt
- 1/4 teaspoon pepper
- 2 cups cubed cooked turkey
- 1/4 cup chopped water chestnuts
- 2 tablespoons chopped green onion
- 2 tubes (one 8 ounces, one 4 ounces) refrigerated crescent rolls
- 2 tablespoons butter, melted
- 2 tablespoons seasoned bread crumbs

1 In a large bowl, beat the cream cheese, milk, dill, celery salt and pepper until smooth. Stir in the turkey, water chestnuts and onion.

2 Separate crescent dough into six rectangles; seal perforations. Spoon 1/3 cup turkey mixture onto the center of each rectangle; bring edges into center and pinch to seal.

3 Place on a baking sheet. Brush with butter; sprinkle with bread crumbs. Bake at 375° for 15-20 minutes or until golden brown. **YIELD:** 6 servings.

CHICKEN AND SHELLS DINNER

Prep: 15 min. **Bake:** 20 min.

Like most kids, mine love macaroni and cheese. The addition of chicken and peas makes this a meal-in-one they never refuse.
LeeAnn McCue // Charlotte, North Carolina

- 1 package (12 ounces) shells and cheese dinner mix
- 1/4 cup chopped onion
- 4 tablespoons butter, *divided*
- 2 cups cubed cooked chicken
- 1 package (10 ounces) frozen peas, thawed
- 2/3 cup mayonnaise
- 1/3 cup seasoned bread crumbs

1 Prepare dinner mix according to package directions. Meanwhile, in a small skillet, saute onion in 2 tablespoons butter until tender. Stir the chicken, peas, mayonnaise and sauteed onion into dinner mix.

2 Transfer to a greased 1-1/2-qt. baking dish. Melt remaining butter; toss with bread crumbs. Sprinkle over top. Bake, uncovered, at 350° for 20-25 minutes or until bubbly. **YIELD:** 4-6 servings.

EDITOR'S NOTE: Reduced-fat or fat-free mayonnaise is not recommended for this recipe.

This classic is remade into a time-saving microwave dish. If you like, use cheddar cheese for the Swiss.

Louise Gilbert // Quesnel, British Columbia

QUICK CHICKEN CORDON BLEU

Prep/Total Time: 25 min.

- 4 boneless skinless chicken breast halves (6 ounces *each*)
- 4 thin slices deli ham
- 2 slices Swiss cheese, halved
- 1/4 cup butter, melted
- 1 envelope seasoned coating mix

1 Flatten the chicken to 1/4-in. thickness. Place the ham and cheese down the center of each; roll up and secure with a toothpick. Place the butter and the coating mix in separate shallow bowls. Dip the chicken in butter, then roll in the coating mix.

2 Place in a greased 2-qt. microwave-safe dish. Cover loosely and microwave on high for 5-7 minutes on each side or until no longer pink. Let stand for 5 minutes. Discard toothpicks. **YIELD:** 4 servings.

EDITOR'S NOTE: This recipe was tested in a 1,100-watt microwave.

SPANISH RICE TURKEY CASSEROLE

Prep: 30 min. Bake: 20 min.

Everyone in my family loves this casserole, even my eighty-year-old grandparents who aren't big fans of Mexican food. Mild green chilies, tender cubes of turkey, tomatoes and lots of cheese make it a mouthwatering delight.

Ann Herren // Pulaski, Tennessee

- 2 packages (6.8 ounces *each*) Spanish rice and vermicelli mix
- 1/4 cup butter, cubed
- 4 cups water
- 1 can (14-1/2 ounces) diced tomatoes, undrained
- 1 can (10 ounces) diced tomatoes and green chilies, undrained
- 3 cups cubed cooked turkey *or* chicken
- 1 can (11 ounces) whole kernel corn, drained
- 1/2 cup sour cream
- 1 cup (4 ounces) shredded Mexican cheese blend, *divided*

1 In a large skillet, saute rice and vermicelli in butter until golden brown. Gradually stir in the water, tomatoes and the contents of rice seasoning packets. Bring to a boil. Reduce heat; cover and simmer for 15-20 minutes or until rice is tender.

2 Meanwhile, in a large bowl, combine the turkey, corn, sour cream and 1/2 cup cheese. Stir in rice mixture.

3 Transfer to a greased 3-qt. baking dish. Sprinkle with remaining cheese (dish will be full). Bake, uncovered, at 375° for 20-25 minutes or until heated through. **YIELD:** 8 servings.

A beautiful chicken and pastry braid delivers both on taste and presentation. It's rich, creamy, full of chicken and veggies, and surrounded with a crispy, flaky crust.
Dana Rabe // West Richland, Washington

CHICKEN 'N' BROCCOLI BRAID

Prep: 25 min. **Bake:** 15 min.

- 2 cups cubed cooked chicken breast
- 1 cup chopped fresh broccoli
- 1 cup (4 ounces) shredded reduced-fat cheddar cheese
- 1/2 cup chopped sweet red pepper
- 2 teaspoons dill weed
- 2 garlic cloves, minced
- 1/4 teaspoon salt
- 1/4 cup reduced-fat mayonnaise
- 1/4 cup reduced-fat plain yogurt
- 2 tubes (8 ounces *each*) refrigerated reduced-fat crescent rolls
- 1 egg white, lightly beaten
- 1 tablespoon slivered almonds

1 In a large bowl, combine the first seven ingredients. Stir in mayonnaise and yogurt. Unroll both tubes of crescent dough onto an ungreased baking sheet; press together, forming a 15-in. x 12-in. rectangle. Seal seams and perforations. Spoon filling lengthwise down the center third of dough.

2 On each long side, cut dough 3 in. toward the center at 1-1/2-in. intervals, forming strips. Bring one strip from each side over filling; pinch ends to seal. Repeat. Pinch ends of loaf to seal.

3 Brush with egg white; sprinkle with almonds. Bake at 375° for 15-20 minutes or until crust is golden brown and filling is heated through. **YIELD:** 8 servings.

TIP

This pretty braiding technique is very easy to do. Use a clean, plastic ruler to help you space out each cut. Then use a sharp knife or scissors to cut the dough. Start at one end of the dough and working your way to the other end, pinch each set of strips together.

You'll loved the great flavor of this moist chicken dish. Cook up a little extra for a delicious salad topping or tasty sandwich. Either way, you're going to like it!

LaDonna Reed // Ponca City, Oklahoma

GARLIC CHICKEN BREASTS
Prep/Total Time: 25 min.

1/2 cup grated Parmesan cheese
1 envelope garlic and herb *or* Italian salad dressing mix
2 boneless skinless chicken breast halves (6 ounces *each*)

1 In a large resealable plastic bag, combine cheese and dressing mix. Add chicken; shake to coat.

2 Place chicken in a greased 8-in. square baking dish. Bake, uncovered, at 400° for 20-25 minutes or until a meat thermometer reads 170°. **YIELD:** 2 servings.

TURKEY LATTICE PIE
Prep: 20 min. **Bake:** 20 min.

With its pretty lattice crust, this cheesy baked dish is as eye-catching as it is delicious. It's simple to make, too, since it uses convenient crescent roll dough. It's a fun and different way to dress up leftover turkey.

Lorraine Naig // Emmetsburg, Iowa

3 tubes (8 ounces *each*) refrigerated crescent rolls
4 cups cubed cooked turkey
1-1/2 cups (6 ounces) shredded cheddar *or* Swiss cheese
3 cups frozen chopped broccoli, thawed and drained
1 can (10-3/4 ounces) condensed cream of chicken soup, undiluted
1-1/3 cups milk
2 tablespoons Dijon mustard
1 tablespoon dried minced onion
1/2 teaspoon salt
Dash pepper
1 egg, lightly beaten

1 Unroll two tubes of crescent roll dough; separate into rectangles. Place the rectangles in an ungreased 15-in. x 10-in. x 1-in. baking pan. Press onto the bottom and 1/4 in. up the sides of the pan to form a crust, sealing the seams and perforations.

2 Bake at 375° for 5-7 minutes or until light golden brown. Meanwhile, in a large bowl, combine the turkey, cheese, broccoli, soup, milk, mustard, onion, salt and pepper. Spoon over crust.

3 Unroll remaining dough; divide into rectangles. Seal perforations. Cut each rectangle into four 1-in. strips. Using strips, make a lattice design on top of turkey mixture. Brush with egg. Bake 17-22 minutes longer or until top crust is golden brown and filling is bubbly. **YIELD:** 12-16 servings.

CRANBERRY CHICKEN AND WILD RICE

Prep: 10 min. **Bake:** 40 min.

Tender chicken is baked in a sweet-tart cranberry sauce for this elegant, but easy-to-prepare entree. I love that I can do other things while it bakes.

Evelyn Lewis // Independence, Missouri

- 6 boneless skinless chicken breast halves (4 ounces *each*)
- 1-1/2 cups hot water
- 1 package (6.2 ounces) fast-cooking long grain and wild rice mix
- 1 can (16 ounces) whole-berry cranberry sauce
- 1 tablespoon lemon juice
- 1 tablespoon reduced-sodium soy sauce
- 1 tablespoon Worcestershire sauce

1 Place the chicken in a 13-in. x 9-in. baking dish coated with cooking spray. In a small bowl, combine the water and rice mix with contents of seasoning packet. Pour around chicken.

2 In a small bowl, combine the cranberry sauce, lemon juice, soy sauce and Worcestershire sauce; pour over chicken. Cover and bake at 350° for 40-50 minutes or until a meat thermometer reads, 170°. **YIELD:** 6 servings.

TIP

If you have any leftovers of this dish, save it for lunch. Place the rice and chicken in separate covered containers and refrigerate for up to 2 days. Reheat each in the microwave until heated through.

CHICKEN SATAY WRAPS
Prep/Total Time: 15 min.

- 2 tablespoons olive oil
- 2 tablespoons creamy peanut butter
- 2 green onions, chopped
- 1 teaspoon reduced-sodium soy sauce
- 1/4 teaspoon pepper
- 2 cups sliced cooked chicken
- 1 cup coleslaw mix
- 4 flour tortillas (8 inches), room temperature

1 In a large bowl, whisk the oil, peanut butter, onions, soy sauce and pepper until combined. Add the chicken and toss to coat. Sprinkle 1/4 cup coleslaw mix over each tortilla; top with chicken mixture. Roll up tightly. **YIELD:** 4 servings.

TURKEY BROCCOLI HOLLANDAISE
Prep: 25 min. **Bake:** 25 min.

This delectable dish is a great way to use extra turkey. The original recipe called for Thanksgiving leftovers, but my family loves it so much that I prepare this version all year long.
Pamela Yoder // Elkhart, Indiana

- 1 cup fresh broccoli florets
- 1 package (6 ounces) stuffing mix
- 1 envelope hollandaise sauce mix
- 2 cups cubed cooked turkey *or* chicken
- 1 can (2.8 ounces) french-fried onions

1 In a large saucepan, place 1 in. of water. Add broccoli and bring to a boil. Reduce heat; cover and simmer for 5-8 minutes or until broccoli is crisp-tender. Meanwhile, prepare the stuffing and sauce mixes according to the package directions.

2 Spoon stuffing into a greased 11-in. x 7-in. baking dish. Top with turkey. Drain broccoli; arrange over turkey. Spoon sauce over the top; sprinkle with onions. Bake, uncovered, at 325° for 25-30 minutes or until heated through. **YIELD:** 6 servings.

I first served these hens at Thanksgiving one year when only a few of us gathered to celebrate the holiday. They're so yummy, they often grace our table throughout the year. The wild rice stuffing offers a flavor my family always enjoys.

Jenny Holliday // Roanoke, Alabama

STUFFED CORNISH HENS

Prep: 20 min. **Bake:** 65 min. + standing

- 1 package (6.2 ounces) fast-cooking long grain and wild rice mix
- 2 celery ribs, chopped
- 1 small onion, chopped
- 2 tablespoons butter, *divided*
- 1 can (10-3/4 ounces) condensed cream of mushroom soup, undiluted
- 1 can (4 ounces) mushroom stems and pieces, drained
- 4 Cornish game hens (20 ounces *each*)
- 1/4 teaspoon salt
- 1/4 teaspoon pepper

1 Cook rice according to package directions. In a small skillet, saute celery and onion in 1 tablespoon butter until tender. Stir in the soup, mushrooms and prepared rice.

2 Sprinkle inside and outside of hens with salt and pepper. Stuff with rice mixture. Place on a rack in a greased shallow roasting pan; cover with foil.

3 Bake at 350° for 40 minutes. Remove foil. Melt remaining butter; brush over hens. Bake 25-35 minutes longer or until juices run clear and a meat thermometer reads 180° for hens and 165° for stuffing. Let stand for 10 minutes before serving. **YIELD:** 4 servings.

FIESTA CHICKEN 'N' STUFFING

Prep/Total Time: 20 min.

My mother gave me this recipe at my bridal shower, and I've been making it ever since. Mom knew that every new bride needs recipes for good food that is super easy to make.

Angela Peppers // Memphis, Tennessee

- 3 eggs
- 3/4 cup milk
- 2 cups crushed stuffing mix
- 1-1/2 cups cubed cooked chicken
- 1 large tomato, chopped
- 3 tablespoons chopped green chilies
- 3 tablespoons chopped green onions
Sour cream and salsa, optional

1 In a large bowl, combine eggs and milk. Stir in the stuffing mix, chicken, tomato, chilies and onions.

2 Transfer to a greased microwave-safe 9-in. pie plate. Microwave, covered, on high for 2 minutes; stir. Microwave for another 2 minutes; stir.

3 Cook 1-1/2 to 2 minutes longer or until set and a meat thermometer reads 160°. Let stand for 5 minutes before serving. Garnish with sour cream and salsa if desired. **YIELD:** 4 servings.

EDITOR'S NOTE: This recipe was tested in a 1,100-watt microwave.

All you need is one skillet to make this delectable, scaled-down dinner. It's an easy way to dress up packaged noodles and sauce, plus cleanup is a breeze.

Margery Bryan // Moses Lake, Washington

MUSHROOM CHICKEN ALFREDO

Prep/Total Time: 30 min.

- 1/2 pound boneless skinless chicken breasts, cut into 2-inch cubes
- 1 tablespoon butter
- 1 cup sliced fresh mushrooms
- 1 small onion, sliced
- 1-3/4 cups water
- 1/2 cup 2% milk
- 1 package (4.4 ounces) quick-cooking noodles and Alfredo sauce mix

Minced fresh parsley, optional

1 In a large nonstick skillet, cook chicken in butter for 6 minutes or until meat is no longer pink. Remove and keep warm. In the same skillet, saute mushrooms and onion until tender.

2 Stir in water and milk; bring to a boil. Stir in contents of noodles and sauce mix; boil for 8 minutes or until noodles are tender.

3 Return chicken to the pan; heat through. Garnish with parsley if desired. **YIELD:** 3 servings.

TASTY TURKEY SKILLET

Prep: 10 min. **Cook:** 35 min.

I like using boxed rice and pasta mixes as the basis for quick meals. This colorful dish is simple to cook on the stovetop using fried rice mix, tender turkey and convenient frozen vegetables.

Betty Kleberger // Florissant, Missouri

- 1 pound turkey breast tenderloins, cut into 1/4-inch strips
- 1 package (6.2 ounces) fried rice mix
- 1 tablespoon butter
- 2 cups water
- 1/8 teaspoon cayenne pepper
- 1-1/2 cups frozen corn, thawed
- 1 cup frozen broccoli cuts, thawed
- 2 tablespoons chopped sweet red pepper, optional

1 In a nonstick skillet coated with cooking spray, cook turkey over medium heat until no longer pink; drain. Remove turkey and keep warm.

2 Set aside seasoning packet from rice. In the same skillet, saute rice in butter until lightly browned. Stir in the water, cayenne and contents of seasoning packet.

3 Bring to a boil. Reduce heat; cover and simmer for 15 minutes. Stir in the corn, broccoli, red pepper if desired and turkey. Return to a boil. Reduce heat; cover and simmer for 6-8 minutes or until the rice and vegetables are tender. **YIELD:** 4-6 servings.

I rely on a baking mix, canned soup and frozen vegetables for this spirit-warming family favorite. I like to serve it with cranberry sauce.
Martha Evans // Omaha, Nebraska

EASY CHICKEN POTPIE

Prep: 20 min. **Bake:** 40 min.

- 1 can (10-3/4 ounces) reduced-fat reduced-sodium condensed cream of chicken soup, undiluted
- 1 can (10-3/4 ounces) reduced-fat reduced-sodium condensed cream of mushroom soup, undiluted
- 1/2 cup plus 2/3 cup fat-free milk, *divided*
- 1/2 teaspoon dried thyme
- 1/4 teaspoon pepper
- 1/8 teaspoon poultry seasoning
- 2 packages (16 ounces *each*) frozen mixed vegetables, thawed
- 1-1/2 cups cubed cooked chicken breast
- 1-1/2 cups reduced-fat biscuit/baking mix

1 In a large bowl, combine the soups, 1/2 cup milk, thyme, pepper and poultry seasoning. Stir in the vegetables and chicken.

2 Transfer to a 13-in. x 9-in. baking dish coated with cooking spray. In a small bowl, stir the biscuit mix and remaining milk just until blended. Drop by 12 rounded tablespoonfuls onto chicken mixture.

3 Bake, uncovered, at 350° for 40-50 minutes or until filling is bubbly and biscuits are golden brown. **YIELD:** 6 servings.

SPANISH RICE EMPANADAS

Prep: 25 min. **Bake:** 20 min.

The shells for this main course call for refrigerated pie crust, which are folded into pockets. Inside, you'll find tender pieces of chicken and rice accented with Spanish spices. Delicious!
Sheila Bradshaw // Powell, Ohio

- 1 package (5.6 *or* 6.8 ounces) Spanish rice and vermicelli mix
- 1-1/2 cups cubed cooked chicken
- 1 cup (4 ounces) shredded cheddar cheese
- 1/2 cup sliced green onions
- 1/4 cup chopped ripe olives
- 2 packages (15 ounces *each*) refrigerated pie pastry
- 1 egg yolk
- 1 tablespoon water

1 Prepare Spanish rice according to package directions, omitting the butter or oil. In a large bowl, combine the chicken, cheese, onions and olives. Stir in prepared rice.

2 Roll each sheet of pastry into a 12-in. circle; place on greased baking sheets. Spoon rice mixture over half of each circle; spread to within 1 in. of edges. Fold pastry over filling; crimp edges to seal. Beat egg yolk and water; brush over tops.

3 Bake at 400° for 20-25 minutes or until golden brown. Cut empanadas in half to serve. **YIELD:** 8 servings.

These savory golden chicken breasts make a delightful weeknight mainstay that's sure to please every family member. Coated in an oniony-bread-crumb mixture, the recipe's ready in no time and tastes wonderful over a bed of broccoli-cheddar rice.

Clara Coulston Minney
Washington Court House, Ohio

COUNTRY-STYLE CHICKEN
Prep: 15 min. **Bake:** 20 min.

    6 boneless skinless chicken breast halves
       (6 ounces *each*)
    1 egg
    1 tablespoon water
  3/4 cup dry bread crumbs
  1/4 cup grated Parmesan cheese
    1 envelope onion soup mix
    1 tablespoon butter, melted
    1 package (4.7 ounces) broccoli cheddar rice and
       sauce mix

1 Flatten chicken to 1/2-in. thickness. In a shallow bowl, beat egg and water. In another shallow bowl, combine the bread crumbs, Parmesan cheese and soup mix. Dip chicken in egg mixture, then coat with crumb mixture. Place in a greased 15-in. x 10-in. x 1-in. baking pan; drizzle with butter.

2 Bake, uncovered, at 350° for 20-25 minutes or until meat is no longer pink. Meanwhile, prepare rice according to package directions. Serve with chicken. **YIELD:** 6 servings.

HOT TURKEY SANDWICHES
Prep/Total Time: 15 min.

I like to team these tasty sandwiches with a salad or green beans for a pretty meal that's really filling. They're also a great way to use up holiday leftovers. And try substituting cranberry or turkey stuffing mix for savory variety.

Margery Bryan // Moses Lake, Washington

    1 package (6 ounces) chicken stuffing mix
    4 slices white bread, toasted
    1 pound thinly sliced deli turkey
    1 cup turkey gravy

1 Prepare stuffing mix according to package directions. Place the toast on a large microwave-safe plate; top each with turkey, stuffing and gravy. Microwave, uncovered, on high for 30-40 seconds or until heated through. **YIELD:** 4 servings.

EDITOR'S NOTE: This recipe was tested in a 1,100-watt microwave.

SPICY WARM CHICKEN SALAD

Prep/Total Time: 30 min.

This hearty main-dish salad makes a great cool-weather entree. It's colorful, delicious and filled with the kind of heat that's great after a chilly football game or hike. Best of all, you can have it on the table in half an hour!

Iola Egle // Bella Vista, Arkansas

1 envelope onion soup mix
4 boneless skinless chicken breast halves
(4 ounces *each*)
2 tablespoons olive oil
1 can (15 ounces) pinto beans, rinsed and drained
1 cup frozen corn
1/2 cup picante sauce
1 can (4 ounces) chopped green chilies
1/4 cup chopped green onions
1/2 cup sour cream
1/2 cup jalapeno pepper jelly
1 tablespoon lemon juice
2 cups chopped iceberg lettuce
2 cups torn romaine
1 small sweet red pepper, thinly sliced
1/4 cup minced fresh cilantro
2 jalapeno peppers, seeded and chopped, optional

1 Rub soup mix over both sides of chicken. In a large skillet, cook chicken in oil over medium heat for 8-10 minutes on each side or until a meat thermometer reads 170°. Remove and keep warm.

2 In the same skillet, combine the beans, corn and picante sauce. Cook and stir over medium heat for 2-3 minutes or until heated through. Stir in chilies and onions; set aside. In a small bowl, combine the sour cream, pepper jelly and lemon juice; set aside.

3 Toss lettuce and romaine; divide among four salad plates. Slice chicken; arrange on greens. Place red pepper slices and bean mixture around chicken. Drizzle with sour cream mixture; sprinkle with cilantro. Serve with jalapenos if desired. **YIELD:** 4 servings.

EDITOR'S NOTE: When cutting hot peppers, disposable gloves are recommended. Avoid touching your face.

CHICKEN FAJITA SPAGHETTI

Prep/Total Time: 20 min.

This tasty dinner has been a great time-saver for me. I usually cut up the chicken, onion and peppers while our two young children are napping. Then, just before my husband gets home from work, I toss everything into the skillet while the pasta is cooking on another burner.

Heather Brown // Frisco, Texas

- 8 ounces uncooked spaghetti
- 1 pound boneless skinless chicken breasts, cut into strips
- 1 tablespoon canola oil
- 1 small onion, sliced
- 1 small sweet red pepper, julienned
- 1 small sweet yellow pepper, julienned
- 1 can (4 ounces) chopped green chilies
- 1/2 cup water
- 1/2 cup taco sauce
- 1 envelope fajita seasoning mix

1 Cook the spaghetti according to package directions. Meanwhile, in a large skillet, cook chicken in oil over medium heat for 4-5 minutes on each side or until meat is no longer pink; remove and keep warm.

2 In the same skillet, saute onion and peppers until tender. Add the chicken, chilies, water, taco sauce and fajita seasoning; heat through. Drain spaghetti; toss with chicken mixture. **YIELD:** 6 servings.

TIP

This chicken dish will be great over any sturdy pasta, such as fettuccine, rotini, penne or bow tie. If your family likes some heat to their food, add some chopped jalapeno in with the sweet peppers and use hot taco sauce.

The flavorful filling in these wraps has a definite kick, but you can adjust the chilies and peppers to suit your taste. I like to serve them alongside Spanish rice.
Melissa Green // Louisville, Kentucky

TACO CHICKEN WRAPS

Prep/Total Time: 30 min.

- 1 can (10 ounces) diced tomatoes and green chilies, drained
- 1 can (9-3/4 ounces) chunk white chicken, drained
- 1 cup (4 ounces) shredded cheddar-Monterey Jack cheese
- 2 tablespoons diced jalapeno pepper
- 2 teaspoons taco seasoning
- 6 flour tortillas (6 inches), warmed

Taco sauce and sour cream, optional

1 In a small bowl, combine the tomatoes, chicken, cheese, jalapeno and taco seasoning. Place about 1/3 cupful down the center of each tortilla. Roll up and place seam side down in a greased 11-in. x 7-in. baking dish.

2 Bake, uncovered, at 350° for 10-15 minutes or until heated through. Serve with taco sauce and sour cream if desired. **YIELD:** 6 servings.

EDITOR'S NOTE: When cutting hot peppers, disposable gloves are recommended. Avoid touching your face.

SPINACH TURKEY BURGERS

Prep/Total Time: 20 min.

When you're looking for a change-of-pace burger, these pretty sandwiches will satisfy the need. Instead of beef, the burgers are filled with spinach and turkey for a succulent switch to the usual grilled fare.
C. A. Hedges // Clarence Center, New York

- 1 cup stuffing mix, finely crushed
- 1/3 cup chicken broth
- 1/2 teaspoon Italian seasoning
- 1/4 teaspoon salt
- 1/4 teaspoon pepper
- 1 package (10 ounces) frozen chopped spinach, thawed and squeezed dry
- 1 pound ground turkey
- 4 sandwich buns, split

Cheese slices, lettuce leaves and tomato slices, optional

1 In a large bowl, combine the stuffing mix, broth, Italian seasoning, salt, pepper and half of the spinach (save remaining spinach for another use). Crumble turkey over mixture and mix well. Shape into four 3/4-in.-thick patties.

2 Grill, uncovered, over medium-hot heat or broil 3-4 in. from the heat for 3-4 minutes on each side or until a meat thermometer reads 165° and juices run clear. Serve on buns with cheese, lettuce and tomato if desired. **YIELD:** 4 servings.

TACO NOODLE DISH

Prep: 20 min. **Bake:** 10 min. + standing

I got creative while we were housebound during a snowstorm one winter...and used ingredients I had on hand to come up with this hearty casserole. Later, I modified it so it has less fat and fewer calories.

Judy Munger // Warren, Minnesota

- 2 cups uncooked yolk-free wide noodles
- 2 pounds lean ground turkey
- 1 can (8 ounces) tomato sauce
- 1/2 cup water
- 1 can (4 ounces) chopped green chilies
- 1 envelope reduced-sodium taco seasoning
- 1 teaspoon onion powder
- 1 teaspoon chili powder
- 1/2 teaspoon garlic powder
- 1 cup (4 ounces) shredded reduced-fat cheddar cheese
- 2 cups shredded lettuce
- 1 cup diced fresh tomatoes
- 1/3 cup sliced ripe olives, drained
- 1/2 cup taco sauce
- 1/2 cup fat-free sour cream

1 Cook the noodles according to package directions. Meanwhile, in a large nonstick skillet, cook the turkey over medium heat until no longer pink; drain. Stir in the tomato sauce, water, green chilies, taco seasoning, onion powder, chili powder and garlic powder. Bring to a boil. Reduce heat; simmer, uncovered, for 5 minutes.

2 Drain noodles; place in an 11-in. x 7-in. baking dish coated with cooking spray. Spread the turkey mixture over the top. Sprinkle with cheese. Bake, uncovered, at 350° for 10-15 minutes or until cheese is melted. Let stand for 10 minutes.

3 Top with the lettuce, tomatoes, olives and taco sauce. Dollop each serving with 1 tablespoon of sour cream. **YIELD:** 8 servings.

I still have the card for this recipe that a friend gave me over 25 years ago—the stains on it attest to its frequent use! The chicken turns out juicy and moist, and the sauce makes a tasty gravy.
Norma Harder // Saskatoon, Saskatchewan

BARBECUED CHICKEN
Prep: 20 min. **Bake:** 55 min.

    1 broiler/fryer chicken (4 to 5 pounds), cut up
    1 tablespoon canola oil
  1/2 cup chicken broth
  1/2 cup ketchup
  1/4 cup cider vinegar
    1 tablespoon brown sugar
  1/2 teaspoon curry powder
  1/2 teaspoon paprika
  1/4 teaspoon salt
  1/4 teaspoon ground mustard
  1/8 teaspoon chili powder
Pinch pepper
    2 tablespoons onion soup mix

1 In a large skillet, brown chicken on all sides in oil in batches; drain. Place the chicken in a greased 13-in. x 9-in. baking dish and an 8-in. square baking dish.

2 Combine the broth, ketchup, vinegar, brown sugar, curry powder, paprika, salt, mustard, chili powder and pepper; pour over chicken. Sprinkle with soup mix. Cover and bake at 350° for 55-65 minutes or until the chicken juices run clear. **YIELD:** 4-6 servings.

PEPPER JACK STUFFED CHICKEN
Prep: 20 min. **Bake:** 25 min.

The spicy cheese and Mexican seasoning give plenty of zip to these tender chicken rolls. Round out the meal with rice pilaf and pineapple tidbits.
Taste of Home Test Kitchen

    2 ounces pepper Jack cheese
    2 boneless skinless chicken breast halves
      (4 ounces *each*)
    1 teaspoon Mexican *or* taco seasoning
    1 tablespoon canola oil

1 Cut cheese into two 2-1/4-in. x 1-in. x 3/4-in. strips. Flatten chicken to 1/4-in. thickness. Place a strip of cheese down the center of each chicken breast half; fold chicken over cheese and secure with toothpicks. Rub Mexican seasoning over chicken.

2 In a large skillet, brown chicken in oil on all sides. Transfer to a greased 8-in. square baking dish. Bake, uncovered, at 350° for 25-30 minutes or until meat is no longer pink. Discard toothpicks. **YIELD:** 2 servings.

PEACHY CHICKEN
Prep/Total Time: 25 min.

- 4 boneless skinless chicken breast halves (4 ounces *each*)
- 1 tablespoon canola oil
- 1 tablespoon butter
- 1 can (15-1/4 ounces) sliced peaches, undrained
- 1/2 cup packed brown sugar
- 1/2 cup orange juice
- 1 envelope onion soup mix
- Hot cooked rice, optional

1 In a large skillet, brown chicken in oil and butter over medium heat; remove and keep warm. Stir in the peaches with juice, brown sugar, orange juice and soup mix. Bring to a boil; cook and stir for 2 minutes. Reduce heat; return chicken to the pan. Simmer, uncovered, for 15-20 minutes or until a thermometer reads 170°. Serve over rice if desired. **YIELD:** 4 servings.

HERBED TURKEY BREASTS
Prep: 15 min. + marinating **Cook:** 3-1/2 hours

Tender, moist turkey breast is enhanced with an array of flavorful herbs in this comforting slow-cooked entree.
Laurie Mace // Los Ososo, California

- 2 cans (14-1/2 ounces *each*) chicken broth
- 1 cup lemon juice
- 1/2 cup packed brown sugar
- 1/2 cup fresh sage
- 1/2 cup minced fresh thyme
- 1/2 cup lime juice
- 1/2 cup cider vinegar
- 1/2 cup olive oil
- 2 envelopes onion soup mix
- 1/4 cup Dijon mustard
- 2 tablespoons minced fresh marjoram
- 3 teaspoons paprika
- 2 teaspoons garlic powder
- 2 teaspoons pepper
- 1 teaspoon salt
- 2 boneless turkey breasts (2 pounds *each*)

1 In a blender, process the first 15 ingredients in batches until blended. Pour 3-1/2 cups marinade into a large resealable plastic bag; add the turkey. Seal bag and turn to coat; refrigerate for 8 hours or overnight. Cover and refrigerate remaining marinade.

2 Drain and discard marinade from turkey. Place turkey in a 5-qt. slow cooker; add reserved marinade. Cover and cook on high for 3-1/2 to 4-1/2 hours or until juices run clear and a meat thermometer reads 170°. **YIELD:** 14-16 servings.

This skillet supper comes together with leftover cooked chicken and a packaged mix. After I prepared this rice, I served the extras on tortillas with cheese and sour cream the next day. Both meals were a hit.
Debra Rzodkiewicz // Erie, Pennsylvania

MEXICAN RICE WITH CHICKEN
Prep: 5 min. **Cook:** 30 min.

- 1 package (6.4 ounces) Mexican-style rice and vermicelli mix
- 2 tablespoons butter
- 1-3/4 cups water
- 1 can (14-1/2 ounces) diced tomatoes with onions, undrained
- 2 cups cubed cooked chicken
- 1 jalapeno pepper, seeded and chopped

1 In a large skillet, cook and stir rice and pasta mix in butter until lightly browned, about 5 minutes. Add the water, tomatoes and contents of rice seasoning packet. Bring to a boil. Reduce heat; cover and cook for 10 minutes.

2 Add chicken and jalapeno. Cover and cook for 8-10 minutes or until rice is tender and liquid is absorbed. **YIELD:** 4 servings.

EDITOR'S NOTE: When cutting hot peppers, disposable gloves are recommended. Avoid touching your face.

CHICKEN WITH LEEK SAUCE
Prep/Total Time: 25 min.

This entree, with its rich, creamy and elegant sauce takes less than a half hour from start to table.
Vicki Atkinson // Kamas, Utah

- 1/2 cup all-purpose flour
- 1/8 teaspoon paprika
- 1/8 teaspoon pepper
- 4 boneless skinless chicken breast halves (6 ounces *each*)
- 2 tablespoons canola oil
- 3 tablespoons leek soup mix
- 1 cup water
- 1/2 cup sour cream
- 1-1/2 teaspoons minced chives

1 In a large resealable plastic bag, combine the flour, paprika and pepper. Add chicken, two pieces at a time, and shake to coat. In a large skillet, cook chicken in oil over medium heat for 6-7 minutes on each side or until a meat thermometer reads 170°.

2 Meanwhile, in a small saucepan, bring soup mix and water to a boil, stirring frequently. Reduce heat; simmer, uncovered, for 5 minutes, stirring occasionally. Remove from the heat; stir in sour cream and chives. Serve with chicken. **YIELD:** 4 servings.

CHICKEN FRICASSEE WITH DUMPLINGS

Prep: 20 min. **Cook:** 1 hour 25 min.

  1 **bay leaf**
  9 **whole peppercorns**
  4 **whole cloves**
1/3 **cup all-purpose flour**
1-1/2 **teaspoons salt**
  1 **teaspoon dried marjoram**
  1 **broiler/fryer chicken (3 to 4 pounds), cut up**
  2 **to 4 tablespoons butter**
  6 **large carrots, cut into 1-inch pieces**
1-1/2 **cups chopped onions**
  2 **celery ribs, cut into 1-inch pieces**
  1 **can (14-1/2 ounces) chicken broth**
  1 **cup water**
DUMPLINGS:
1-1/2 **cups biscuit/baking mix**
  2 **tablespoons minced chives**
  1 **egg, lightly beaten**
1/4 **cup milk**
  2 **tablespoons all-purpose flour**
1/2 **cup half-and-half cream**

1 Place the bay leaf, peppercorns and cloves on a double thickness of cheesecloth; bring up corners of cloth and tie with string to form a bag. Set aside. In a large resealable bag, combine flour, salt and marjoram. Add chicken, a few pieces at a time, and shake to coat.

2 In a Dutch oven, brown chicken in batches in butter. Remove and keep warm. In the drippings, saute the carrots, onions and celery for 5-6 minutes or until onions begin to brown. Stir in the broth, water and spice bag. Bring to a boil; add chicken. Reduce heat; cover and simmer for 40 minutes or until chicken juices run clear. Discard spice bag.

3 For dumplings, in a small bowl, combine biscuit mix and chives. Combine egg and milk; add to biscuit mix just until moistened. Drop by heaping tablespoonfuls onto simmering chicken mixture. Cook, uncovered, for 10 minutes. Cover and cook 10 minutes longer or until a toothpick inserted into dumplings comes out clean.

4 Using a slotted spoon, carefully remove chicken and dumplings; keep warm. Combine flour and cream until smooth; stir into cooking juices. Bring to a boil; cook and stir for 2 minutes or until thickened. Serve with chicken and dumplings. **YIELD:** 6-8 servings.

seafood

CORN BREAD-TOPPED SALMON

Prep: 15 min. **Bake:** 30 min.

- 2 cans (10-3/4 ounces *each*) condensed cream of mushroom soup, undiluted
- 1/4 cup milk
- 1 can (14-3/4 ounces) salmon, drained, bones and skin removed
- 1-1/2 cups frozen peas, thawed
- 1 package (8-1/2 ounces) corn bread/muffin mix
- 1 jar (4 ounces) diced pimientos, drained
- 1/4 cup finely chopped green pepper
- 1 teaspoon finely chopped onion
- 1/2 teaspoon celery seed
- 1/4 teaspoon dried thyme

1 In a large saucepan, bring soup and milk to a boil; add salmon and peas. Pour into a greased shallow 2-1/2-qt. baking dish. Prepare corn bread batter according to the package directions; stir in the remaining ingredients. Spoon over salmon mixture.

2 Bake, uncovered, at 400° for 30-35 minutes or until a toothpick inserted in the corn bread comes out clean. **YIELD:** 6-8 servings.

ANGEL HAIR TUNA

Prep/Total Time: 20 min.

This recipe came from a dear friend, and it quickly became a favorite standby in my household. Simply toss together a green salad and toast some garlic bread for a complete meal.

Collette Burch // Edinburg, Texas

- 2 packages (5.1 ounces *each*) angel hair pasta with Parmesan cheese dinner mix
- 1 can (12 ounces) tuna, drained and flaked
- 1/2 teaspoon Italian seasoning
- 3/4 cup crushed butter-flavored crackers (about 15)
- 1/4 cup butter, melted

1 Prepare pasta dinner mixes according to package directions. Stir in the tuna and Italian seasoning.

2 Transfer to a large serving bowl; cover and let stand for 5 minutes to thicken. Toss cracker crumbs and butter; sprinkle over the top. Serve immediately. **YIELD:** 4 servings.

WEEKNIGHT CATFISH WRAPS

Prep: 10 min. + chilling **Cook:** 10 min.

I like to tuck catfish "nuggets" and a convenient coleslaw mix into tortillas with tasty results. The fish gets a slight kick from the Creole seasoning.

Monica Perry // Boise, Idaho

1-1/2 cups coleslaw mix
   2 tablespoons finely chopped onion
 1/8 teaspoon pepper
   1 teaspoon Creole *or* Cajun seasoning, *divided*
 1/4 cup coleslaw salad dressing
   2 tablespoons pancake mix
 1/2 pound catfish fillets, cut into 2-inch pieces
   1 teaspoon canola oil
   4 flour tortillas (6 inches), warmed

1 Combine the coleslaw mix, onion, pepper and 1/4 teaspoon seasoning. Stir in the dressing. Cover and refrigerate for at least 30 minutes.

2 In a resealable plastic bag, combine the pancake mix and remaining seasoning. Add fish and toss to coat. In a small skillet, cook fish in oil over medium heat for 6 minutes or until lightly browned on each side and fish flakes easily with a fork. Spoon coleslaw mixture onto tortillas; top with fish and roll up. **YIELD:** 2 servings.

TIP

Catfish is a mild-flavored fish with a medium texture, so it will hold up well in this recipe. Pollack and haddock can be used in place of the catfish with equally good results.

Shrimp, pepper and a tasty lemon sauce dress up a packaged broccoli rice mix in this speedy main course. I found the recipe years ago and have served it numerous times, always with success. It's a cinch to double for company, and guests always rave about it.
Lynn Corsaro // Florence, Colorado

LEMON GARLIC SHRIMP
Prep/Total Time: 30 min.

1 package (6-1/2 ounces) broccoli au gratin rice and vermicelli mix
1 pound uncooked medium shrimp, peeled and deveined
1 medium sweet red pepper, julienned
3 green onions, cut into 1/2-inch pieces
1 teaspoon minced garlic
1/2 teaspoon Italian seasoning
1 tablespoon butter
2 teaspoons cornstarch
1/2 cup chicken broth
1 tablespoon lemon juice
1 teaspoon grated lemon peel, *divided*

1 Prepare rice mix according to the package directions. Meanwhile, in a large skillet, saute the shrimp, red pepper, onions, garlic and Italian seasoning in butter until shrimp turn pink.

2 Combine the cornstarch, broth and lemon juice until smooth; stir into shrimp mixture. Bring to a boil; cook and stir for 1-2 minutes or until thickened. Stir 1/2 teaspoon lemon peel into prepared rice. Serve with shrimp mixture; sprinkle with remaining lemon peel. **YIELD:** 4 servings.

SEAFOOD POTPIES
Prep: 15 min. Bake: 30 min.

You'll really like this recipe if you favor crab and shrimp. It's an old family favorite, and it tastes gourmet even though it's so easy to make. All my friends love it!
Carol Hickey // Lake St. Louis, Missouri

1 sheet refrigerated pie pastry
1 can (6 ounces) crabmeat, drained, flaked and cartilage removed
1 can (4-1/4 ounces) tiny shrimp, rinsed and drained
1/2 cup chopped celery
1/2 cup mayonnaise
1/4 cup chopped green pepper
2 tablespoons diced pimientos
1 tablespoon lemon juice
1-1/2 teaspoons chopped onion
1/4 teaspoon seafood seasoning
1/4 cup shredded cheddar cheese

1 On a lightly floured surface, roll out pastry to 1/8-in. thickness. Cut out two 7-in. circles (discard scraps or save for another use). Press pastry circles onto the bottom and up the sides of two ungreased 10-oz. custard cups. Place on a baking sheet. Bake at 425° for 7-10 minutes or until golden brown. Reduce heat to 375°.

2 Combine the crab, shrimp, celery, mayonnaise, green pepper, pimientos, lemon juice, onion and seafood seasoning. Spoon into hot shells. Sprinkle with cheese. Bake for 20-25 minutes or until bubbly and cheese is melted. **YIELD:** 2 servings.

The mildness of the fish contrasts perfectly with the deep flavor of pesto. It literally takes 5 minutes to get the fish fillets ready for the oven, so you can start on your choice of side dishes; just about anything goes well with this fish.

April Showalter // Milwaukee, Wisconsin

PESTO HALIBUT
Prep/Total Time: 20 min.

- 2 tablespoons olive oil
- 1 envelope pesto sauce mix
- 1 tablespoon lemon juice
- 6 halibut fillets (4 ounces *each*)

1 Combine the oil, sauce mix and lemon juice; brush over both sides of fillets.

2 Place in a greased 13-in. x 9-in. baking dish. Bake, uncovered, at 450° for 12-15 minutes or until fish flakes easily with a fork. **YIELD:** 6 servings.

ASPARAGUS CRAB OMELETS
Prep/Total Time: 30 min.

Impress your weekend guests with this springtime treatment for eggs. It makes an elegant breakfast, brunch or even lunch dish made with crab, asparagus and a lemon-colored hollandaise sauce that is prepared from a convenient mix.

Dave Eddy // Miles City, Montana

- 1 envelope (1-1/4 ounces) hollandaise sauce mix
- 3 teaspoons canola oil, *divided*
- 8 eggs
- 2 tablespoons milk
- Salt, pepper and garlic powder to taste
- 2 cups (8 ounces) shredded cheddar cheese, *divided*
- 2 cups cut fresh asparagus, cooked, *divided*
- 2 cups flaked imitation crabmeat, coarsely chopped, *divided*
- Minced chives

1 Prepare hollandaise sauce according to the package directions; set aside and keep warm.

2 In a 10-in. nonstick skillet, heat 1-1/2 teaspoons oil over medium-high heat. Whisk the eggs, milk, salt, pepper and garlic powder. Add half of the egg mixture to skillet (mixture should set immediately at edges).

3 As eggs set, push cooked edges toward the center, letting uncooked portion flow underneath. When the eggs are set, sprinkle 1/2 cup cheese on one side. Layer with 1 cup asparagus, 1 cup crab and 1/2 cup cheese; fold omelet in half. Cover and cook for 1-2 minutes or until the cheese is melted. Invert omelet onto a plate. Repeat for second omelet. Serve with hollandaise sauce. Garnish with chives. **YIELD:** 2-4 servings.

An easy-to-make rice mix is turned into a tasty meal with the addition of asparagus and shrimp. You can even add chicken or any variety of green vegetables to suit your taste.
Taste of Home Test Kitchen

CARIBBEAN RICE 'N' SHRIMP
Prep/Total Time: 25 min.

- 1 package (8 ounces) Caribbean rice mix
- 6 cups water
- 1/2 pound fresh asparagus, trimmed and cut into 1-inch pieces
- 1 pound uncooked medium shrimp, peeled and deveined
- 1 medium tomato, chopped

1 Prepare the rice mix according to package directions, omitting chicken.

2 Meanwhile, in a large saucepan, bring water to a boil. Add asparagus; cover and cook for 2 minutes.

3 Stir in shrimp; cook for 2-3 minutes or until shrimp turn pink. Drain. Add asparagus, shrimp and tomato to rice; toss gently. **YIELD:** 4 servings.

GOLDEN TUNA CASSEROLE
Prep: 20 min. **Bake:** 25 min.

Mushrooms, green peppers and onion are added to boxed macaroni and cheese in this comforting take on the classic tuna bake. It is a delicious, hearty and quick-to-fix dinner. I serve it with a tossed salad and hot rolls.

Helen Suter // Richmond, Texas

- 1 package (7-1/4 ounces) macaroni and cheese mix
- 1/2 cup chopped onion
- 1/4 cup chopped green pepper
- 1/3 cup butter
- 3/4 cup milk
- 1 can (10-3/4 ounces) condensed cream of celery soup, undiluted
- 1 can (6 ounces) tuna, drained
- 1 jar (4-1/2 ounces) sliced mushrooms, drained
- 1 jar (2 ounces) diced pimientos, drained

1 Set aside the cheese sauce packet. In a large saucepan, cook the macaroni according to the package directions; drain and set aside.

2 In the same pan, saute onion and green pepper in butter. Return macaroni to the pan. Add milk and contents of cheese sauce packet; stir until smooth. Stir in the soup, tuna, mushrooms and pimientos.

3 Pour into a greased 2-qt. baking dish. Cover and bake at 350° for 25-30 minutes or until bubbly. **YIELD:** 4-6 servings.

The combination of tender salmon, fresh cucumber sauce and a crisp, flaky crust makes this impressive dish perfect for special occasions. Mom likes to decorate the pastry with a star or leaf design for holidays.
Kimberly Laabs // Hartford, Wisconsin

PUFF PASTRY SALMON BUNDLES
Prep: 20 min. **Bake:** 25 min.

- 2 packages (17.3 ounces *each*) frozen puff pastry, thawed
- 8 salmon fillets (6 ounces *each*), skin removed
- 1 egg
- 1 tablespoon water
- 2 cups shredded cucumber
- 1 cup (8 ounces) sour cream
- 1 cup mayonnaise
- 1 teaspoon dill weed
- 1/2 teaspoon salt

1 On a lightly floured surface, roll each pastry sheet into a 12-in. x 10-in. rectangle. Cut each pastry sheet into two 10-in. x 6-in. rectangles. Place a salmon fillet in the center of each rectangle.

2 Beat egg and water; lightly brush over pastry edges. Bring opposite corners of pastry over each fillet; pinch seams to seal tightly. Place seam side down in a greased 15-in. x 10-in. x 1-in. baking pan; brush with remaining egg mixture.

3 Bake at 400° for 25-30 minutes or until pastry is golden brown. In a small bowl, combine the cucumber, sour cream, mayonnaise, dill and salt. Serve with bundles. **YIELD:** 8 servings.

BUSY-DAY BAKED FISH
Prep/Total Time: 30 min.

An onion soup and sour cream mixture really adds zip to this delectable fish entree. Your family would never guess that it's so fast and simple to prepare.
Beverly Krueger // Yamhill, Oregon

- 1 cup (8 ounces) sour cream
- 2 tablespoons onion soup mix
- 1-1/2 cups seasoned bread crumbs
- 2-1/2 pounds fresh *or* frozen fish fillets, thawed
- 1/4 cup butter, melted
- 1/3 cup shredded Parmesan cheese

1 In a shallow bowl, combine sour cream and soup mix. Place bread crumbs in another shallow bowl. Cut fish into serving-size pieces; coat with sour cream mixture, then roll in crumbs.

2 Place in two greased 13-in. x 9-in. baking dishes. Drizzle with butter. Bake, uncovered, at 425° for 12 minutes. Sprinkle with cheese; bake 2-6 minutes longer or until fish flakes easily with a fork. **YIELD:** 6-8 servings.

We find ourselves pressed for time on many evenings, so this dish is a lifesaver. I get a head start using a biscuit/baking mix and canned tuna. Instead of the American cheese, consider Swiss cheese.

Elizabeth Montgomery // Taylorville, Illinois

TUNA BISCUIT SQUARES
Prep/Total Time: 30 min.

- 2/3 cup milk
- 1/3 cup mayonnaise
- 1/3 cup ranch salad dressing
- 4 cups biscuit/baking mix
- 2 cans (6-1/2 ounces *each*) tuna, drained and flaked
- 1/3 cup chopped celery
- 3 tablespoons finely chopped onion
- 2 tablespoons sweet pickle relish
- 1/4 teaspoon garlic powder
- 6 to 8 slices process American cheese

Tomato slices, optional

1 In a large bowl, combine milk, mayonnaise and salad dressing. Stir in biscuit mix until blended. On a lightly floured surface, knead dough 5-8 times. Pat into a greased 13-in. x 9-in. baking pan. Bake at 450° for 12-15 minutes or until lightly browned.

2 Meanwhile, combine the tuna, celery, onion, relish and garlic powder. Spread over crust; top with cheese. Bake for 4 minutes longer or until cheese is melted. Garnish with tomato if desired. **YIELD:** 6 servings.

FISH WITH FLORENTINE RICE
Prep/Total Time: 25 min.

A handful of ingredients is all you'll need to prepare the speedy skillet supper. The entire dinner cooks in one pan and eliminates the hassle of breading and frying the fish.

Margrit Eagen // Crestwood, Missouri

- 1 package (6.9 ounces) chicken-flavored rice mix
- 2 tablespoons butter
- 2-3/4 cups water
- 1 package (10 ounces) frozen chopped spinach
- 1 pound orange roughy *or* tilapia fillets
- 1/4 cup slivered almonds, toasted

1 Set rice seasoning packet aside. In a large skillet, saute rice mix in butter. Add the water, spinach and contents of seasoning packet. Bring to a boil. Reduce heat; cover and simmer for 10 minutes.

2 Top with the fish fillets. Cover and simmer for 5-10 minutes or until fish flakes easily with a fork. Sprinkle with almonds. **YIELD:** 4 servings.

CRAB CAKES WITH LIME SAUCE

Prep/Total Time: 25 min.

Reel in a breezy taste of the seashore with these delectable, crispy-coated crab. The refreshing, lip-smacking lime sauce adds a delightful summery tang to this old-fashioned favorite.

Marjie Gaspar // Oxford, Pennsylvania

- 2 cans (6 ounces *each*) crabmeat, drained, flaked and cartilage removed
- 1 green onion, chopped
- 1 tablespoon Dijon mustard
- 1 teaspoon Italian salad dressing mix
- 1-1/2 cups crushed butter-flavored crackers (about 37), *divided*
- 1 cup mayonnaise, *divided*
- 2 tablespoons lime juice, *divided*
- 1/4 cup canola oil
- 1/4 cup sour cream
- 1-1/2 teaspoons grated lime peel

1 Combine the crab, onion, mustard, dressing mix, 1 cup cracker crumbs, 1/2 cup mayonnaise and 1 tablespoon lime juice. Shape into six patties; coat with remaining cracker crumbs.

2 In a large skillet, heat oil over medium heat. Cook the crab cakes for 3-4 minutes on each side or until they are lightly browned.

3 For lime sauce, in a small bowl, combine the sour cream, lime peel, and remaining mayonnaise and lime juice until blended. Serve with crab cakes. **YIELD:** 3 servings.

When my neighbor prepared these large full-flavored sandwiches, I had to have the recipe. Strips of catfish are treated to a zesty Cajun cornmeal breading, then served on a bun with packaged broccoli coleslaw mix dressed in a homemade sauce.

Mildred Sherrer // Fort Worth, Texas

CATFISH PO'BOYS

Prep/Total Time: 30 min.

- 2 tablespoons fat-free mayonnaise
- 1 tablespoon fat-free sour cream
- 1 tablespoon white wine vinegar
- 1 teaspoon sugar
- 2 cups broccoli coleslaw mix
- 1/4 cup cornmeal
- 2 teaspoons Cajun seasoning
- 1/2 teaspoon salt
- 1/8 teaspoon cayenne pepper
- 2 tablespoons fat-free milk
- 1 pound catfish fillets, cut into 2-1/2-inch strips
- 2 teaspoons olive oil
- 4 kaiser rolls, split

1 In a small bowl, whisk the mayonnaise, sour cream, vinegar and sugar until smooth. Add coleslaw mix; toss to coat. Set aside.

2 In a large resealable plastic bag, combine the cornmeal, Cajun seasoning, salt and cayenne. Place the milk in a shallow bowl. Dip a few pieces of fish at a time in milk mixture, then place in bag; seal and shake to coat.

3 In a large nonstick skillet, cook catfish over medium heat in oil for 4-5 minutes on each side or until fish flakes easily with a fork and coating is golden brown. Spoon coleslaw onto rolls; top with catfish. **YIELD:** 4 servings.

SIMPLE SEAFOOD ALFREDO

Prep/Total Time: 20 min.

After making the pasta mix, simply add seafood to create a meal with a fancy flair. This light and easy recipe came together because I wanted a quick-fix meal that tasted like real seafood Alfredo.
Verna Knox // Live Oak, Florida

- 1 package (4.4 ounces) quick-cooking noodles and Alfredo sauce mix
- 1 package (8 ounces) imitation lobster *or* crabmeat
- 1/2 pound frozen cooked small shrimp, thawed

1 Prepare the noodle mix according to package directions. Stir in lobster and shrimp; heat through. **YIELD:** 3 servings.

This rich and creamy pasta dish with three types of seafood comes together in moments. When I serve it to guests, they say I shouldn't have worked so hard. I never tell them what a breeze it is to assemble.

Renae Rossow // Union, Kentucky

ALFREDO SEAFOOD FETTUCCINE

Prep/Total Time: 20 min.

- 8 ounces uncooked fettuccine
- 1 envelope Alfredo sauce mix
- 1 package (8 ounces) imitation crabmeat
- 6 ounces bay scallops
- 6 ounces uncooked medium shrimp, peeled and deveined
- 1 tablespoon plus 1-1/2 teaspoons butter
- 1/8 to 1/4 teaspoon garlic powder

1 Cook the fettuccine according to package directions. Meanwhile, prepare the Alfredo sauce according to package directions.

2 In a large skillet, saute the crab, scallops and shrimp in butter for 2-3 minutes or until scallops are opaque and shrimp turn pink. Stir into Alfredo sauce. Season with garlic powder. Cook and stir for 5-6 minutes or until thickened. Drain fettuccine; top with seafood mixture. **YIELD:** 4 servings.

PERCH FILLETS

Prep/Total Time: 30 min.

Friends will never guess that lemon-lime soda and pancake mix are the secret ingredients behind these tasty perch fillets in a golden coating. If perch isn't available, try substituting haddock.

Connie Tibbetts // Wilton, Maine

- 1-1/2 cups lemon-lime soda
- 1 pound perch fillets
- 2 cups pancake mix
- 1/4 teaspoon pepper
- Oil for frying

1 Pour soda into a shallow bowl; add fish fillets and let stand for 15 minutes. In another shallow bowl, combine pancake mix and pepper. Remove fish from soda and coat with pancake mix.

2 In a large skillet, heat 1/4 in. of oil over medium-high heat. Fry fish for 2-3 minutes on each side or until fish flakes with a fork. Drain on paper towels. **YIELD:** 4 servings.

While I was in college, my roommates and I loved the taste of ranch dressing so much that it was our condiment of choice for almost everything. So I created these rich, delectable crab enchiladas with ranch dressing mix as my secret ingredient.

Kelly Mockler // Madison, Wisconsin

CHEESY CRAB ENCHILADAS

Prep: 20 min. **Bake:** 30 min.

- 2 packages (8 ounces *each*) cream cheese, softened
- 1 envelope ranch salad dressing mix
- 3 tablespoons plus 1/4 cup milk, *divided*
- 1 small red onion, diced
- 2 garlic cloves, minced
- 2 tablespoons butter
- 1 pound fresh, frozen *or* canned crabmeat, flaked and cartilage removed
- 2 cans (2-1/2 ounces *each*) sliced ripe olives, drained
- 1 can (4 ounces) chopped green chilies
- 1/2 teaspoon pepper
- 1/4 teaspoon salt
- 2 cups (8 ounces) shredded Monterey Jack cheese, *divided*
- 8 flour tortillas (8 inches), warmed
- 1/2 cup shredded Colby cheese

Chopped green onions and tomatoes, shredded lettuce and additional sliced ripe olives, optional

1 In a large bowl, combine the cream cheese, dressing mix and 3 tablespoons milk until smooth. Set aside 3/4 cup for topping.

2 In a large skillet, saute onion and garlic in butter until tender. Stir in the crab, olives, chilies, pepper and salt. Fold crab mixture and 1-1/2 cups Monterey Jack into remaining cream cheese mixture.

3 Spoon about 2/3 cup down the center of each tortilla. Roll up and place seam side down in a greased 13-in. x 9-in. baking dish. Combine remaining milk and reserved cream cheese mixture until blended; pour over tortillas.

4 Sprinkle with Colby and remaining Monterey Jack. Cover and bake 350° for 25 minutes. Uncover; bake 5-10 minutes longer or until heated through. Serve with the green onions, tomatoes, lettuce and olives if desired. **YIELD:** 8 enchiladas.

meatless

CALYPSO BURRITOS

Prep/Total Time: 30 min.

When I build a burrito, I like to use a bounty of beans, veggies, cheese and salsa. My husband doesn't notice he's not getting meat. Serve them with sour cream, chopped tomatoes and avocado. Leftovers make a great taco salad topping.

Darlene Deeg // Vernon, British Columbia

- 2 small zucchini, shredded
- 2 medium carrots, shredded
- 1 medium onion, finely chopped
- 1 tablespoon canola oil
- 1 can (16 ounces) kidney beans, rinsed and drained
- 1 can (15 ounces) black beans, rinsed and drained
- 1-1/2 cups frozen corn, thawed
- 3/4 cup salsa
- 2 tablespoons reduced-sodium taco seasoning
- 2 teaspoons ground cumin
- 1 cup (4 ounces) shredded part-skim mozzarella cheese
- 1/4 cup minced fresh cilantro
- 8 flour tortillas (8 inches), warmed

1 In a large skillet over medium heat, cook and stir the zucchini, carrots and onion in oil for 3-5 minutes or until tender. Stir in the beans, corn, salsa, taco seasoning and cumin. Cook and stir for 5-7 minutes or until vegetables are tender.

2 Remove from the heat. Stir in cheese and cilantro. Spoon about 2/3 cupful filling off center on each tortilla. Fold sides and ends over filling and roll up. **YIELD:** 8 servings.

Served with a green salad and garlic bread, this is the easiest dinner I prepare for my family. They love the four-ingredient main dish and think I worked on it for hours.
Lisa Blackwell // Henderson, North Carolina

ITALIAN BOW TIE BAKE
Prep: 20 min. **Bake:** 15 min.

  8 **ounces uncooked bow tie pasta**
  1 **jar (16 ounces) garlic and onion spaghetti sauce**
  1 **envelope Italian salad dressing mix**
  2 **cups (8 ounces) shredded part-skim mozzarella cheese**

1 Cook pasta according to package directions; drain. In a large bowl, combine the spaghetti sauce and salad dressing mix. Add pasta; toss to coat.

2 Transfer to a greased shallow 2-qt. baking dish. Sprinkle with cheese. Bake, uncovered, at 400° for 15-20 minutes or until heated through. **YIELD:** 4 servings.

ROASTED VEGGIE WRAPS
Prep: 15 min. **Cook:** 25 min.

Give roasted veggies an Italian accent with salad dressing mix and shredded mozzarella, then fold them into flour tortillas. My husband and I really enjoy the assortment of vegetables in these handheld sandwiches.
Jeanette Simec // Ottawa, Illinois

    1 **envelope Parmesan Italian salad dressing mix**
1/4 **cup water**
1/4 **cup red wine vinegar**
    2 **tablespoons olive oil**
    1 **medium sweet red pepper, sliced**
    1 **cup julienned carrots**
    1 **cup quartered fresh mushrooms**
    1 **cup fresh broccoli florets**
    1 **medium onion, sliced and separated into rings**
    1 **medium yellow summer squash, sliced**
    6 **flour tortillas (8 inches)**
1-1/2 **cups (6 ounces) shredded part-skim mozzarella cheese**
Salsa, optional

1 In a small bowl, whisk together the dressing mix, water, vinegar and oil. Place vegetables in a large bowl; drizzle with dressing and toss to coat.

2 Spread vegetables in two 15-in. x 10-in. x 1-in. baking pans coated with cooking spray. Bake, uncovered, at 425° for 20-25 minutes or until the vegetables are tender, stirring occasionally.

3 Spoon about 3/4 cup roasted vegetables off center on each tortilla; sprinkle each with 1/4 cup cheese. Place on a baking sheet.

4 Broil 4-6 in. from the heat for 2 minutes or until cheese is melted. Fold sides and one end of tortilla over filling and roll up. Serve with salsa if desired. **YIELD:** 6 servings.

Although this pizza doesn't have sauce, it gets unforgettable flavor from a blend of cheeses, vegetables and garlic. Using frozen bread dough appeals to folks who don't care to bake.

Davis Johns // Hurst, Texas

FOUR-CHEESE PIZZA
Prep: 15 min. **Bake:** 25 min.

- 1 loaf (16 ounces) frozen bread dough, thawed
- 1 large sweet red pepper, chopped
- 1 large green pepper, chopped
- 1 cup (4 ounces) shredded part-skim mozzarella cheese
- 3/4 cup shredded Swiss cheese
- 1/2 cup grated Parmesan cheese
- 1/2 cup crumbled feta cheese
- 2 tablespoons minced fresh parsley
- 1 tablespoon minced fresh basil *or* 1 teaspoon dried basil
- 3 plum tomatoes, thinly sliced
- 1 tablespoon olive oil
- 2 garlic cloves, minced

1 On a lightly floured surface, roll dough into a 15-in. circle. Transfer to a greased 14-in. pizza pan; build up edges slightly. Prick dough several times with a fork. Bake at 400° for 8-10 minutes or until lightly browned. Remove from the oven.

2 Reduce heat to 375°. Sprinkle the chopped peppers, cheeses, parsley and basil over crust. Arrange tomato slices over top. Combine oil and garlic; brush over tomatoes.

3 Bake for 15-20 minutes or until cheese is melted. Let stand for 5 minutes before cutting. **YIELD:** 8 slices.

GRILLED CHEESE IN A PAN
Prep: 15 min. **Bake:** 30 min.

My cousin served this dish at a shower years ago, and my daughter and I immediately asked for the recipe. If you don't have all of the exact cheeses it calls for, you can switch a couple and it still tastes absolutely delicious.

Mary Ann Wendt // Ephrata, Washington

- 1 tube (8 ounces) refrigerated crescent rolls
- 4 cups (1 cup *each*) shredded Muenster, Monterey Jack, Swiss and cheddar cheese
- 1 package (8 ounces) cream cheese, sliced
- 1 egg, lightly beaten
- 1 tablespoon butter, melted
- 1 tablespoon sesame seeds

1 Unroll the crescent roll dough; divide in half. Seal perforations. Line an ungreased 8-in. square baking pan with half of the dough. Layer with the Muenster, Monterey Jack, Swiss, cheddar and cream cheese. Pour egg over all.

2 Top with remaining dough. Brush with butter; sprinkle with sesame seeds. Bake, uncovered, at 350° for 30-35 minutes or until golden brown. **YIELD:** 9 servings.

My family loves Mexican food, so I created this easy recipe one summer when our garden was bursting with zucchini.
Linda Taylor // Lenexa, Kansas

SPICY ZUCCHINI QUESADILLAS
Prep/Total Time: 25 min.

  1 large onion, chopped
1/2 cup chopped sweet red pepper
  1 teaspoon plus 2 tablespoons butter, softened, *divided*
  2 cups shredded zucchini
  2 tablespoons taco seasoning
  8 flour tortillas (8 inches)
  8 ounces pepper Jack cheese, shredded
Salsa, sour cream and pickled jalapeno pepper slices

1 In a large skillet, saute onion and red pepper in 1 teaspoon butter for 3 minutes. Stir in zucchini and taco seasoning; saute 3-4 minutes longer or until vegetables are tender. Remove from the heat.

2 Spread remaining butter over one side of each tortilla. Place tortillas butter side down on a griddle. Sprinkle about 1/4 cup cheese and 1/4 cup zucchini mixture over half of each tortilla; fold over.

3 Cook over low heat for 1-2 minutes on each side or until cheese is melted. Serve with salsa, sour cream and jalapenos. **YIELD:** 4 servings.

GINGER PLUM STIR-FRY
Prep/Total Time: 30 min.

Here's a great way to get in your vegetables. I lightened up the original recipe by using soy crumbles instead of sausage. I serve it over cooked rice.
Evelyn Joan Brewer // Bluffton, Indiana

  4 teaspoons cornstarch
1/2 teaspoon ground ginger
3/4 cup vegetable broth
1/4 cup reduced-sodium soy sauce
1/4 cup plum sauce
  1 small sweet red pepper, cut into chunks
  1 garlic clove, minced
  2 teaspoons canola oil
  1 cup sliced fresh mushrooms
  1 package (16 ounces) coleslaw mix
1/4 cup thinly sliced green onions
  1 package (12 ounces) frozen vegetarian meat crumbles

1 In a small bowl, combine cornstarch and ginger. Stir in the broth until smooth. Stir in the soy sauce and plum sauce until blended; set aside.

2 In a large nonstick skillet or wok coated with cooking spray, stir-fry red pepper and garlic in oil for 2 minutes. Add mushrooms; stir-fry 2 minutes longer. Add coleslaw mix and onions; stir-fry for 2 minutes.

3 Add vegetarian meat crumbles. Stir broth mixture; gradually stir into skillet. Bring to a boil; cook and stir for 1-2 minutes or until thickened and crumbles are heated through. **YIELD:** 4 servings.

RUSTIC PHYLLO VEGETABLE PIE

Prep: 30 min. **Bake:** 50 min. + standing

- 1 egg, lightly beaten
- 2 cups cooked long grain rice
- 1 cup (8 ounces) 1% cottage cheese
- 1 cup (4 ounces) shredded part-skim mozzarella cheese, *divided*
- 1 tablespoon lemon juice
- 1 teaspoon grated lemon peel
- 1 medium onion, chopped
- 4 garlic cloves, minced
- 1 tablespoon olive oil
- 2 packages (10 ounces *each*) fresh spinach, torn
- 1/2 cup golden raisins
- 1/4 teaspoon ground cinnamon
- 1/8 teaspoon salt
- 12 sheets phyllo dough (14 inches x 9 inches)
- Butter-flavored cooking spray
- 1-1/2 cups meatless spaghetti sauce

1 In a large bowl, combine the egg, rice, cottage cheese, 1/2 cup mozzarella, lemon juice and peel; set aside. In a Dutch oven, saute onion and garlic in oil until tender. Add the spinach, raisins, cinnamon and salt. Cook and stir until spinach is wilted, about 3 minutes. Remove from the heat; stir in remaining mozzarella.

2 Spritz one sheet of phyllo dough with butter-flavored spray. Place in a 9-in. deep-dish pie plate coated with cooking spray, allowing short sides of dough to hang over edges. (Keep remaining phyllo covered with plastic wrap and a damp towel to prevent it from drying out.)

3 Place remaining phyllo sheets in pie plate in a crisscross fashion resembling the spokes of a wheel, spritzing between layers with butter-flavored spray. Spread half of rice mixture into crust; layer with half of spinach mixture and half of spaghetti sauce. Repeat layers.

4 Gently fold edges of dough over filling, leaving center of pie uncovered. Spritz with butter-flavored spray. Cover loosely with foil; bake at 350° for 45 minutes. Uncover; bake 5-10 minutes longer or until filling reaches 160°. Let stand for 10 minutes before cutting.
YIELD: 6 servings.

Here's a creamy and delicious, vegetarian main dish. It's easy to assemble and looks like you really fussed. Serve with a leafy salad, crusty garlic bread and thirst-quenching iced tea.

Debbie Herbert // Seymour, Indiana

SPINACH-STUFFED SHELLS
Prep: 25 min. **Bake:** 25 min.

  15 uncooked jumbo pasta shells
   1 envelope white sauce mix
   1 cup (8 ounces) 4% cottage cheese
 1/2 cup shredded part-skim mozzarella cheese
   1 egg white
 1/2 teaspoon dried basil
 1/4 teaspoon garlic powder
Dash pepper
   1 package (10 ounces) frozen chopped spinach, thawed and squeezed dry
   1 tablespoon shredded Parmesan cheese

1 Cook the pasta according to package directions. Meanwhile, prepare white sauce according to package directions; set aside.

2 In a small bowl, combine the cottage cheese, mozzarella, egg white, basil, garlic powder, pepper and half of the spinach (save remaining spinach for another use). Pour half of the white sauce into a greased 11-in. x 7-in. baking dish.

3 Drain pasta and rinse in cold water; stuff each shell with 2 tablespoons spinach mixture. Arrange over sauce. Top with remaining white sauce.

4 Cover and bake at 375° for 25 minutes or until heated through. Sprinkle with Parmesan cheese. **YIELD:** 5 servings.

BROCCOLI TORTELLINI ALFREDO
Prep/Total Time: 20 min.

I indulge my weakness for fettuccine Alfredo with this trimmed-down tortellini. It has the same rich flavor without the heaviness. Nutmeg adds a lovely accent to the sauce.

Mitzi Sentiff // Annapolis, Maryland

   1 package (9 ounces) refrigerated cheese tortellini
 3/4 pound fresh broccoli florets
   1 envelope Alfredo sauce mix
1-1/2 cups fat-free milk
   2 teaspoons reduced-fat butter
 1/8 teaspoon ground nutmeg

 1/4 cup shredded Parmesan cheese
 1/4 teaspoon pepper

1 Cook tortellini according to package directions, adding broccoli during the last few minutes. Meanwhile, in a small saucepan, whisk the sauce mix and milk. Add butter and nutmeg; bring to a boil. Reduce heat; simmer, uncovered, for 2 minutes, stirring constantly.

2 Drain tortellini and broccoli; place in a large bowl. Stir in the Alfredo sauce, Parmesan cheese and pepper. **YIELD:** 4 servings.

EDITOR'S NOTE: This recipe was tested with Land O'Lakes light stick butter.

SOUTHWEST LASAGNA ROLLS

Prep: 20 min. **Bake:** 35 min.

We love this south-of-the-border lasagna. The cheesy dish comes together fast with a carton of vegetarian chili, and it makes a great entree served with a green salad and baked tortilla chips.

Trisha Kruse // Eagle, Idaho

- 8 lasagna noodles
- 1 can (15 ounces) fat-free vegetarian chili
- 1 carton (15 ounces) reduced-fat ricotta cheese
- 1 cup (4 ounces) shredded reduced-fat Mexican cheese blend
- 1 can (4 ounces) chopped green chilies
- 1 teaspoon taco seasoning
- 1/4 teaspoon salt
- 1 jar (16 ounces) salsa

1 Cook lasagna noodles according to package directions; drain. In a large bowl, combine the chili, cheese, chilies, taco seasoning and salt. Spread about 1/2 cup on each noodle; carefully roll up. Place seam side down in a 13-in. x 9-in. baking dish coated with cooking spray.

2 Cover and bake at 350° for 25 minutes. Uncover; top with salsa. Bake 10 minutes longer or until heated through. **YIELD:** 8 servings.

TIP

By using fat-free and lower-fat items for this dish, the calories come in at 259 and there is only 6 grams of fat and 3 grams of saturated fat in a serving.

sides

When I tried out these roasted potato wedges on my family, it was love at first taste. Since I generally have the onion soup mix and seasonings on hand, the recipe couldn't be easier. Spice amounts can be altered to your brood's liking.

Irene Marshall // Nampa, Idaho

CHILI-SEASONED POTATO WEDGES

Prep: 10 min. **Bake:** 35 min.

- 1 tablespoon onion soup mix
- 1 tablespoon chili powder
- 1/4 teaspoon salt
- 1/4 teaspoon garlic powder
- 1/4 teaspoon pepper
- 4 large baking potatoes
- 2 tablespoons canola oil

1 In a large resealable plastic bag, combine the soup mix, chili powder, salt, garlic powder and pepper. Cut each potato into eight wedges; place in the bag and shake to coat potatoes.

2 Arrange in a single layer in a greased 15-in. x 10-in. x 1-in. baking pan. Drizzle with oil. Bake, uncovered, at 425° for 12-20 minutes on each side or until crisp. **YIELD:** 8 servings.

TRIPLE-CHEESE BROCCOLI PUFF

Prep: 15 min. **Bake:** 50 min. + standing

On our Christmas morning menu is this rich-tasting souffle. Like any puffy souffle, it will settle a bit after you remove the dish from the oven, but the pretty golden top is still very attractive. I often add some cubed ham.

Maryellen Hays // Wolcottville, Indiana

- 1 cup sliced fresh mushrooms
- 1 tablespoon butter
- 1 package (3 ounces) cream cheese, softened
- 6 eggs
- 1 cup milk
- 3/4 cup biscuit/baking mix
- 3 cups frozen chopped broccoli, thawed
- 2 cups (8 ounces) shredded Monterey Jack cheese
- 1 cup (8 ounces) 4% cottage cheese
- 1/4 teaspoon salt

1 In a small skillet, saute mushrooms in butter until tender; set aside. In a large bowl, beat the cream cheese, eggs, milk and biscuit mix just until combined. Stir in the broccoli, cheeses, salt and mushrooms.

2 Pour into a greased round 2-1/2-qt. baking dish. Bake, uncovered, at 350° for 50-60 minutes or until a thermometer reads 160°. Let stand for 10 minutes before serving. **YIELD:** 6-8 servings.

VEGGIE SPIRAL SALAD

Prep/Total Time: 20 min.

My husband and son detested pasta salad before I came up with this one. There were no leftovers the very first time I served it, and now it's a summertime family favorite! Filled with fresh, crunchy radishes and celery, juicy tomatoes and cucumbers, this nutritious recipe is one to try with your gang.

Melody Loyd // Parowan, Utah

- 1 cup uncooked tricolor spiral pasta
- 1/2 cup chopped seeded cucumber
- 1/2 cup thinly sliced celery
- 1/2 cup chopped red onion
- 1/2 cup sliced radishes
- 1/2 cup chopped tomatoes
- 1/2 cup sliced ripe olives, drained
- 1/2 cup shredded Swiss cheese
- 1/8 teaspoon garlic powder
- 1/8 teaspoon pepper
- 1 tablespoon Italian salad dressing mix
- 2 tablespoons plus 1-1/2 teaspoons cider vinegar
- 2 tablespoons olive oil

1 Cook the pasta according to package directions. Meanwhile, in a large bowl, combine the cucumber, celery, onion, radishes, tomatoes, olives, cheese, garlic powder and pepper. Drain pasta and rinse in cold water; stir into vegetable mixture.

2 In a bowl, whisk together the dressing mix, vinegar and oil. Drizzle over the salad and toss to coat. Serve immediately or refrigerate. **YIELD:** 5 servings.

TIP

You can easily beef up this pasta salad. Buy hard salami at the deli counter and ask them to cut it into thick slices, about 1/4 in. thick. Then chop or dice it when you get home and toss it into the salad. Or, halve slices of pepperoni and add to the salad.

Green beans get a makeover with help from fresh mushrooms, ranch salad dressing mix and crumbled bacon. For added convenience, I sometimes use canned mushrooms when fixing this side dish.

Nicole Orr // Columbus, Ohio

GREEN BEANS WITH A TWIST
Prep/Total Time: 15 min.

- 1 package (16 ounces) frozen
  French-style green beans
- 1 cup sliced fresh mushrooms
- 2 tablespoons butter
- 1 envelope ranch salad dressing mix
- 4 bacon strips, cooked and crumbled

1 In a large skillet, saute beans and mushrooms in butter. Sprinkle with dressing mix; toss to coat. Just before serving, sprinkle with bacon. **YIELD**: 4-6 servings.

TWICE-BAKED RANCH POTATOES
Prep: 15 min. + freezing **Cook**: 30 min. + standing

I make the most of leftover mashed potatoes to create these creamy stuffed potatoes. You can enjoy two and store the other two in the freezer. They warm up nicely in the microwave.

Janice Arnold // Gansevoort, New York

- 4 large baking potatoes (about 2-1/4 pounds)
- 1 package (3 ounces) cream cheese, softened
- 2 tablespoons milk
- 1 envelope (1 ounce) ranch salad dressing mix
- 1-1/2 cups mashed potatoes
- 1/4 cup shredded cheddar cheese

1 Scrub and pierce potatoes; place on a microwave-safe plate. Microwave, uncovered, on high for 13-15 minutes or until tender, turning several times. Let stand for 10 minutes.

2 Meanwhile, in a small bowl, combine cream cheese and milk until smooth; beat in the salad dressing mix. Add mashed potatoes and mix well.

3 Cut a thin slice from the top of each potato; scoop out pulp, leaving a thin shell. Add pulp to the cream cheese mixture and mash. Spoon into potato shells. Top with cheese. Place two potatoes on a microwave-safe plate. Microwave, uncovered, on high for 3-1/2 to 4-1/2 minutes or until heated through. Place remaining potatoes on a baking sheet. Freeze overnight or until thoroughly frozen; transfer to a freezer bag. May be frozen for up to 3 months.

4 **TO USE FROZEN POTATOES**: Place the potatoes on a microwave-safe plate. Microwave, uncovered, at 50% power for 8-9 minutes or until heated through. **YIELD**: 4 servings.

EDITOR'S NOTE: This recipe was tested in a 1,100-watt microwave.

*Despite my sometimes hectic schedule, I enjoy
cooking for family and friends. This recipe is
one of my favorites.*
            Pam Holloway // Marion, Louisiana

CORN BREAD SALAD

Prep: 15 min. **Bake:** 20 min. + cooling

  1 package (8-1/2 ounces) corn bread/muffin mix
  2 cans (11 ounces *each*) Mexicorn, drained, *divided*
  3 medium tomatoes, diced
3/4 cup chopped green pepper
  1 medium onion, chopped
  1 cup mayonnaise
  4 bacon strips, cooked and crumbled

1 Prepare corn bread batter according to the package
directions; stir in one can of Mexicorn. Bake according
to package directions. Cool and crumble.

2 In a large bowl, combine the crumbled corn bread,
tomatoes, green pepper, onion and remaining corn. Add
the mayonnaise; toss to coat. Sprinkle with the bacon.
Serve or refrigerate. **YIELD:** 10-12 servings.

ONION-STUFFED ACORN SQUASH

Prep: 25 min. **Bake:** 50 min.

*Acorn squash are such a treat this time of year, especially when
dressed up for the holidays with a special stuffing. I found this
recipe in an old cookbook that was handed down to me.*
            Barb Zamowski // Rockford, Illinois

  3 small acorn squash, halved and seeded
  1 egg, lightly beaten
1/4 teaspoon salt
1/8 teaspoon pepper
  1 teaspoon chicken bouillon granules
  2 tablespoons boiling water
1/4 cup chopped onion
  2 tablespoons butter
  1 cup crushed sage stuffing mix

1 Invert squash in a greased 15-in. x 10-in. x 1-in. baking
pan. Fill pan with hot water to a depth of 1/4 in. Bake,
uncovered, at 400° for 30 minutes or until tender.
When cool enough to handle, scoop out pulp, leaving a
1/4-in. shell (pulp will measure about 3 cups). Place
shells cut side up in a greased 15-in. x 10-in. x 1-in. baking
pan; set aside.

2 In a large bowl, combine the pulp, egg, salt and pepper.
Dissolve bouillon in water; add to squash mixture. In a
small saucepan, saute onion in butter until tender; stir in
stuffing mix. Set aside 1/4 cup for topping; add
remaining stuffing mixture to squash mixture. Bake,
uncovered, at 400° for 20 minutes or until heated
through. **YIELD:** 6 servings.

SQUASH STUFFING CASSEROLE

Prep: 15 min. **Cook:** 4 hours

My friends just rave about this creamy side dish. It's a snap to jazz up summer squash, zucchini and carrots with canned soup and stuffing mix.

Pamela Thorson // Hot Springs, Arkansas

1/4 cup all-purpose flour
1 can (10-3/4 ounces) condensed cream of chicken soup, undiluted
1 cup (8 ounces) sour cream
2 medium yellow summer squash, cut into 1/2-inch slices
1 small onion, chopped
1 cup shredded carrots
1 package (8 ounces) stuffing mix
1/2 cup butter, melted

1 In a bowl, combine the flour, soup and sour cream until blended. Add the vegetables and gently stir to coat.

2 Combine the stuffing mix and butter; sprinkle half into a 5-qt. slow cooker. Top with vegetable mixture and remaining stuffing mixture. Cover and cook on low for 4-5 hours or until vegetables are tender. **YIELD:** 8 servings.

TIP

You can also make use of your garden's bounty of zucchini in this dish. Use it for part or all of the yellow summer squash.

There's plenty of saucy cheese flavor in this simple pasta dish. Taco seasoning and canned chilies give it a zippy Southwestern flair. Make it as spicy as you like by using mild or hot chilies and regular or spicy taco seasoning. Save the rest of the taco seasoning packet to use for another dish.
Aaron Werner // Oconomowoc, Wisconsin

CHILI CHEDDAR PENNE

Prep/Total Time: 25 min.

1-1/3 cups uncooked penne pasta
    4 teaspoons butter
    4 teaspoons all-purpose flour
    1 cup milk
    2 cups (8 ounces) shredded cheddar cheese
    4 teaspoons taco seasoning
  1/4 teaspoon salt
  2/3 cup frozen corn, thawed
  2/3 cup chopped fresh tomatoes
    1 can (4 ounces) chopped green chilies, drained
Sliced avocado, optional

1 Cook pasta according to package directions. Meanwhile, in a large saucepan, melt butter over medium heat. Stir in flour until smooth; gradually add milk. Bring to a boil; cook and stir for 2 minutes or until thickened. Reduce heat to medium. Stir in the cheese, taco seasoning and salt. Cook and stir for 2-3 minutes or until cheese is melted.

2 Drain pasta; stir into cheese sauce. Cook and stir for 3 minutes or until heated through. Stir in the corn, tomatoes and chilies just until combined. Garnish with avocado if desired. **YIELD:** 6 servings.

TEXAS TWO-STEP SLAW

Prep/Total Time: 20 min.

This quick and colorful slaw is laced with ranch dressing. It's a family favorite and comes together in minutes, but for those with time to plan ahead, chilling for an hour helps to blend the flavors.
Sharon Wencel // Austin, Texas

    3 cups coleslaw mix
  1/4 cup Mexicorn, drained
    1 jalapeno pepper, seeded and chopped
    2 tablespoons chopped red onion
    1 tablespoon minced fresh cilantro
  1/2 cup shredded cheddar cheese
  1/2 cup ranch salad dressing
1-1/2 teaspoons lime juice
  1/2 teaspoon ground cumin

1 In a large bowl, combine the first six ingredients. In a small bowl, combine the salad dressing, lime juice and cumin. Pour over the coleslaw and toss to coat. Refrigerate until serving. **YIELD:** 8 servings.

EDITOR'S NOTE: When cutting hot peppers, disposable gloves are recommended. Avoid touching your face.

Broccoli, cauliflower, green beans and red pepper give traditional potato salad a new twist. It's a fresh-tasting dish that makes a nice addition to all your meals.
Sally Burek // Fenton, Michigan

SALLY'S POTATO SALAD
Prep: 20 min. + chilling **Cook:** 20 min.

   6 medium red potatoes, cubed
1-1/2 cups chopped celery
1-1/2 cups fresh broccoli florets
   3/4 cup cut fresh green beans, blanched
   1/2 cup fresh cauliflowerets
   1/2 cup julienned sweet red pepper
   1/4 cup fat-free Italian salad dressing
   1/2 cup reduced-fat mayonnaise
     2 teaspoons reduced-fat ranch salad dressing mix
   1/4 teaspoon pepper

1 Place potatoes in a large saucepan and cover with water. Bring to a boil. Reduce heat; cover and simmer for 15-20 minutes or until tender.

2 Meanwhile, in a large bowl, combine the celery, broccoli, beans, cauliflower, red pepper and Italian dressing. Drain potatoes and add to the vegetable mixture. Combine the mayonnaise, salad dressing mix and pepper; pour over the vegetable mixture and toss to coat. Cover and chill for at least 2 hours. **YIELD:** 16 servings.

FLAVORFUL ONIONY ASPARAGUS
Prep/Total Time: 20 min.

As a working mom with four children, I don't have much time to cook big meals during the week. But on Sundays, when I make a special meal, this is our favorite way to enjoy asparagus.
Kathy Mitchell // Tinley Park, Illinois

   2 pounds fresh asparagus, trimmed
   1/4 cup butter, cubed
     1 tablespoon onion soup mix
   1/2 cup shredded part-skim mozzarella cheese

1 Place asparagus in a steamer basket. Place in a large saucepan or skillet over 1 in. of water; bring to a boil. Cover and steam for 4-5 minutes or until crisp-tender.

2 In a small saucepan, melt butter. Add soup mix. Cook and stir for 1 minute or until heated through. Remove asparagus to a serving dish. Drizzle with butter mixture; sprinkle with cheese. **YIELD:** 8-10 servings.

As the caretaker for a private home, I sometimes cook for the young family who lives there. Although I'm an old-fashioned cook, my job has me trying new flavors. Everyone likes these grilled vegetables.

Jan Oeffler // Danbury, Wisconsin

ONION-BASIL GRILLED VEGETABLES

Prep: 25 min. **Cook:** 25 min.

- 3 medium ears fresh corn, cut into 3 pieces
- 1 pound medium red potatoes, quartered
- 1 cup fresh baby carrots
- 1 large green pepper, cut into 1-inch pieces
- 1 large sweet red pepper, cut into 1-inch pieces
- 1 envelope onion soup mix
- 3 tablespoons minced fresh basil *or*
  1 tablespoon dried basil
- 1 tablespoon olive oil
- 1/4 teaspoon pepper
- 1 tablespoon butter

1 In a large bowl, combine the first nine ingredients. Toss to coat. Place on a double thickness of heavy-duty foil (about 28 in. x 18 in.). Dot with butter. Fold foil around vegetable mixture and seal tightly. Grill, covered, over medium heat for 25-30 minutes or until potatoes are tender, turning once. **YIELD:** 6 servings.

CITRUS RICE PILAF

Prep/Total Time: 30 min.

Food doesn't have to be made from scratch to have great homemade flavor. Here, packaged rice mix gets added flair from crunchy snow peas and water chestnuts.

Taste of Home Test Kitchen

- 1 package (6.9 ounces) chicken-flavored rice and vermicelli mix
- 2 tablespoons butter
- 2-3/4 cups water
- 1 package (6 ounces) frozen snow peas
- 1 can (8 ounces) sliced water chestnuts, drained
- 1 to 2 tablespoons orange marmalade
- 1/4 teaspoon pepper

1 In a large skillet, saute rice mix in butter until golden brown. Stir in water and contents of rice seasoning packet. Bring to a boil. Reduce heat; cover and simmer for 15 minutes. Stir in peas, water chestnuts, marmalade and pepper. Cover and cook for 3-4 minutes or until rice and vegetables are tender. **YIELD:** 4 servings.

My family's not big on traditional pasta salad made with mayonnaise, so when I served this colorful version that uses Italian dressing, it was a big hit. This crowd-pleaser is loaded with vegetables, beans and tricolor pasta.
Felicia Fiocchi // Vineland, New Jersey

PICNIC PASTA SALAD
Prep/Total Time: 25 min.

- 1 package (12 ounces) tricolor spiral pasta
- 1 package (10 ounces) refrigerated tricolor tortellini
- 1 jar (7-1/2 ounces) marinated artichoke hearts, undrained
- 1/2 pound fresh broccoli florets (about 1-3/4 cups)
- 12 ounces provolone cheese, cubed
- 12 ounces hard salami, cubed
- 1 medium sweet red pepper, chopped
- 1 medium green pepper, chopped
- 1 can (15 ounces) garbanzo beans *or* chickpeas, rinsed and drained
- 2 cans (2-1/4 ounces *each*) sliced ripe olives, drained
- 1 medium red onion, chopped
- 4 garlic cloves, minced
- 2 envelopes Italian salad dressing mix

1 Cook spiral pasta and tortellini according to package directions. Drain and rinse in cold water. Place in a large bowl; add the artichokes, broccoli, provolone cheese, salami, peppers, beans, olives, onion and garlic.

2 Prepare salad dressing according to package directions; pour over salad and toss to coat. Serve immediately or cover and refrigerate. **YIELD:** 14-16 servings.

SAUSAGE CORN BREAD DRESSING
Prep/Total Time: 25 min.

I like to dress up stuffing mix with pork sausage and jarred mushrooms to create this in-a-dash dressing. The hearty side dish is terrific with chicken, turkey or pork.
Ruby Harman // Carrollton, Missouri

- 1 pound bulk pork sausage
- 3-1/2 cups water
- 1 jar (7 ounces) sliced mushrooms, drained
- 2 packages (6 ounces *each*) corn bread stuffing mix

1 In a large skillet, brown the sausage; drain. Add water and mushrooms. Bring to a boil. Remove from the heat; add the stuffing mix. Cover and let stand for 5 minutes. **YIELD:** 8 servings.

VEGETABLE SPIRAL STICKS

Prep/Total Time: 30 min.

I love to serve these savory wrapped vegetable sticks for parties or special occasions. They're a simple but impressive appetizer or side.

Teri Albrecht // Mt. Airy, Maryland

- 3 medium carrots
- 12 fresh asparagus spears, trimmed
- 1 tube (11 ounces) refrigerated breadsticks
- 1 egg white, lightly beaten
- 1/4 cup grated Parmesan cheese
- 1/2 teaspoon dried oregano

1 Cut carrots lengthwise into quarters. In a large skillet, bring 2 in. of water to a boil. Add carrots; cook for 3 minutes. Add asparagus; cook 2-3 minutes longer. Drain and rinse with cold water; pat dry.

2 Cut each piece of breadstick dough in half. Roll each piece into a 7-in. rope. Wrap one rope in a spiral around each vegetable. Place on a baking sheet coated with cooking spray; tuck ends of dough under vegetables to secure.

3 Brush with egg white. Combine cheese and oregano; sprinkle over sticks. Bake at 375° for 12-14 minutes or until golden brown. Serve warm. **YIELD:** 2 dozen.

EDITOR'S NOTE: This recipe was tested with Pillsbury refrigerated breadsticks.

TIP

You can omit the Parmesan cheese and oregano and sprinkle the dough with sesame seeds or poppy seeds before baking.

GLAZED FRUIT BOWL
Prep/Total Time: 30 min.

This quick-to-fix fruit salad combines summer favorites such as cantaloupe, honeydew and strawberries into a refreshing side dish. You can substitute other fruits if you like.

Christine Wilson // Sellersville, Pennsylvania

- 2 cans (20 ounces *each*) unsweetened pineapple chunks
- 2 packages (3 ounces *each*) cook-and-serve vanilla pudding mix
- 2-1/2 cups orange juice
- 1 small cantaloupe, cubed
- 3-1/2 cups cubed honeydew
- 2 cups fresh strawberries, halved
- 2 cups fresh blueberries
- 2 cups seedless grapes
- 2 medium firm bananas, sliced

1 Drain pineapple, reserving 1 cup juice; set pineapple aside. (Discard remaining juice or save for another use.)

2 In a large saucepan, combine the pudding mix, pineapple juice and orange juice. Cook and stir over medium heat until mixture boils and thickens. Remove from the heat; cool.

3 In a large bowl, combine the pineapple, melons, berries, grapes and bananas. Drizzle with pudding mixture. Refrigerate until serving. **YIELD:** 25 servings.

This vegetable combination makes a delightful side dish or weekend brunch specialty. It's long been a favorite with my children. I like it because it's so easy to put together and can easily be lightened up by using reduced-fat ingredients.

Jacque Capurro // Anchorage, Alaska

VEGGIE CHEESE CASSEROLE

Prep: 10 min. **Bake:** 35 min.

    3 cups frozen chopped broccoli, thawed and drained
1/2 cup biscuit/baking mix
    1 cup (8 ounces) sour cream
    1 cup (8 ounces) 4% cottage cheese
    2 eggs
1/4 cup butter, melted
1/4 teaspoon salt
    1 large tomato, thinly sliced and halved
1/4 cup grated Parmesan cheese

1 Arrange the broccoli in a greased 8-in. square baking dish; set aside.

2 In a large bowl, beat the biscuit mix, sour cream, cottage cheese, eggs, butter and salt; pour over broccoli. Arrange tomato slices over the top; sprinkle with Parmesan cheese.

3 Bake, uncovered, at 350° for 35-40 minutes or until a thermometer reads 160°. Let stand for 5 minutes before cutting. **YIELD:** 9 servings.

SKILLET RANCH VEGETABLES

Prep/Total Time: 20 min.

Celebrate the last garden harvest with this satisfying side dish. Simply cook carrots, squash and zucchini in oil that's been spiced up with ranch dressing mix. You'll be able to dish out hot and hearty helpings in minutes!

Taste of Home Test Kitchen

    1 tablespoon canola oil
    1 envelope buttermilk ranch salad dressing mix
    2 medium carrots, thinly sliced
    2 medium yellow squash, sliced
    2 medium zucchini, sliced

1 In a skillet, combine the oil and salad dressing mix. Add carrots; cook over medium heat for 4-5 minutes or until crisp-tender. Add squash and zucchini; cook 4-5 minutes longer or until all of the vegetables are tender. Remove with a slotted spoon to serving dish. **YIELD:** 4 servings.

This sparking salad has a popular flavor combination...cherry and cola. It's always been a hit when I serve it.

Judy Nix // Toccoa, Georgia

CHERRY COKE SALAD

Prep: 10 min. + chilling

    1 can (20 ounces) crushed pineapple
  1/2 cup water
    2 packages (3 ounces *each*) cherry gelatin
    1 can (21 ounces) cherry pie filling
  3/4 cup cola

1 Drain pineapple, reserving juice; set fruit aside. In a saucepan or microwave, bring pineapple juice and water to a boil. Add gelatin; stir until dissolved. Stir in pie filling and cola.

2 Pour into a serving bowl. Refrigerate until slightly thickened. Fold in reserved pineapple. Refrigerate until firm. **YIELD:** 10-12 servings.

BACON RANCH POTATOES

Prep: 10 min. **Bake:** 35 min.

When I prepare mashed potatoes, I often make extras, just so we can have this casserole the next day.

Kathryn Hostetler // West Farmington, Ohio

    6 cups mashed potatoes (prepared with
      milk and butter)
    1 cup (8 ounces) 4% cottage cheese
  1/2 cup milk
    1 medium onion, finely chopped
    2 tablespoons ranch salad dressing mix
    1 pound sliced bacon, cooked and crumbled
    2 cups (8 ounces) shredded Monterey Jack cheese
    1 cup crushed butter-flavored crackers
      (about 25 crackers)
  1/4 cup butter, melted

1 In a large bowl, combine the potatoes, cottage cheese, milk, onion and dressing mix. Spread in a greased 3-qt. baking dish. Top with bacon and cheese.

2 Combine cracker crumbs and butter; sprinkle over top. Bake, uncovered, at 350° for 35-40 minutes or until bubbly. **YIELD:** 8-10 servings.

Since this dish is one of my favorites, my mother would always make it for me when I did not feel well. Just smelling it simmer made me feel better, along with her tender loving care.

Viola Stutz // Greenwood, Delaware

STEWED TOMATOES WITH DUMPLINGS

Prep/Total Time: 20 min.

    1 can (14-1/2 ounces) diced tomatoes, undrained
    1 tablespoon sugar
    1/4 teaspoon salt
    1/4 teaspoon pepper
    2 tablespoons butter
    1/2 cup biscuit/baking mix
    3 tablespoons milk

1 In a large saucepan, combine the tomatoes, sugar, salt, pepper and butter. Bring to a boil over medium heat, stirring occasionally.

2 Combine biscuit mix and milk. Drop batter in four mounds onto the tomatoes. Reduce heat; cover and simmer for 10 minutes or until a toothpick inserted in a dumpling comes out clean (do not lift cover while simmering). **YIELD:** 2 servings.

PECAN TOSSED SALAD

Prep/Total Time: 10 min.

This light and refreshing salad comes together in a snap. Toasting the pecans really gives them a rich flavor. Sometimes I double the dressing and just refrigerate the rest for later use.

Bonnie Gluhanich // Muskegon, Michigan

    1/2 cup olive oil
    1/4 cup balsamic vinegar
    2 tablespoons water
    1 envelope Italian salad dressing mix
    1 package (10 ounces) ready-to-serve salad greens
    1/3 cup pecan halves, toasted
    1/4 cup shredded Parmesan cheese

1 In a jar with a tight-fitting lid, combine the oil, vinegar, water and salad dressing mix; shake well. In a large salad bowl, combine greens, pecans and Parmesan. Just before serving, shake dressing and pour over salad; toss to coat. **YIELD:** 6 servings.

Oregon's fertile Willamette Valley produces a lot of hazelnuts, and this is one of my favorite ways to use them. I came up with this vegetable side dish while experimenting in the kitchen.

Florence Snyder // Hillsboro, Oregon

BROCCOLI-HAZELNUT BAKE
Prep: 20 min. **Bake:** 25 min.

- 8 cups chopped fresh broccoli *or* 2 packages (10 ounces *each*) chopped frozen broccoli
- 5 tablespoons butter, *divided*
- 3 tablespoons all-purpose flour
- 1-1/2 cups milk
- 2 teaspoons chicken bouillon granules
- 1 cup herb-seasoned stuffing mix
- 1/4 cup water
- 2/3 cup chopped hazelnuts *or* filberts, toasted

1 In a large saucepan, bring 1 in. of water and broccoli to a boil. Reduce heat; cover and simmer for 5-6 minutes or until crisp-tender.

2 In a saucepan, melt 3 tablespoons butter over medium heat. Stir in flour until blended. Gradually add milk and bouillon, stirring constantly. Cook and stir until thickened and bubbly; cook and stir 2 minutes longer.

3 Drain broccoli; add to sauce; gently toss to coat. Pour into a greased 9-in. square baking dish. In large bowl, combine the stuffing mix, water and nuts. Melt the remaining butter; pour over stuffing mixture and toss to coat. Spoon over broccoli. Bake, uncovered, at 350° for 25-30 minutes. **YIELD:** 6 servings.

CREAMY CORN
Prep/Total Time: 30 min.

I make this recipe often because it only takes minutes to prepare and really hits the spot on chilly or rainy days. Cheese and cream-style corn really turn the seasoned noodles into a comforting sensation.

Carol White // Vernona, Illinois

- 1 package (4.3 ounces) quick-cooking noodles and butter herb sauce mix
- 1 can (14-3/4 ounces) cream-style corn
- 2 ounces process cheese (Velveeta), cubed

1 Prepare noodles and sauce mix according to package directions. When the noodles are tender, stir in corn and cheese; cook and stir until cheese is melted. Let stand for 5 minutes. **YIELD:** 6-8 servings.

FRUITED GELATIN SALAD

Prep: 30 min. + chilling

I've found this salad to be perfect for potlucks and special occasions. It cuts nicely into squares and can be served on lettuce leaves if you like.

Norma Warner // Hot Springs Village, Arkansas

- 2 packages (3 ounces *each*) orange gelatin
- 2 cups boiling water
- 1 cup apricot nectar
- 1 cup pineapple juice
- 1 can (15 ounces) apricot halves, drained and mashed
- 1 can (8 ounces) crushed pineapple, drained
- 4 cups miniature marshmallows

TOPPING:
- 1/2 cup sugar
- 2 tablespoons all-purpose flour
- 1/2 cup apricot nectar
- 1/2 cup pineapple juice
- 1 egg, lightly beaten
- 2 tablespoons butter
- 1 cup heavy whipping cream
- 1 cup (4 ounces) shredded cheddar cheese

1 In a large bowl, dissolve gelatin in boiling water. Stir in the juices, apricots and pineapple. Transfer to a 13-in. x 9-in. dish coated with cooking spray. Refrigerate for 30 minutes or until geletin is partially set. Sprinkle with the marshmallows; refrigerate.

2 For topping, combine sugar and flour in a saucepan. Gradually whisk in juices. Bring to a boil over medium heat; cook and stir for 2 minutes or until thickened. Removed from the heat. Stir a small amount into egg; return all to the pan, stirring constantly. Cook and stir until a thermometer reads 160° and mixture is thickened. Remove from the heat; stir in butter. Cool to room temperature.

3 In a small bowl, beat cream on high speed until stiff peaks form. Gently fold into custard. Spread over gelatin; sprinkle with cheese. Refrigerate 1 hour or until chilled. **YIELD:** 12-16 servings.

A colorful mix of zucchini, onion, celery, green pepper and tomato is at its best in this simple side dish. Mom came up with this recipe as a way to use up her garden vegetables. It has the flavor of summer.

Sue Gronholz // Columbus, Wisconsin

MOM'S VEGETABLE MEDLEY
Prep/Total Time: 20 min.

- 2 celery ribs, chopped
- 1 medium green pepper, chopped
- 2 tablespoons chopped onion
- 2 tablespoons butter
- 3 small zucchini, quartered lengthwise and sliced
- 1 medium tomato, chopped
- 1 tablespoon onion soup mix

1 In a large skillet, saute the celery, green pepper and onion in butter for 6-8 minutes. Add zucchini; cook and stir over medium heat until tender. Add tomato and soup mix; cook and stir until tomato is tender. **YIELD:** 8 servings.

BROCCOLI ROLL-UPS
Prep/Total Time: 20 min.

It takes only three ingredients and less than half an hour to fix these tasty snacks. What a great way to eat your vegetables!

Taste of Home Test Kitchen

- 1 tube (4 ounces) refrigerated crescent rolls
- 1 slice process American cheese, quartered
- 4 frozen broccoli spears, thawed and patted dry

1 Separate crescent dough into four triangles. Place a piece of cheese and a broccoli spear along the wide edge of each triangle; roll up dough. Place point side down on an ungreased baking sheet. Bake at 375° for 12-15 minutes or until golden brown. **YIELD:** 4 servings.

I came up with this recipe when I had some leftover taco seasoning mix. I used it to spice up oven fries...and they were an immediate hit with my family!

Linda Tepper // Clifton Park, New York

SPICY ROASTED POTATOES

Prep/Total Time: 30 min.

    3 medium red potatoes, cut into 1-inch pieces
    1 tablespoon taco seasoning
    1 tablespoon canola oil

1 In a large resealable plastic bag, combine all ingredients; shake to coat. Place potatoes in a 9-in. square baking pan coated with cooking spray. Bake, uncovered, at 450° for 25-30 minutes or until tender, stirring once. **YIELD:** 2 servings.

CRAN-RASPBERRY SAUCE

Prep: 20 min. + chilling

Sweet raspberries mellow the cranberries' tart flavor in this rave-winning cranberry sauce. It's an ideal accompaniment to Thanksgiving and Christmas meals when cranberry sauce is a popular side dish.

Madeline Farina // Leola, Pennsylvania

    1 package (12 ounces) fresh *or* frozen cranberries
    1 cup cranberry juice
  1/2 cup water
  1/4 cup sugar
    1 package (3 ounces) raspberry gelatin
    1 cup ice cubes
    2 cups fresh *or* frozen raspberries

1 In a large saucepan, combine the cranberries, cranberry juice, water and sugar. Bring to a boil. Reduce heat; simmer, uncovered, for 10 minutes or until cranberries pop. Stir in gelatin until dissolved.

2 Remove from the heat. Add ice cubes; stir until melted. Gently fold in raspberries. Cool to room temperature. Cover and refrigerate overnight. **YIELD:** 4 cups.

WILD RICE BARLEY SALAD

Prep/Total Time: 30 min.

I like this chilled salad because it's out of the ordinary. The rice is tossed with barley, green pepper, olives and cranberries, then coated with a tangy vinaigrette.

Mared Metzger Beling // Eagle River, Alaska

- 1 package (6 ounces) long grain and wild rice mix
- 1 cup cooked barley
- 1/2 cup chopped green pepper
- 1/2 cup sliced ripe olives
- 1/4 cup dried cranberries

DRESSING:
- 1/4 cup balsamic vinegar
- 2 tablespoons minced fresh basil
- 1 tablespoon chopped green onion
- 2 garlic cloves, minced
- 1/2 teaspoon pepper
- 1/3 cup olive oil

1 Cook rice according to package directions. In a large serving bowl, combine the rice, barley, green pepper, olives and cranberries.

2 In a blender, combine the vinegar, basil, green onion, garlic and pepper. While processing, gradually add oil in a steady stream.

3 Drizzle over salad and toss to coat. Cover and refrigerate until chilled. **YIELD:** 4-6 servings.

soups

CHICKEN SOUP WITH POTATO DUMPLINGS

Prep: 25 min. **Cook:** 40 min.

- 1/4 cup chopped onion
- 2 garlic cloves, minced
- 1 tablespoon canola oil
- 6 cups chicken broth
- 2 cups cubed cooked chicken
- 2 celery ribs, chopped
- 2 medium carrots, sliced
- 1/4 teaspoon dried sage leaves

DUMPLINGS:

- 1-1/2 cups biscuit/baking mix
- 1 cup cold mashed potatoes (with added milk)
- 1/4 cup milk
- 1 tablespoon chopped green onion
- 1/8 teaspoon pepper

1 In a large saucepan, saute onion and garlic in oil for 3-4 minutes or until onion is tender. Stir in the broth, chicken, celery, carrots and sage. Bring to a boil. Reduce heat; cover and simmer for 10-15 minutes or until vegetables are tender.

2 In a small bowl, combine the dumpling ingredients. Drop heaping tablespoonfuls of batter onto simmering soup. Cover and simmer for 20 minutes or until a toothpick inserted in a dumpling comes out clean (do not lift cover while simmering). **YIELD:** 5 servings.

HEARTY TORTELLINI SOUP

Prep: 5 min. **Cook:** 30 min.

Once you brown the sausage, it's a snap to throw in the other ingredients and let them simmer. Frozen tortellini is added minutes before serving for a savory soup that tastes like you spent hours making it.

Diana Lauhon // Minerva, Ohio

- 3 uncooked Italian sausage links (1/2 to 3/4 pound)
- 4 cups water
- 2 cans (14-1/2 ounces *each*) Italian stewed tomatoes
- 1 can (10-1/2 ounces) condensed French onion soup, undiluted
- 2 cups broccoli coleslaw mix
- 2 cup frozen cut green beans
- 2 cups frozen cheese tortellini
- Grated Parmesan cheese, optional

1 Cut sausage into 3/4-in. pieces; brown in a Dutch oven or stockpot. Drain. Add the water, tomatoes, soup, coleslaw mix and beans; bring to a boil. Reduce heat; cover and simmer for 20-25 minutes or until vegetables are tender.

2 Uncover; add tortellini. Cook for 3-5 minutes or until pasta is tender. Garnish with cheese if desired. **YIELD:** 10-12 servings (about 3 quarts).

ITALIAN WEDDING SOUP

Prep: 30 min. **Cook:** 45 min.

I enjoyed a similar soup for lunch at work one day and decided to re-create it at home. I love the combination of meatballs, vegetables and pasta.

Noelle Myers // Grand Forks, North Dakota

- 2 eggs, lightly beaten
- 1/2 cup seasoned bread crumbs
- 1 pound ground beef
- 1 pound bulk Italian sausage
- 3 medium carrots, sliced
- 3 celery ribs, diced
- 1 large onion, chopped
- 3 garlic cloves, minced
- 4-1/2 teaspoons olive oil
- 4 cans (14-1/2 ounces *each*) reduced-sodium chicken broth
- 2 cans (14-1/2 ounces *each*) beef broth
- 1 package (10 ounces) frozen chopped spinach, thawed and squeezed dry
- 1/4 cup minced fresh basil
- 1 envelope onion soup mix
- 4-1/2 teaspoons ketchup
- 1/2 teaspoon dried thyme
- 3 bay leaves
- 1-1/2 cups uncooked penne pasta

1 In a large bowl, combine the eggs and bread crumbs. Crumble beef and sausage over mixture; mix well. Shape into 3/4-in. balls.

2 Place meatballs on a greased rack in a foil-lined 15-in. x 10-in. x 1-in. baking pan. Bake at 350° for 15-18 minutes or until no longer pink. Meanwhile, in a Dutch oven, saute carrots, celery, onion and garlic in oil until tender. Stir in the broths, spinach, basil, soup mix, ketchup, thyme and bay leaves.

3 Drain meatballs on paper towels. Bring soup to a boil; add meatballs. Reduce heat; simmer, uncovered, for 30 minutes. Add pasta; cook 13-15 minutes longer or until tender, stirring occasionally. Discard bay leaves before serving. **YIELD:** 10 servings (2-1/2 quarts).

I found this recipe a few years ago and made a few changes to suit our tastes. We love this creamy soup because it starts with a package of macaroni and cheese, and it's ready in a jiffy.

Nancy Daugherty // Cortland, Ohio

MAC 'N' CHEESE SOUP

Prep/Total Time: 30 min.

> 1 package (14 ounces) deluxe macaroni and cheese dinner mix
> 9 cups water, *divided*
> 1 cup fresh broccoli florets
> 2 tablespoons finely chopped onion
> 1 can (10-3/4 ounces) condensed cheddar cheese soup, undiluted
> 2-1/2 cups milk
> 1 cup chopped fully cooked ham

1 Set aside cheese sauce packet from macaroni and cheese mix. In a large saucepan, bring 8 cups water to a boil. Add the macaroni; cook for 8-10 minutes or until tender.

2 Meanwhile, in another large saucepan, bring remaining water to a boil. Add broccoli and onion; cook for 3 minutes. Stir in soup, milk, ham and contents of cheese sauce packet; heat through. Drain macaroni; stir into soup. **YIELD:** 8 servings.

SANTA FE CHILI

Prep: 20 min. Cook: 4 hours

This colorful and hearty chili is perfect for heartwarming, holiday get-togethers. My family has been enjoying it for years.

Laura Manning // Lilburn, Georgia

> 2 pounds ground beef
> 1 medium onion, chopped
> 2 cans (16 ounces *each*) kidney beans, rinsed and drained
> 2 cans (15 ounces *each*) black beans, rinsed and drained
> 2 cans (15 ounces *each*) pinto beans, rinsed and drained
> 2 cans (11 ounces *each*) shoepeg corn
> 1 can (14-1/2 ounces) whole tomatoes, diced
> 1 can (10 ounces) diced tomatoes and green chilies
> 1 can (11-1/2 ounces) V8 juice
> 2 envelopes ranch salad dressing mix
> 2 envelopes taco seasoning
> Sour cream, shredded cheddar cheese and corn chips, optional

1 In a skillet, cook beef and onion over medium heat until meat is no longer pink; drain. Transfer to a 5-qt. slow cooker. Stir in the beans, corn, tomatoes, juice, salad dressing mix and taco seasoning.

2 Cover and cook on high for 4 hours or until heated through. Serve with sour cream, cheese and corn chips if desired. **YIELD:** 4 quarts (16 servings).

Homemade taste makes this chunky soup a favorite of mine. We enjoy it with hot bread in winter and with salad in summer.
Elaine Bickford // Las Vegas, Nevada

TURKEY NOODLE SOUP

Prep: 10 min. **Cook:** 35 min.

    2 cans (14-1/2 ounces *each*) chicken broth
    3 cups water
1-3/4 cups sliced carrots
  1/2 cup chopped onion
    2 celery ribs, sliced
    1 package (12 ounces) frozen egg noodles
    3 cups chopped cooked turkey
    1 package (10 ounces) frozen peas
    2 envelopes chicken gravy mix
  1/2 cup cold water

1 In a large saucepan, bring the broth, water, carrots, onion and celery to a boil. Reduce heat; cover and simmer for 4-6 minutes or until vegetables are crisp-tender. Add the noodles. Simmer, uncovered for 20 minutes or until noodles are tender.

2 Stir in turkey and peas. Combine gravy mixes and cold water until smooth; stir into soup. Bring to a boil; cook and stir for 2 minutes or until thickened. **YIELD:** 7 servings.

HAMBURGER RICE SOUP

Prep: 10 min. **Cook:** 35 min.

The aroma of this soup simmering on the stove makes the kitchen smell so good. The second helping tastes even better than the first! If there are any leftovers, I pop them in the freezer.
Jean Fisher // Waynesboro, Pennsylvania

    1 pound ground beef
  1/2 cup chopped onion
   14 cups water
    1 can (28 ounces) diced tomatoes, undrained
    1 envelope onion soup mix
    3 tablespoons Worcestershire sauce
    1 tablespoon salt
    1 teaspoon brown sugar
    1 teaspoon celery salt
  1/8 teaspoon pepper
  1/2 cup uncooked long grain rice

1 In a stockpot or Dutch oven, cook beef and onion over medium heat until meat is no longer pink; drain.

2 Add the water, tomatoes, soup mix, Worcestershire sauce, salt, brown sugar, celery salt and pepper; bring to a boil. Add rice. Reduce heat; cover and simmer for 20-25 minutes or until rice is tender. **YIELD:** 20 servings (5 quarts).

VEGETABLE SOUP WITH DUMPLINGS

Prep: 25 min. **Cook:** 40 min.

Not only is this hearty soup my family's favorite meatless recipe, but it's a complete meal-in-one. It's loaded with vegetables, and the fluffy carrot dumplings are a great change of pace at dinnertime.

Karen Mau // Jacksboro, Tennessee

1-1/2 cups chopped onions
    4 medium carrots, sliced
    3 celery ribs, sliced
    2 tablespoons canola oil
    3 cups vegetable broth
    4 medium potatoes, peeled and sliced
    4 medium tomatoes, chopped
    2 garlic cloves, minced
 1/2 teaspoon salt
 1/2 teaspoon pepper
 1/4 cup all-purpose flour
 1/2 cup water
    1 cup chopped cabbage
    1 cup frozen peas

CARROT DUMPLINGS:

2-1/4 cups reduced-fat biscuit/baking mix
    1 cup shredded carrots
    1 tablespoon minced fresh parsley
    1 cup cold water
   10 tablespoons shredded reduced-fat cheddar cheese

1 In a Dutch oven, cook the onions, carrots and celery in oil for 6-8 minutes or until crisp-tender. Stir in the broth, potatoes, tomatoes, garlic, salt and pepper. Bring to a boil. Reduce heat; cover and simmer for 15-20 minutes or until vegetables are tender.

2 In a small bowl, combine flour and water until smooth; stir into vegetable mixture. Bring to a boil; cook and stir for 2 minutes or until thickened. Stir in cabbage and peas.

3 For dumplings, in a small bowl, combine baking mix, carrots and parsley. Stir in water until moistened. Drop in 10 mounds onto simmering soup. Cover and simmer for 15 minutes or until a toothpick inserted in a dumpling comes out clean (do not lift cover while simmering). Garnish with cheese. **YIELD:** 10 servings.

This tasty soup has a surprisingly short simmering time. Leftover turkey has never tasted so good! If you don't have frozen mixed vegetables on hand, stir in extra veggies from your Thanksgiving meal until heated through.

Taste of Home Test Kitchen

TURKEY RICE SOUP

Prep: 10 min. **Cook:** 30 min.

- 1/2 cup sliced fresh mushrooms
- 1/2 cup chopped onion
- 2 teaspoons canola oil
- 2 cans (14-1/2 ounces *each*) chicken broth
- 2 cups water
- 1/2 cup apple juice, optional
- 1 package (6 ounces) long grain and wild rice mix
- 2-1/2 cups cubed cooked turkey
- 2 cups frozen mixed vegetables

1 In a large saucepan, saute mushrooms and onion in oil for 3 minutes. Stir in the broth, water and apple juice if desired. Bring to a boil. Stir in rice mix. Reduce heat; cover and simmer for 20 minutes.

2 Stir in turkey and vegetables; cook 5 minutes longer or until rice and vegetables are tender. **YIELD:** 6 servings.

POTLUCK PASTA SOUP

Prep: 15 min. **Cook:** 1 hour 25 min.

In an attempt to duplicate a soup served at an Italian restaurant, I came up with this recipe. Friends and family are willing dinner guests when it's on the menu.

Marilyn Foss // Beaverton, Ohio

- 1-1/2 pounds ground beef
- 8 cups water
- 2 cans (14-1/2 ounces *each*) Italian stewed tomatoes
- 2 cups diced carrots
- 1-1/2 cups diced celery
- 1 cup chopped onion
- 1 can (8 ounces) tomato sauce
- 1 envelope onion soup mix
- 1 tablespoon sugar
- 1 teaspoon Italian seasoning
- 2 garlic cloves, minced
- 2 bay leaves
- 1/2 teaspoon pepper
- 3 cups cooked elbow macaroni
- 1 can (15 ounces) garbanzo beans, rinsed and drained
- 1/2 cup chopped green pepper

1 In a Dutch oven or stockpot, cook beef over medium heat until no longer pink; drain. Add the water, tomatoes, carrots, celery, onion, tomato sauce, soup mix and seasonings; bring to a boil. Reduce heat; simmer, uncovered, for 1 hour.

2 Stir in the macaroni, beans and green pepper; heat through. Discard bay leaves. **YIELD:** 20 servings (5 quarts).

Chock-full of potatoes, Italian sausage and spinach, this hearty soup is sure to disappear fast. Not only is it delicious and quick, but it freezes well. Adjust the amount of broth to suit your family's preference.

Bonita Krugler // Anderson, Indiana

SPINACH SAUSAGE SOUP
Prep/Total Time: 30 min.

- 1 pound bulk Italian sausage
- 4 cans (14-1/2 ounces *each*) chicken broth
- 8 small red potatoes, quartered and thinly sliced
- 1 envelope Italian salad dressing mix
- 2 cups fresh spinach *or* frozen chopped spinach

1 In a large skillet, brown sausage over medium heat until no longer pink. Meanwhile, in a Dutch oven, combine the broth, potatoes and salad dressing mix. Bring to a boil; cover and simmer for 10 minutes or until potatoes are tender.

2 Drain sausage. Add sausage and spinach to broth mixture; heat through. **YIELD**: 10 servings (2-1/2 quarts).

BLACK BEAN POTATO CHILI
Prep: 5 min. **Cook**: 3 hours 20 min. + standing

Although I was always interested in cooking, I never got a chance to do much of it until I got married. I used to only rely on cookbooks, but over time, I became more confident and started creating my own recipes. This is one I'm especially proud of.

Giovanna Garver // Paonia, Colorado

- 1 pound dried black beans
- 6 cups water
- 1 can (28 ounces) diced tomatoes, undrained
- 1 pound ground beef, cooked and drained
- 4 medium potatoes, peeled and cubed
- 2 medium onions, chopped
- 1 can (16 ounces) enchilada sauce
- 1 envelope chili seasoning
- 1 tablespoon sugar
- 2 teaspoons salt
- 1 teaspoon garlic powder

1 Place the beans in a stockpot or Dutch oven; add water to cover by 2 in. Bring to a boil; boil for 2 minutes. Remove from the heat; cover and let stand for 1-4 hours or until beans are softened. Drain and discard liquid.

2 Add 6 cups water to the beans; bring to a boil. Reduce heat; cover and simmer for 2 hours or until beans are almost tender.

3 Add remaining ingredients. Cover and simmer for 1 hour or until soup reaches desired consistency. **YIELD**: 12 servings (3 quarts).

MEXICAN CHICKEN SOUP

Prep: 10 min. **Cook:** 3 hours

This zesty dish is loaded with chicken, corn and black beans in a mildly spicy red broth. As a busy mom, I'm always looking for dinner recipes that can be prepared in the morning. The kids love the taco-like taste of this easy soup.

Marlene Kane // Lainesburg, Michigan

1-1/2   **pounds boneless skinless chicken breasts, cubed**
   2   **teaspoons canola oil**
 1/2   **cup water**
   1   **envelope reduced-sodium taco seasoning**
   1   **can (32 ounces) V8 juice**
   1   **jar (16 ounces) salsa**
   1   **can (15 ounces) black beans, rinsed and drained**
   1   **package (10 ounces) frozen corn, thawed**
   6   **tablespoons reduced-fat cheddar cheese**
   6   **tablespoons reduced-fat sour cream**
   2   **tablespoons minced fresh cilantro**

1 In a large nonstick skillet, saute chicken in oil until no longer pink. Add water and taco seasoning; simmer until chicken is well coated.

2 Transfer to a 5-qt. slow cooker. Stir in the V8 juice, salsa, beans and corn. Cover and cook on low for 3-4 hours or until heated through. Serve with cheese, sour cream and cilantro. **YIELD:** 6 servings.

TIP

This taco-flavored soup is fun to garnish. Just treat it like a taco and let your imagination go wild. You can top it with chopped ripe olives, avocado, green onion or tomato. You can also top with toasted or fried strips of flour tortillas.

This hearty three-bean soup is very easy to fix. You can add a can of green chilies if you like it hotter. I increase the amount of tomatoes and beans for large church get-togethers.

Sharon Thompson // Hunter, Kansas

TACO BEAN SOUP
Prep: 15 min. **Cook:** 45 min.

- 1 pound bulk pork sausage
- 1 pound ground beef
- 1 envelope taco seasoning
- 4 cups water
- 2 cans (16 ounces *each*) kidney beans, rinsed and drained
- 2 cans (15 ounces *each*) pinto beans, rinsed and drained
- 2 cans (15 ounces *each*) garbanzo beans *or* chickpeas, rinsed and drained
- 2 cans (14-1/2 ounces *each*) stewed tomatoes
- 2 cans (14-1/2 ounces *each*) Mexican diced tomatoes, undrained
- 1 jar (16 ounces) chunky salsa

Sour cream, shredded cheddar cheese and sliced ripe olives, optional

1 In a Dutch oven, cook sausage and beef over medium heat until no longer pink; drain. Add taco seasoning and mix well. Stir in the water, beans, tomatoes and salsa. Bring to a boil. Reduce heat; simmer, uncovered, for 30 minutes or until heated through, stirring occasionally. Garnish with sour cream, cheese and olives if desired. **YIELD:** 12-14 servings.

NAVY BEAN VEGETABLE SOUP
Prep: 15 min. **Cook:** 9 hours

My family likes bean soup, so I came up with this robust version. The leftovers freeze well for first-rate future meals.

Eleanor Mielke // Mitchell, South Dakota

- 4 medium carrots, thinly sliced
- 2 celery ribs, chopped
- 1 medium onion, chopped
- 2 cups cubed fully cooked ham
- 1-1/2 cups dried navy beans
- 1 package (1.70 ounces) vegetable soup mix
- 1 envelope onion soup mix
- 1 bay leaf
- 1/2 teaspoon pepper
- 8 cups water

1 In a 5-qt. slow cooker, combine the vegetables, ham, beans, soup mixes, bay leaf and pepper. Stir in water. Cover and cook on low for 9-10 hours or until beans are tender. Discard bay leaf. **YIELD:** 12 servings.

I always like to try new and different things. So I added a package of leek soup mix to my potato soup, and my family loved it. It was even a hit with my picky teenagers.

Terri Day // Rochester, Washington

POTATO LEEK SOUP

Prep/Total Time: 30 min.

2 cups water
2 medium potatoes, peeled and diced
2 bacon strips, cooked and crumbled
2 cups milk
3/4 cup mashed potato flakes
1 package (1.8 ounces) leek soup and dip mix
Shredded cheddar cheese

1 In a large saucepan, bring the water, potatoes and bacon to a boil. Reduce heat; cover and simmer for 10-15 minutes or until potatoes are tender.

2 Reduce heat to low. Stir in the milk, potato flakes and soup mix. Cook and stir for 5 minutes or until heated through. Sprinkle with cheese. **YIELD:** 5 servings.

CREAM OF WILD RICE SOUP

Prep: 15 min. **Cook:** 25 min.

I used to make this soup on the evening when we would pick out our Christmas tree. But my husband enjoys it so much, I now make it throughout the year.

Tammy Bailey // Hastings, Minnesota

1 package (6 ounces) long grain and wild rice mix
1 cup chopped onion
4-1/2 teaspoons butter
4-1/2 teaspoons all-purpose flour
1/2 teaspoon ground mace
Pinch white pepper
3 cans (14-1/2 ounces *each*) chicken broth
2 cups half-and-half cream
1/2 cup white wine *or* additional chicken broth

1 Prepare rice mix according to package directions.

2 In a large saucepan, saute onion in butter until tender. Stir in the flour, mace and white pepper until blended. Gradually stir in the broth, cream, wine and cooked rice. Bring to a boil, stirring constantly. **YIELD:** 10 servings (2-1/2 quarts).

MEXICAN BEAN SOUP

Prep: 20 min. **Cook:** 45 min.

For our family's fall birthday bash, I make a big pot of this soup and serve it with plenty of oven-fresh corn bread.

Vivian Christian // Stephenville, Texas

- 2 pounds ground beef
- 1 medium onion, chopped
- 4 cups water
- 3 cans (14-1/2 ounces *each*) diced tomatoes, undrained
- 2 cans (15-1/2 ounces *each*) hominy, drained
- 2 cans (15-1/2 ounces *each*) ranch-style *or* chili beans
- 1 can (16 ounces) kidney beans, rinsed and drained
- 1 can (4 ounces) chopped green chilies
- 2 envelopes taco seasoning
- 1 envelope (1 ounce) original ranch dressing mix
- 2 tablespoons brown sugar
- 1/4 teaspoon cayenne pepper

Shredded cheddar cheese and sour cream, optional

1 In a Dutch oven or stockpot, brown beef and onion; drain. Add the water, tomatoes, hominy, beans, chilies, taco seasoning, dressing mix, sugar and cayenne; bring to a boil. Reduce heat; cover and simmer for 30 minutes. Garnish with cheese and sour cream if desired. **YIELD:** 14-16 servings (4 quarts).

TIP

To turn this into a hearty, meatless soup, omit the ground beef, and saute the onion in a little canola oil. Add vegetarian meat crumbles (look for them in the frozen food section of your supermarket) to the pan along with the water.

I love soup and serve it often. My sister gave me this delicious recipe. It can be cooked up in no time, and it also freezes well.

Martha Pollock // Oregonia, Ohio

BROCCOLI WILD RICE SOUP

Prep: 5 min. **Cook:** 30 min.

   5 **cups water**
   1 **package (6 ounces) long grain and wild rice mix**
   1 **can (10-3/4 ounces) reduced-fat reduced-sodium condensed cream of chicken soup, undiluted**
1-1/2 **cups fat-free milk**
   1 **package (8 ounces) fat-free cream cheese, cubed**
1/4 **teaspoon salt**
   3 **cups frozen chopped broccoli, thawed**

   1 **large carrot, shredded**
1/4 **cup sliced almonds, toasted**

1 In a large saucepan, combine the water and rice mix with contents of seasoning packet; bring to a boil. Reduce heat; cover and simmer for 20 minutes.

2 Add the soup, milk, cream cheese and salt; stir until cheese is melted. Add broccoli and carrot; cook over medium-low heat for 5-6 minutes or until vegetables and rice are tender. Sprinkle with almonds. **YIELD:** 6 servings.

CHUNKY TURKEY CHILI

Prep: 30 min. **Cook:** 2 hours

When I needed a hearty dish for a benefit cook-off at work, I decided on this recipe but substituted ground turkey for the beef. Everyone raved about the great flavor, and many people requested the recipe.

Judith Southcombe // Aurora, Colorado

5 **pounds ground turkey**
6 **cups chopped celery**
2 **medium green peppers, chopped**
2 **large onions, chopped**

2 **cans (28 ounces *each*) crushed tomatoes**
2 **cups water**
2 **envelopes (1-3/4 ounces *each*) chili seasoning**
1 **to 2 tablespoons chili powder**
2 **cans (16 ounces *each*) kidney beans, rinsed and drained**

1 In a Dutch oven over medium heat, brown turkey; drain. Add celery, peppers and onions; cook and stir for 5 minutes. Add the tomatoes, water, chili seasoning and chili powder; bring to a boil. Reduce heat; cover and simmer for 2 hours. Add beans; heat through. **YIELD:** 24 servings (6 quarts).

BEEF VEGETABLE SOUP

Prep: 10 min. **Cook:** 4 hours

- 1 pound lean ground beef
- 1 medium onion, chopped
- 2 garlic cloves, minced
- 4 cups picante V8 juice
- 2 cups coleslaw mix
- 1 can (14-1/2 ounces) Italian stewed tomatoes
- 1 package (10 ounces) frozen corn
- 1 package (9 ounces) frozen cut green beans
- 2 tablespoons Worcestershire sauce
- 1 teaspoon dried basil
- 1/4 teaspoon pepper

1 In a large nonstick skillet, cook the beef, onion and garlic over medium heat until meat is no longer pink; drain. Transfer to a 5-qt. slow cooker. Stir in the remaining ingredients. Cover and cook on high for 4-5 hours or until heated through. **YIELD:** 9 servings.

LENTIL AND BROWN RICE SOUP

Prep: 20 min. **Cook:** 45 min.

The first time I made this soup, I thought our teenage son would turn up his nose. Much to my delight—and surprise—he loved every bite! I know you will, too.
Janis Plourde // Smooth Rock Falls, Ontario

- 2 quarts water
- 3/4 cup dried lentils, rinsed
- 1/2 cup uncooked brown rice
- 1 envelope onion soup mix
- 1 can (14-1/2 ounces) diced tomatoes, undrained
- 1 medium carrot, diced
- 1/2 cup diced celery
- 1 tablespoon minced fresh parsley
- 4 chicken bouillon cubes
- 1/2 teaspoon dried basil
- 1/2 teaspoon dried oregano
- 1/2 teaspoon salt
- 1/2 teaspoon pepper
- 1/4 teaspoon dried thyme
- 1 tablespoon cider vinegar, optional

1 In a Dutch oven or stockpot, combine all ingredients except vinegar; bring to a boil. Reduce heat; cover and simmer for 35-45 minutes or until lentils and rice are tender, stirring occasionally. Stir in vinegar if desired. **YIELD:** 12-14 servings (3-1/2 quarts).

CHILI WITH CORN BREAD TOPPING

Prep: 20 min. **Bake:** 15 min.

- 1/3 **pound lean ground beef**
- 1/4 **cup chopped onion**
- 1 **can (15 ounces) chili with beans**
- 1/2 **cup water**
- 3/4 **cup corn bread/muffin mix**
- 3 **tablespoons 2% milk**
- 2 **tablespoons beaten egg**
- 1/3 **cup shredded cheddar cheese**
- 1/4 **cup frozen corn, thawed**

1 In a large skillet, cook beef and onion over medium heat until meat is no longer pink; drain. Stir in chili and water. Bring to a boil. Reduce heat; cover and simmer for 10 minutes. Pour into two 2-cup baking dishes.

2 In a small bowl, combine the corn bread mix, milk and egg. Stir in cheese and corn just until combined. Spread batter evenly over chili. Bake at 400° for 15-18 minutes or until topping is golden brown. **YIELD:** 2 servings.

TURKEY BARLEY TOMATO SOUP

Prep: 15 min. **Cook:** 40 min.

This low-calorie soup is so quick to prepare and tastes so good. It's a real stomach-filler and warms us up on cold winter days.
Denise Kilgore // Lino Lakes, Minnesota

- 1 **pound lean ground turkey**
- 3/4 **cup sliced *or* baby carrots**
- 1 **medium onion, chopped**
- 1 **celery rib, chopped**
- 1 **garlic clove, minced**
- 1 **envelope reduced-sodium taco seasoning, *divided***
- 3-1/2 **cups water**
- 1 **can (28 ounces) Italian diced tomatoes, undrained**
- 3/4 **cup quick-cooking barley**
- 1/2 **teaspoon minced fresh oregano *or* 1/8 teaspoon dried oregano**

1 In a Dutch oven, cook the turkey, carrots, onion, celery, garlic and 1 tablespoon taco seasoning over medium heat until meat is no longer pink. Stir in the water, tomatoes and remaining taco seasoning; bring to a boil. Reduce heat; cover and simmer for 20 minutes.

2 Add barley; cover and simmer for 15-20 minutes longer or until barley is tender. Stir in oregano. **YIELD:** 6 servings.

Here's a Western twist on traditional turkey dumpling soup. I especially like this recipe because it's fast, easy and uses up leftover turkey or chicken.

Lisa Williams // Steamboat Springs, Colorado

SOUTHWESTERN TURKEY DUMPLING SOUP

Prep: 15 min. **Cook:** 30 min.

- 1 can (15 ounces) tomato sauce
- 1 can (14-1/2 ounces) diced tomatoes, undrained
- 1-3/4 cups water
- 1 envelope chili seasoning
- 3 cups diced cooked turkey *or* chicken
- 1 can (16 ounces) kidney beans, rinsed and drained
- 1 can (15 ounces) black beans, rinsed and drained
- 1 can (15-1/4 ounces) whole kernel corn, drained
- 1-1/2 cups biscuit/baking mix
- 1/2 cup cornmeal
- 3/4 cup shredded cheddar cheese, *divided*
- 2/3 cup milk

1 In a Dutch oven, combine the tomato sauce, tomatoes, water, chili seasoning and turkey; bring to a boil. Reduce heat; cover and simmer for 10 minutes, stirring occasionally. Add beans and corn.

2 In a large bowl, combine biscuit mix, cornmeal and 1/2 cup of cheese; stir in the milk. Drop by heaping tablespoonfuls onto the simmering soup. Cover and cook for 12-15 minutes or until dumplings are firm. Sprinkle with remaining cheese; cover and simmer 1 minute longer or until the cheese is melted. Serve immediately. **YIELD**: 6-8 servings (2-1/2 quarts).

POTATO SHRIMP CHOWDER

Prep/Total Time: 25 min.

With only three ingredients, this chowder couldn't be any simpler! I like recipes that get me out of the kitchen in a flash. I often serve this dish with crackers or hot bread and a green salad.
Martha Castille // Opelousas, Louisiana

- 1 package (11 ounces) cream of potato soup mix
- 1 cup frozen mixed vegetables
- 1 pound frozen cooked small shrimp, thawed

1 In a large saucepan, prepare soup mix according to package directions, adding the mixed vegetables.

2 Stir in shrimp; cook 5-6 minutes longer or until heated through. **YIELD**: 12 servings (3 quarts).

breads

GARLIC BUBBLE LOAF

Prep: 10 min. + rising **Bake:** 30 min.

- 1/4 cup butter, melted
- 1 tablespoon dried parsley flakes
- 1 teaspoon garlic powder
- 1/4 teaspoon garlic salt
- 1 loaf (1 pound) frozen white bread dough, thawed

1 In a small bowl, combine the butter, parsley, garlic powder and garlic salt. Cut dough into 1-in. pieces; dip into butter mixture. Layer in a greased 9-in. x 5-in. loaf pan. Cover and let rise until doubled, about 1 hour.

2 Bake at 350° for 30 minutes or until golden brown. Serve warm. **YIELD:** 1 loaf.

PLUM COFFEE LOAF

Prep: 30 min. + rising **Bake:** 20 min. + cooling

I've baked this moist bread for so long that I don't recall where I got the recipe. A simple-to-make plum filling and hot roll mix make it easy to whip up on Christmas morning.

Janet Snider // Kalamazoo, Michigan

- 1 package (16 ounces) hot roll mix
- 2 tablespoons butter, melted
- 1 can (30 ounces) purple plums, drained, halved and pitted
- 1/4 cup sugar
- 1/4 teaspoon ground cinnamon
- 1/8 teaspoon ground cloves

GLAZE:
- 1 cup confectioners' sugar
- 1/4 teaspoon almond extract
- 1 to 2 tablespoons milk
- 1/3 cup slivered almonds

1 Prepare and knead hot roll mix according to package directions. Place in a greased bowl, turning once to grease top. Cover and let rise in a warm place until doubled, about 30 minutes.

2 Punch dough down. Turn onto a lightly floured surface; roll into a 15-in. x 10-in. rectangle. Brush with butter. Place plums cut side down lengthwise down the center third of rectangle. Combine the sugar, cinnamon and cloves; sprinkle over plums.

3 Fold both long sides of dough over filling; pinch seam to seal and tuck ends under. Place a greased baking sheet on work surface next to loaf. Carefully slide loaf onto baking sheet. With a sharp knife, make slashes 1 in. apart across top of loaf. Cover and let rise until doubled, about 30 minutes.

4 Bake at 350° for 20-25 minutes or until golden brown. Remove from pan to a wire rack to cool.

5 For glaze, combine the confectioners' sugar, extract and enough milk to achieve desired consistency. Drizzle over warm loaf. Sprinkle with almonds. **YIELD:** 1 loaf.

APPLE STREUSEL MUFFINS

Prep: 20 min. **Bake:** 15 min.

I was looking for something warm to make for my daughter before school on a rainy morning. So I jazzed up a boxed muffin mix with a chopped apple, walnuts, brown sugar and a fast-to-fix vanilla glaze. The tasty results really hit the spot.
Elizabeth Calabrese // Yucaipa, California

- 1 package (6-1/2 ounces) apple cinnamon muffin mix
- 1 large tart apple, peeled and diced
- 1/3 cup chopped walnuts
- 3 tablespoons brown sugar
- 4-1/2 teaspoons all-purpose flour
- 1 tablespoon butter, melted

GLAZE:

- 3/4 cup confectioners' sugar
- 1/2 teaspoon vanilla extract
- 1 to 2 tablespoons milk

1 Prepare muffin mix according to package directions; fold in apple. Fill greased muffin cups three-fourths full. In a small bowl, combine the walnuts, brown sugar, flour and butter; sprinkle over batter.

2 Bake at 400° for 15-20 minutes or until a toothpick inserted near the center comes out clean. Cool for 5 minutes before removing from pan to a wire rack.

3 In a small bowl, combine the confectioners' sugar, vanilla and enough milk to achieve desired consistency; drizzle over warm muffins. Serve warm. **YIELD:** 6 muffins.

TIP

Don't have a toothpick to test the muffins for doneness? Then use a strand of dry, uncooked spaghetti. It works as well as a toothpick.

A packaged hot roll mix speeds along preparation of this delightful bread. Let it cool completely before slicing...if you can wait that long! It's great with beef stew in the winter. Yum!

Lois Schneider // Madison, Wisconsin

SWISS ONION LOAF

Prep: 25 min. + rising **Bake:** 25 min. + cooling

- 1 cup (4 ounces) shredded Swiss cheese
- 2 tablespoons dried minced onion
- 1 package (16 ounces) hot roll mix
- 1 tablespoon butter, melted

1 In a large bowl, combine cheese and minced onion with the contents of the roll mix and yeast packets. Prepare mix according to package directions.

2 Turn onto a floured surface; knead until smooth and elastic, about 6-8 minutes. Shape into a 5-in. ball and place on a greased baking sheet. Cover and let rise in a warm place for 30 minutes or until doubled.

3 Bake at 375° for 25-30 minutes or until golden brown. Brush with butter. Remove to a wire rack to cool. **YIELD:** 1 loaf (16 servings).

CHERRY PISTACHIO BREAD

Prep: 15 min. **Bake:** 40 min. + cooling

This bread echos the colors of Christmas with the red maraschino cherries and green pistachio pudding mix. But its pleasant taste makes it appropriate any time of year.

Rose Harman // Hays, Kansas

- 1 package (18-1/4 ounces) yellow cake mix
- 1 package (3.4 ounces) instant pistachio pudding mix
- 4 eggs
- 1 cup (8 ounces) sour cream
- 1/4 cup canola oil
- 2 tablespoons water
- 4 drops green food coloring, optional
- 3/4 cup halved maraschino cherries
- 1/2 cup chopped pecans
- 1/4 cup sugar
- 1 teaspoon ground cinnamon

1 In a bowl, combine cake and pudding mixes. Combine eggs, sour cream, oil, water and food coloring if desired; add to dry ingredients. Beat until blended (batter will be thick). Fold in cherries and the pecans.

2 Combine the sugar and cinnamon; sprinkle 1 tablespoon over the bottom and up the sides of two greased 8-in. x 4-in. loaf pans. Add batter; sprinkle with the remaining cinnamon-sugar.

3 Bake at 350° for 40-50 minutes or until a toothpick inserted near the center comes out clean. Cool for 10 minutes before removing from pans to wire racks. **YIELD:** 2 loaves (16 slices each).

For a simple treat, bake these sweet fruit-topped rolls that call for just six ingredients. They're so yummy, your family may request them for breakfast, too.

Taste of Home Test Kitchen

STRAWBERRY BREADSTICK ROLLS

Prep/Total Time: 30 min.

- 2 cups sliced fresh strawberries
- 5 teaspoons sugar, *divided*
- 1 tube (11 ounces) refrigerated breadsticks
- 2 tablespoons butter, melted
- 2 tablespoons brown sugar
- 2 tablespoons maple syrup

1 In a small bowl, combine strawberries and 2 teaspoons sugar; set aside. On a lightly floured surface, unroll breadstick dough (do not separate). Seal perforations; brush dough with butter. Combine brown sugar and remaining sugar; sprinkle over dough. Reroll, starting with a short end. Cut along seam lines.

2 Place rolls cut side down on a greased baking sheet. Bake at 375° for 11-13 minutes or until golden brown. Brush with syrup. Serve with reserved strawberry mixture. **YIELD:** 6 servings.

EDITOR'S NOTE: This recipe was tested with Pillsbury refrigerated breadsticks.

CHEDDAR GARLIC BISCUITS

Prep/Total Time: 25 min.

I get a lot of recipes from friends, and this one is no exception. Biscuit mix is combined with a little minced onion, garlic powder and cheese to create these golden drop biscuits that bake in a flash.

Frances Poste // Wall, South Dakota

- 2 cups biscuit/baking mix
- 1/2 cup shredded cheddar cheese
- 1/2 teaspoon dried minced onion
- 2/3 cup milk
- 1/4 cup butter, melted
- 1/2 teaspoon garlic powder

1 In a large bowl, combine the biscuit mix, cheese and onion. Stir in the milk until a soft dough forms; stir 30 seconds longer.

2 Drop by rounded tablespoonfuls 2 in. apart onto ungreased baking sheets. Bake at 450° for 8-10 minutes or until golden brown. Combine the butter and garlic powder; brush over the biscuits. Serve warm. **YIELD:** 15 biscuits.

Bursting with poppy seeds, these luscious muffins are filled and drizzled with lots of lemony flavor. They're great with coffee or tea and couldn't be much easier to whip up.
Donna Gonda // North Canton, Ohio

LEMON POPPY SEED MUFFINS
Prep/Total Time: 30 min.

- 2 cups biscuit/baking mix
- 1 package (3.4 ounces) instant lemon pudding mix
- 1/4 cup poppy seeds
- 1/4 teaspoon grated lemon peel
- 2 eggs
- 1 cup milk
- 1/4 cup canola oil
- 3/4 cup confectioners' sugar
- 1 tablespoon lemon juice

1 In a large bowl, combine the baking mix, pudding mix, poppy seeds and lemon peel. In another bowl, combine the eggs, milk and oil; stir into dry ingredients just until moistened. Fill greased or paper-lined muffin cups two-thirds full.

2 Bake at 375° for 20-25 minutes or until a toothpick comes out clean. Cool for 5 minutes before removing from pan to a wire rack.

3 In a small bowl, combine confectioners' sugar and lemon juice; drizzle over muffins. **YIELD**: 1 dozen.

WALNUT BACON BREAD
Prep: 10 min. **Bake**: 50 min. + cooling

Talk about something frugal and easy...this is it! The recipe uses a biscuit mix, so I have time to make the bread regularly.
Barbara Nowakowski // North Tonawanda, New York

- 3 cups biscuit/baking mix
- 1 cup milk
- 2 eggs, lightly beaten
- 2 tablespoons dried minced onion
- Dash hot pepper sauce
- 3/4 cup shredded cheddar cheese
- 12 bacon strips, cooked and crumbled
- 1/2 cup chopped walnuts

1 In a large bowl, combine the biscuit mix, milk, eggs, onion and pepper sauce just until moistened. Stir in the cheese, bacon and walnuts. Spread into a greased 9-in. x 5-in. loaf pan.

2 Bake at 350° for 48-52 minutes or until a toothpick inserted near the center comes out clean. Cool for 10 minutes before removing from pan to a wire rack to cool completely. **YIELD**: 1 loaf.

Try this delicious, but quick way to make focaccia using frozen bread dough.
Taste of Home Test Kitchen

RED ONION FOCACCIA

Prep: 15 min. **Bake:** 30 min. + cooling

- 3 frozen bread dough rolls, thawed
- 1/2 teaspoon olive oil
- 2 red onion slices, separated into rings
- 1/2 teaspoon Italian seasoning
- 2 tablespoons shredded Parmesan cheese
- 1 tablespoon butter, melted
- 1/8 teaspoon garlic salt

1 On a lightly floured surface, knead dough together. Roll out dough into a 7-in. circle. Place on greased 7-1/2-in. pizza pan or baking sheet. Brush with oil. Top with the onion slices. Sprinkle with Italian seasoning and Parmesan cheese. Bake at 350° for 28-32 minutes or until golden brown.

2 In a small bowl, combine the butter and garlic salt; brush over warm foccacia. Remove from pan to a wire rack. Cool for 10 minutes before cutting. **YIELD:** 2 servings.

ONION POTATO ROLLS

Prep: 25 min. **Bake:** 15 min.

As a 4-H judge, I sampled a variation of these light, golden rolls at our county fair. With a touch of onion, it's a real blue-ribbon recipe that wins raves whenever I serve it.
Fancheon Resler // Bluffton, Indiana

- 2 packages (1/4 ounce *each*) active dry yeast
- 1/2 cup warm water (110° to 115°)
- 1 cup warm milk (110° to 115°)
- 1 cup mashed potato flakes
- 1/2 cup butter, softened
- 1/2 cup packed brown sugar
- 2 eggs
- 1 envelope onion soup mix
- 1 teaspoon salt
- 2 cups whole wheat flour
- 2-1/2 to 3 cups all-purpose flour
- TOPPING:
- 1 egg, lightly beaten
- 1/4 cup dried minced onion

1 In a large bowl, dissolve yeast in warm water. Beat in the milk, potato flakes, butter, sugar, eggs, soup mix, salt and whole wheat flour. Stir in enough all-purpose flour to form a soft dough.

2 Turn onto a floured surface; knead until smooth and elastic, about 6-8 minutes. Place in a greased bowl, turning once to grease top. Cover and let rise in a warm place until doubled, about 1 hour.

3 Punch dough down; divide into 18 pieces. Shape each into a ball. Place 2 in. apart on greased baking sheets. Cover and let rise until doubled, about 30 minutes.

4 Brush egg over rolls. Sprinkle with dried onion. Bake at 350° for 15-18 minutes or until golden brown. Remove from pan to wire racks to cool. **YIELD:** 1-1/2 dozen.

These delightful Danish are so quick to fix, you don't even have to uncoil the refrigerated breadsticks. We prefer them with cherry pie filling, but you can use peach or blueberry instead.

Margaret McNeil
Germantown, Tennessee

CHERRY DANISH
Prep/Total Time: 30 min.

  2 tubes (11 ounces *each*) refrigerated breadsticks
1/3 cup butter, melted
  1 tablespoon sugar
  1 cup cherry pie filling
  1 cup confectioners' sugar
1-1/2 teaspoons water

1 Separate each tube of breadsticks into six sections but leave coiled. Place in a greased 15-in. x 10-in. x 1-in. baking pan. Brush generously with butter and sprinkle with sugar.

2 Make an indentation in the top of each coil; fill with about 1 tablespoon of pie filling. Bake at 400° for 15-20 minutes or until golden brown. Cool on a wire rack. Combine the confectioners' sugar and water; drizzle over the warm rolls. **YIELD:** 1 dozen.

EDITOR'S NOTE: This recipe was tested with Pillsbury refrigerated breadsticks.

NEVER-FAIL YEAST ROLLS
Prep: 20 min. + rising **Bake:** 15 min.

This simple recipe produces sweet, tender rolls and requires no kneading. It's the perfect way for a child to make an impressive contribution to a meal. It's also nice for an adult who wants homemade rolls without the usual fuss.

Karen Gentry // Eubank, New York

  1 package (1/4 ounce) active dry yeast
1-1/2 cups warm water (110° to 115°)
3-1/4 cups all-purpose flour
  1 package (9 ounces) yellow *or* white cake mix
1/2 teaspoon salt
Melted butter

1 In a large bowl, dissolve yeast in warm water. Beat in the flour, dry cake mix and salt (do not knead). Place in a greased bowl, turning once to grease the top. Cover and let rise in a warm place until doubled, about 1 hour.

2 Punch dough down; divide in half. Roll each portion into a 12-in. circle; cut each circle into 12 wedges. Roll up, beginning at the wide end; place point side down on greased baking sheets. Brush with butter. Cover and let rise until doubled, about 25 minutes.

3 Bake at 350° for 12-15 minutes or until golden brown. Remove from the pan to wire racks. Serve warm. **YIELD:** 2 dozen.

Hot roll mix gives me a head start when making this savory bread. I usually make it with a big pot of chili and serve thick, warm slices for dunking.

Katie Dreibelbis
State College, Pennsylvania

CHEDDAR CHILI BRAID

Prep: 20 min. + rising **Bake:** 30 min.

- 1 package (16 ounces) hot roll mix
- 1 cup warm water (120° to 130°)
- 2 eggs
- 2 cups (8 ounces) shredded cheddar cheese
- 2 tablespoons canned chopped green chilies, drained
- 2 tablespoons grated Parmesan cheese

1 In a large bowl, combine the contents of the roll mix and yeast packets; stir in the water, one egg, cheddar cheese and chilies. Turn onto a floured surface; knead dough until smooth and elastic, about 5 minutes. Cover and let rest for 5 minutes.

2 Divide into thirds. Shape each into a 14-in. rope. Place ropes on a greased baking sheet and braid; pinch ends to seal and tuck under. Cover and let rise in a warm place until doubled, about 30 minutes.

3 Beat remaining egg; brush over dough. Sprinkle with Parmesan cheese. Bake at 375° for 30 minutes or until golden brown. Remove from the pan to a wire rack. **YIELD:** 1 loaf.

ICE CREAM STICKY BUNS

Prep: 10 min. + rising **Bake:** 20 min.

A gooey caramel sauce made with ice cream coats the tender rolls in the breakfast treat. Instead of using a loaf of bread dough, thaw frozen dinner rolls and divide in thirds for faster assembly. For a little crunch, top with chopped pecans before serving.

Sharon Donat // Kalispell, Montana

- 1 cup vanilla ice cream, melted
- 1/2 cup butter, melted
- 1/2 cup sugar
- 1/2 cup packed brown sugar
- 1 loaf (1 pound) frozen bread dough, thawed

1 In a large bowl, combine the ice cream, butter and sugars. Pour into a greased 13-in. x 9-in. baking dish. Cut dough into 36 pieces; arrange in dish. Cover and let rise in a warm place until doubled, about 1 hour.

2 Bake at 375° for 18-22 minutes or until golden brown. Cool for 2 minutes before serving. **YIELD:** 3 dozen.

ORANGE-MASCARPONE BREAKFAST ROLLS

Prep: 25 min. **Bake:** 20 min.

These special rolls are melt-in-your-mouth good and smell wonderful while baking. I came up with these while teaching one of my grandchildren how to make monkey bread.

Pamela Shank // Parkersburg, West Virginia

- 1/4 cup chopped pecans
- 1/4 cup sugar
- 1 teaspoon ground cinnamon
- 2 tablespoons plus 1-1/2 teaspoons Mascarpone cheese, *divided*
- 1 teaspoon grated orange peel
- 1 tube (6 ounces) refrigerated flaky buttermilk biscuits
- 2 tablespoons butter, melted
- 1/2 cup confectioners' sugar
- 2 teaspoons orange juice

1 Sprinkle pecans into a 6-in. round baking pan coated with cooking spray; set aside. In a small bowl, combine sugar and cinnamon. In another bowl, combine 2 tablespoons Mascarpone cheese and the orange peel; set aside.

2 On a lightly floured surface, roll out biscuits into 4-in. circles. Spread 1/2 teaspoon cheese mixture down the center of each circle. Bring dough from opposite sides over filling just until edges meet; pinch to seal. Brush with some of the butter; roll in the sugar mixture. Place seam side down over pecans. Sprinkle with remaining sugar mixture; drizzle with remaining butter.

3 Bake at 350° for 20-25 minutes or until golden brown. Immediately invert onto a serving plate. In a small bowl, combine the confectioners' sugar, orange juice and remaining Mascarpone cheese. Drizzle over rolls. Serve warm. **YIELD:** 5 rolls.

My daughter and I enjoy this tender cake for brunch on the Saturday mornings we spend at home. A delightful hint of orange from the quick bread mix blends well with the other fruit flavors and is a simple treat.
Patricia Clark // Lake Forest, California

PEAR-CRANBERRY COFFEE CAKE

Prep: 20 min. **Bake:** 35 min.

- 1 package (15.6 ounces) cranberry-orange quick bread mix
- 1 can (15 ounces) sliced pears, drained and halved
- 1 teaspoon lemon juice
- 1/3 cup all-purpose flour
- 1/3 cup sugar
- 1/2 teaspoon ground cinnamon
- 2 tablespoons butter, melted

1 Prepare the bread mix according to package directions; pour batter into a greased 9-in. square baking pan. Sprinkle pears with lemon juice; arrange over batter.

2 In a small bowl, combine the flour, sugar and cinnamon; stir in butter until crumbly. Sprinkle over pears.

3 Bake at 375° for 35-40 minutes or until a toothpick inserted near the center comes out clean. Cool on a wire rack. **YIELD:** 9 servings.

QUICK COCONUT MUFFINS

Prep/Total Time: 30 min.

Whether I go to a family event or a church bake sale, people expect me to bring these muffins.
Mary Burrough // Midwest City, Oklahoma

- 1 package (18-1/4 ounces) yellow cake mix
- 1/2 cup butter, softened
- 2/3 cup water
- 3 eggs
- 1 can (8 ounces) crushed pineapple, drained
- 1 cup flaked coconut
- 1 cup chopped pecans
- 1 teaspoon rum extract
- 1 teaspoon coconut extract

1 In a large bowl, beat cake mix and butter. Add the remaining ingredients. Fill greased or paper-lined muffin cups half full.

2 Bake at 350° for 20-25 minutes or until a toothpick inserted near the center comes out clean. Cool for 5 minutes before removing from pans to wire racks. **YIELD:** 2 dozen.

CRANBERRY CREAM CHEESE MUFFINS

Prep: 15 min. **Bake:** 20 min.

The sweet, creamy filling in these cranberry muffins makes them popular at my house. The tender treats also have a crispy sugar topping that is bound to be a hit.

Sharon Hartman // Twin Falls, Idaho

- 1 package (3 ounces) cream cheese, softened
- 4 tablespoons sugar, *divided*
- 1 package (15.6 ounces) cranberry-orange quick bread mix
- 1 cup milk
- 1/3 cup canola oil
- 1 egg

1 In a small bowl, beat cream cheese and 2 tablespoons sugar until smooth; set aside. Place the bread mix in another bowl. Combine the milk, oil and egg; stir into bread mix just until moistened.

2 Fill paper-lined muffin cups one-fourth full with batter. Place 2 teaspoons cream cheese mixture in the center of each; top with remaining batter. Sprinkle with remaining sugar.

3 Bake at 400° for 18-20 minutes or until a toothpick inserted in the muffins comes out clean. Cool for 5 minutes before removing from pan to a wire rack. Serve warm. **YIELD:** 1 dozen.

TIP

If you like the ease and flavor of these muffins, you can serve your family to some other great treats. Try substituting a banana, blueberry or date quick bread mix for the cranberry-orange mix called for in the recipe.

This is the best recipe I have found for cinnamon rolls. They're so moist with a delightful vanilla flavor and yummy frosting. When I serve them to my family, they disappear in no time.

Linda Martin // Warsaw, Indiana

VANILLA CINNAMON ROLLS

Prep: 30 min. + rising **Bake:** 20 min.

2 cups cold milk
1 package (3.4 ounces) instant vanilla pudding mix
2 packages (1/4 ounce *each*) active dry yeast
1/2 cup warm water (110° to 115°)
1/2 cup plus 2 tablespoons butter, melted, *divided*
2 eggs
2 tablespoons sugar
1 teaspoon salt
6 cups all-purpose flour
1/2 cup packed brown sugar
1 teaspoon ground cinnamon

FROSTING:
1 cup packed brown sugar
1/2 cup heavy whipping cream
1/2 cup butter, cubed
2 cups confectioners' sugar

1 In a large bowl, whisk the milk and pudding mix for 2 minutes. Let stand for 2 minutes or until soft set; set aside. In a large bowl, dissolve yeast in warm water. Add 1/2 cup butter, eggs, sugar, salt and 2 cups flour. Beat on medium speed for 3 minutes. Add pudding; beat until smooth. Stir in enough remaining flour to form a soft dough (dough will be sticky).

2 Turn onto a floured surface; knead until smooth and elastic, about 6-8 minutes. Place in a greased bowl, turning once to grease top. Cover and let rise in a warm place until doubled, about 1 hour.

3 Punch dough down. Turn onto a floured surface; divide in half. Roll each portion into an 18-in. x 11-in. rectangle; brush with remaining butter. Combine brown sugar and cinnamon; sprinkle over dough to within 1/2 in. of edges.

4 Roll up jelly-roll style, starting with a long side; pinch seams to seal. Cut each into 16 slices. Place cut side down in two greased 13-in. x 9-in. baking dishes. Cover and let rise until doubled, about 30 minutes.

5 Bake at 350° for 20-25 minutes or until golden brown. Cool on wire racks.

6 Meanwhile, in a large saucepan, combine the brown sugar, cream and butter. Bring to a boil; cook and stir for 2 minutes. Remove from the heat. Beat in confectioners' sugar with a hand mixer until creamy. Frost rolls. Serve warm. **YIELD:** 32 rolls.

With ease of refrigerated bread dough, this tempting cheesy bread has delicious, down-home goodness. You'll find it crisp and golden on the outside, rich and buttery inside.

Judi Messina // Coeur d'Alene, Idaho

SWISS-ONION BREAD RING

Prep: 10 min. **Bake:** 25 min.

2-1/2 teaspoons poppy seeds, *divided*
   2 tubes (11 ounces *each*) refrigerated French bread
   1 cup (4 ounces) shredded Swiss cheese
3/4 cup sliced green onions
   6 tablespoons butter, melted

1 Sprinkle 1/2 teaspoon poppy seeds in a greased 10-in. fluted tube pan. Cut the dough into forty 1-in. pieces; place half in prepared pan. Sprinkle with half of the cheese and onions. Top with 1 teaspoon poppy seeds; drizzle with half of the butter. Repeat layers.

2 Bake at 375° for 30-35 minutes or until golden brown. Immediately invert onto a wire rack. Serve warm. **YIELD:** 1 loaf.

PUMPKIN COFFEE CAKE

Prep: 15 min. **Bake:** 35 min. + cooling

It's tough to resist a second piece of this delightful treat with its comforting flavor. It's a breeze to throw together because it calls for pound cake mix and canned pumpkin.

Sarah Steele // Moulton, Alabama

   1 package (16 ounces) pound cake mix
3/4 cup canned pumpkin
   6 tablespoons water
   2 eggs
   2 teaspoons pumpkin pie spice
   1 teaspoon baking soda

TOPPING:
1/2 cup chopped walnuts
1/2 cup packed brown sugar
1/4 cup all-purpose flour
   3 teaspoons butter, melted

1 In a large bowl, combine the dry cake mix, pumpkin, water, eggs, spice and baking soda; beat on low speed for 30 seconds. Beat on medium for 2 minutes. Pour half of the pumpkin mixture into a greased 9-in. square baking pan.

2 In a small bowl, combine topping ingredients; sprinkle half over the batter. Carefully spread with remaining batter. Sprinkle with remaining topping (pan will be full).

3 Bake at 350° for 35-40 minutes or until a toothpick inserted near the center comes out clean. Cool on a wire rack. **YIELD:** 9 servings.

I think frozen bread dough should be called magic dough because there is so much you can do with it. These flavorful knots are scrumptious with soup or salad.

Liz Lazenby // Victoria, British Columbia

PARADISE BUNS

Prep: 20 min. + rising **Bake:** 15 min.

- 1 loaf (1 pound) frozen bread dough, thawed
- 1 cup (4 ounces) shredded cheddar cheese
- 1/4 cup *each* diced mushrooms, broccoli and sweet red and yellow pepper
- 1 tablespoon chopped green onion
- 1 garlic clove, minced
- 1/2 teaspoon garlic powder

1 Divide bread dough into eight pieces. In a shallow bowl, combine cheese, vegetables, garlic and garlic powder. Roll each piece of dough into an 8-in. rope. Roll in cheese mixture, pressing mixture into dough. Tie into a knot and press vegetables into the dough; tuck the ends under.

2 Place 2 in. apart on greased baking sheets. Cover and let rise until doubled about 30 minutes.

3 Bake at 375° for 15-20 minutes or until golden brown. Remove from pan to a wire rack. **YIELD:** 8 servings.

TWISTER CHEDDAR ROLLS

Prep: 20 min. **Bake:** 15 min.

As flaky as homemade puff pastry, these tasty rolls bring compliments every time I serve them. Because they start with convenient refrigerated crescents, the mouthwatering treats couldn't be quicker or easier for busy holiday cooks!

Jane Birch // Edison, New Jersey

- 2 tubes (8 ounces *each*) refrigerated crescent rolls
- 1-1/2 cups (6 ounces) shredded cheddar cheese
- 1/4 cup chopped green onions
- 1 egg
- 1 teaspoon water
- 2 teaspoons sesame seeds
- 1/2 teaspoon garlic salt *or* garlic powder
- 1/4 teaspoon dried parsley flakes

1 Separate crescent roll dough into eight rectangles; press seams to seal. Combine the cheese and onions; spoon about 3 rounded tablespoonfuls lengthwise down the center of each rectangle to within 1/4 in. of each end. Fold the dough in half lengthwise; firmly press edges to seal. Twist each strip four to five times. Bring ends together to form a ring; pinch to seal. Place on a greased baking sheet.

2 In a small bowl, beat egg and water. Brush over dough. Combine the sesame seeds, garlic salt and parsley; sprinkle over rings.

3 Bake at 375° for 14-16 minutes or until golden brown. Remove from the pan to a wire rack. Serve warm. **YIELD:** 8 rolls.

With its pretty layer of cherries and crunchy streusel topping, this coffee cake is great for breakfast. Or you can even serve it for dessert.

Gail Buss // Westminster, Maryland

CHERRY COFFEE CAKE

Prep: 25 min. **Bake:** 35 min. + cooling

     1 package (18-1/4 ounces) yellow cake mix, *divided*
     1 cup all-purpose flour
     1 package (1/4 ounce) active dry yeast
     2/3 cup warm water (120° to 130°)
     2 eggs, lightly beaten
     1 can (21 ounces) cherry pie filling
     1/3 cup cold butter
GLAZE:
     1 cup confectioners' sugar
     1 tablespoon corn syrup
     1 to 2 tablespoons water

1 In a large bowl, combine 1-1/2 cups cake mix, flour, yeast and water until smooth. Stir in the eggs until blended. Transfer to a greased 13-in. x 9-in. baking dish. Gently spoon pie filling over top. In a small bowl, place remaining cake mix; cut in butter until crumbly. Sprinkle over filling.

2 Bake at 350° for 35-40 minutes or until lightly browned. Cool on a wire rack.

3 Combine the confectioners' sugar, corn syrup and enough water to achieve desired consistency. Drizzle over cake. **YIELD:** 12-16 servings.

MINI ELEPHANT EARS

Prep: 30 min. + thawing

Our kids love to help stretch the pieces of convenient frozen dough to make these ears. After I fry them, the kids brush them with butter and sprinkle on the cinnamon-sugar. Then we all dig in!

Malea Kruse // Huntertown, Indiana

Frozen white dinner roll dough (10 rolls)
Oil for deep-fat frying
     1/2 cup sugar
     1 tablespoon ground cinnamon
     3 tablespoons butter, melted

1 Thaw the dough at room temperature for about 2 hours. Heat oil in an electric skillet or deep-fat fryer to 375°. Combine the sugar and cinnamon; set aside.

2 Stretch each piece of dough into a flat ear shape. Fry, a few at a time, for 1-1/2 minutes per side or until browned. Drain on paper towels. Brush with butter; sprinkle with cinnamon-sugar. **YIELD:** 10 servings.

This wonderful swirled bread is easy to put together...and while it's rising and baking, I make the rest of the meal. Pretty and flavorful, it's great for company or a special holiday. Everyone thinks I bought this special golden loaf at a gourmet bakery!

Deninelle Duncan // Markham, Ontario

HERBED VEGETABLE SPIRAL BREAD

Prep: 15 min. + rising **Bake:** 35 min. + cooling

1/2 cup shredded part-skim mozzarella cheese
1/2 cup canned Mexicorn, drained
1/4 cup grated Parmesan cheese
1/4 cup minced fresh parsley
  2 garlic cloves, minced
  1 teaspoon dried oregano
1/2 teaspoon dried basil
1/2 teaspoon ground cumin
1/4 teaspoon salt
1/8 to 1/4 teaspoon crushed red pepper flakes, optional
  1 loaf (1 pound) frozen bread dough, thawed
  1 tablespoon cornmeal
  1 egg, lightly beaten

1 In a large bowl, combine the mozzarella, corn, Parmesan cheese, parsley, garlic and seasonings; set aside. On a lightly floured surface, roll dough into a 16-in. x 12-in. rectangle. Spread cheese mixture over dough to within 3/4 in. of edges.

2 Roll up jelly-roll style, starting with a long side; pinch seams and ends to seal. Sprinkle a large baking sheet with cornmeal. Place dough seam side down on baking sheet; tuck ends under. Cover and let rise in a warm place until doubled, about 35 minutes.

3 Brush with egg. Bake at 350° for 35-40 minutes or until golden brown and bread sounds hollow when tapped. Remove from pan to a wire rack. Cool for 20 minutes before slicing. Store leftovers in the refrigerator. **YIELD:** 16 slices.

Golden on the outside and tender on the inside, these lovely loaves get a fun flavor boost from ranch dressing. One slice always prompts a second helping or more, so this bread never lasts long.

Cherri Schmidt // Grand Island, Nebraska

RANCH FRENCH BREAD

Prep: 30 min. + rising **Bake:** 20 min. + cooling

> 2 packages (1/4 ounce *each*) active dry yeast
> 1/2 cup warm water (110° to 115°)
> 2 cups warm buttermilk (110° to 115°)
> 1/2 cup sugar
> 1/2 cup butter, softened
> 3 eggs
> 1 to 2 envelopes original ranch salad dressing mix
> 2 teaspoons salt
> 8 to 9 cups all-purpose flour
> Additional butter, melted

1 In a large bowl, dissolve yeast in warm water. Add the buttermilk, sugar, butter, eggs, ranch dressing mix, salt and 4 cups flour; beat until smooth. Stir in enough remaining flour to form a soft dough.

2 Turn onto a floured surface; knead until smooth and elastic, about 6-8 minutes. Place in a greased bowl, turning once to grease top. Cover and let rise in a warm place until doubled, about 1 hour.

3 Punch dough down. Turn onto a lightly floured surface; divide into fourths. Roll each portion into a 14-in. x 12-in. rectangle. Roll up jelly-roll style, starting with a long side; pinch seams to seal and tuck ends under. Place seam side down on two greased baking sheets. With a sharp knife, make five shallow slashes across the top of each loaf. Cover and let rise in a warm place until doubled, about 30 minutes.

4 Bake at 350° for 20-25 minutes or until golden brown. Brush with melted butter. Remove from pans to wire racks to cool. **YIELD:** 4 loaves (14 slices each).

EDITOR'S NOTE: Warmed buttermilk will appear curdled.

BACON-ONION PAN ROLLS

Prep: 15 min. + rising **Bake:** 25 min.

These buttery bacon-filled rolls are a favorite item at family get-togethers. We have to hide them from our two sons-in-law, or there wouldn't be any left for dinner!

Liz Vaughn // Mt. Prospect, Illinois

> 1 loaf (1 pound) frozen bread dough, thawed
> 1/4 cup butter, melted, *divided*
> 1/2 pound sliced bacon, cooked and crumbled
> 1/2 cup chopped onion

1 On a lightly floured surface, roll out dough to 1/4-in. thickness. Cut with a 2-1/2-in. biscuit cutter; brush with 3 tablespoons butter. Place 1 teaspoon of bacon and onion on half of each roll. Fold over and pinch to seal.

2 Place, pinched edge up, in a greased 9-in. square baking pan, forming three rows of six. Brush the tops with the remaining butter. Let rise until doubled, about 30 minutes.

3 Bake at 350° for 25-30 minutes or until golden brown. Cool on a wire rack. **YIELD:** 1-1/2 dozen.

I found this recipe in a newspaper and make it often. I like to bake this coffee cake when unexpected company stops in and I need something speedy to go with a cup of coffee.

Mary Tallman // Arbor Vitae, Wisconsin

LEMON PULL-APART COFFEE CAKE

Prep/Total Time: 30 min.

1/4 cup sugar
1/4 cup chopped walnuts
1/4 cup golden raisins
2 tablespoons butter, melted
2 teaspoons grated lemon peel
1 tube (12 ounces) refrigerated buttermilk biscuits

GLAZE:
1/2 cup confectioners' sugar
1 tablespoon lemon juice

1 In a large bowl, combine the sugar, walnuts, raisins, butter and lemon peel. Separate biscuits and cut each into quarters; toss with sugar mixture. Place in a greased 9-in. round baking pan.

2 Bake at 400° for 20-25 minutes or until golden brown. Immediately invert onto a wire rack. Combine glaze ingredients until smooth; drizzle over warm coffee cake. **YIELD:** 10 servings.

HERBED BISCUIT KNOTS

Prep/Total Time: 20 min.

Shape these simply seasoned biscuits into knots or twist. You'll find that they go well with any entree.

Mary Smith // Columbia, Missouri

1 tube (12 ounces) refrigerated buttermilk biscuits
1/4 cup canola oil
1/2 teaspoon salt
1/2 teaspoon garlic powder
1/2 teaspoon Italian seasoning

1 Cut each biscuit in half. Roll each portion into a 6-in. rope; tie in a loose knot. Place on a greased baking sheet.

2 Bake at 400° for 9-11 minutes or until golden brown. In a small bowl, combine the oil and the seasonings; immediately brush over the warm biscuits. Serve warm. **YIELD:** 20 rolls.

EDITOR'S NOTE: The biscuits can be baked and then frozen for up to 2 months. To serve, reheat them in a 350° oven for 6 to 8 minutes.

PECAN SWEET ROLL RINGS

Prep: 20 min. **Bake:** 15 min.

I rely on tubes of refrigerated crescent roll dough to create these tender treats. Loaded with chopped pecans, cinnamon and nutmeg, the eye-appealing rings feature a sweet glaze.

Jill Cooley // Raleigh, North Carolina

- **2 tubes (8 ounces *each*) refrigerated crescent rolls**
- **4 tablespoons butter, melted, *divided***
- **1/2 cup chopped pecans**
- **1/4 cup sugar**
- **1 teaspoon ground cinnamon**
- **1/2 teaspoon ground nutmeg**
- **1/2 cup confectioners' sugar**
- **2 tablespoons maple syrup**

1 Unroll the crescent dough and separate into eight rectangles; seal perforations. Brush with 2 tablespoons butter. In a small bowl, combine the pecans, sugar, cinnamon and nutmeg.

2 Sprinkle 1 tablespoon over each rectangle; gently press into dough. Roll up jelly-roll style, starting at a long side. Pinch seams to seal. Twist two or three times.

3 Cut six shallow diagonal slits in each roll. Shape each into a ring; pinch ends together. Place on a greased baking sheet; brush with remaining butter.

4 Bake at 375° for 12-14 minutes or until golden brown. Remove from pan to a wire rack.

5 In a small bowl, combine confectioners' sugar and syrup until smooth; drizzle over the warm rolls. **YIELD:** 8 rolls.

I first made this recipe and took it to a church fellowship. One couple liked it so much they now call it "Holly Bread!"

Holly Cummings // Baytown, Texas

BROCCOLI-CHEESE CORN BREAD

Prep: 15 min. **Bake:** 35 min.

- 1 cup chopped onion
- 1 cup butter, cubed
- 2 packages (8-1/2 ounces *each*) corn bread/muffin mix
- 2 cups (8 ounces) shredded cheddar-Monterey Jack cheese
- 6 eggs
- 1-1/2 cups (12 ounces) 4% cottage cheese
- 1 package (9 ounces) frozen broccoli cuts, thawed and drained
- 1 cup fresh *or* frozen corn, thawed
- 2 tablespoons canned jalapeno slices, chopped

1 In a large skillet, saute the onion in butter until tender; set aside. In a large bowl, combine corn bread mix and shredded cheese. In another bowl, beat the eggs, cottage cheese and onion mixture. Stir into corn bread mixture just until moistened. Fold in the broccoli, corn and jalapeno.

2 Transfer to a greased 13-in. x 9-in. baking pan. Bake at 400° for 35-40 minutes or until lightly browned and edges pull away from the sides of the pan. Serve warm. Refrigerate leftovers. **YIELD:** 12-15 servings.

EDITOR'S NOTE: When cutting hot peppers, disposable gloves are recommended. Avoid touching your face.

CHEESY BREADSTICKS

Prep/Total Time: 30 min.

It takes no time at all to turn frozen bread dough into these irresistible breadsticks. Full of cheese flavor, the speedy snacks disappear fast, especially if served with marinara or pizza sauce for dipping.

Taste of Home Test Kitchen

- 1/2 cup grated Parmesan cheese
- 1/4 cup finely shredded cheddar cheese
- 1/2 teaspoon Italian seasoning
- 1/2 teaspoon garlic powder
- 1/8 teaspoon onion powder
- 1 loaf (1 pound) frozen white bread dough, thawed
- 1/4 cup butter, melted

1 In a shallow bowl, combine the first five ingredients; set aside. Divide dough into 16 pieces; roll each into a 6-in. rope. Dip ropes in butter, then roll in cheese mixture.

2 Place 2 in. apart on a greased baking sheet. Let rest for 10 minutes. Bake at 400° for 10-12 minutes or until golden brown. Serve warm. **YIELD:** 16 breadsticks.

With its simple glaze and tasty layer of raisins and nuts, this buttery coffee cake tastes just like a popular store-bought variety. I found the recipe in a church cookbook.

Maxine Winternheimer
Scottsdale, Arizona

CINNAMON-NUT COFFEE CAKE

Prep: 15 min. **Bake:** 40 min. + cooling

    1 cup chopped pecans, *divided*
1/4 cup sugar
1/4 cup raisins
    2 teaspoons ground cinnamon
    1 package (18-1/4 ounces) yellow cake mix
    1 package (3.4 ounces) instant vanilla pudding mix
3/4 cup water
3/4 cup canola oil
    4 eggs
    3 teaspoons butter flavoring
    3 teaspoons vanilla extract

GLAZE:

    1 cup confectioners' sugar
1/2 teaspoon butter flavoring
    4 to 5 teaspoons milk

1 In a small bowl, combine 1/2 cup pecans, sugar, raisins and cinnamon; set aside. In a large bowl, combine the cake mix, pudding mix, water, oil, eggs, butter flavoring, vanilla and remaining pecans; beat on low speed for 30 seconds. Beat on medium for 2 minutes.

2 Pour half the batter into a greased 13-in. x 9-in. baking dish. Sprinkle with reserved pecan mixture. Carefully spread remaining batter over the top. Bake at 350° for 40-45 minutes or until a toothpick comes out clean. Cool on a wire rack.

3 In a small bowl, combine the confectioners' sugar, butter flavoring and enough milk to achieve the desired consistency. Drizzle over coffee cake. **YIELD:** 12 servings.

SURPRISE BANANA MUFFINS

Prep/Total Time: 30 min.

I created these easy muffins after I'd stocked up on too much candy and banana bread mix. My family loves the peanut-butter surprise, and these muffins were a huge hit at a church potluck.

Teresa Heavilin // Kokomo, Indiana

    1 package (14 ounces) banana quick bread and muffin mix
    1 cup milk

1/2 cup canola oil
    2 eggs
  12 miniature peanut butter cups

1 Prepare banana bread batter according to package directions, using milk, oil and eggs. Fill greased muffin cups two-thirds full. Place a peanut butter cup in the center of each; spoon remaining batter over top.

2 Bake at 400° for 15-20 minutes or until a toothpick inserted into muffin comes out clean. Cool for 5 minutes before removing from pan to a wire rack. **YIELD:** 1 dozen.

cookies

CRANBERRY PECAN SANDIES
Prep: 20 min. **Bake:** 15 min./batch

- 1 package (15.6 ounces) cranberry-orange quick bread mix
- 1/2 cup butter, melted
- 1 egg
- 2 tablespoons orange juice
- 3/4 cup chopped pecans
- 30 to 36 pecan halves

ORANGE GLAZE:
- 1 cup confectioners' sugar
- 3 to 4 teaspoons orange juice

1 In a large bowl, combine the bread mix, butter, egg and orange juice. Stir in chopped pecans.

2 Roll into 1-in. balls. Place 2 in. apart on ungreased baking sheets. Flatten with the bottom of a glass coated with cooking spray. Press a pecan half into the center of each cookie.

3 Bake at 350° for 12-14 minutes or until lightly browned. Cool for 1 minute before removing to wire racks. In a small bowl, whisk glaze ingredients. Drizzle over the cookies. **YIELD:** 2-1/2 to 3 dozen.

MACADAMIA COCONUT BARS
Prep: 10 min. **Bake:** 15 min. + cooling

These are absolutely divine. No one will believe that a packaged cookie mix is the main ingredient. Not fond of macadamia nuts? Try pecans, walnuts, almonds or cashews.
Sarah Wilkinson // Bellevue, Nebraska

- 1 package (17-1/2 ounces) sugar cookie mix
- 1 cup vanilla *or* white chips
- 1/2 cup chopped macadamia nuts
- 1/4 cup flaked coconut

1 Prepare cookie mix according to package directions. Stir in chips, nuts and coconut. Spread into a greased 13-in. x 9-in. baking pan.

2 Bake at 375° for 12-15 minutes or until lightly browned around edges. Cool on a wire rack for 25 minutes before cutting. **YIELD:** 3 dozen.

PEANUT BUTTER BROWNIE BARS

Prep: 20 min. **Bake:** 25 min. + chilling

This simple treat will appeal to adults and children alike. Creamy peanut butter, crunchy nuts and crisp cereal make the bars fun to bite into.

Radelle Knappenberger // Oviedo, Florida

- 1 **package fudge brownie mix (13-inch x 9-inch pan size)**
- 12 **peanut butter cups, chopped**
- 1/2 **cup salted peanuts, chopped**
- 2 **cups (12 ounces) semisweet chocolate chips**
- 1-1/4 **cups creamy peanut butter**
- 1 **tablespoon butter**
- 1/8 **teaspoon salt**
- 1-1/2 **cups crisp rice cereal**
- 1 **teaspoon vanilla extract**

1 Prepare brownie batter according to package directions. Spread into a greased 13-in. x 9-in. baking pan. Bake at 350° for 20-25 minutes or until a toothpick inserted near the center comes out with moist crumbs.

2 Sprinkle with peanut butter cups and peanuts. Bake 4-6 minutes longer or until chocolate is melted. Cool on a wire rack.

3 Meanwhile, in a large saucepan, combine the chocolate chips, peanut butter, butter and salt. Cook and stir until chips are melted and mixture is smooth. Remove from the heat; stir in cereal and vanilla. Carefully spread over brownies. Cover and refrigerate for at least 2 hours before cutting. **YIELD:** 3 dozen.

STAMPED BY DESIGN COOKIES

Prep: 25 min. **Bake:** 10 min./batch + cooling

I was afraid if I frosted cookies to give for gifts at Christmastime, they would stick together when stacked in tins. So I came up with this idea to use a foam stamp to create an indented design for the frosting. They're so easy!

Sherry Lee // Columbus, Ohio

> 1 **package (18-1/4 ounces) chocolate *or* white cake mix**
> 2 **eggs**
> 1/4 **cup canola oil**

Sugar

ICING:

> 2 **cups confectioners' sugar**
> 2 **to 3 tablespoons milk**

Assorted food coloring, optional

1 In a large bowl, beat the dry cake mix, eggs and oil until blended. Roll into 1-in. balls; place 2 in. apart on greased baking sheets. Flatten with a glass dipped in sugar.

2 Bake at 350° for 6-8 minutes or until tops are set. Lightly press a 1-1/2-in. cookie cutter onto cookies making a slight indentation. Remove to wire racks to cool completely.

3 In a small bowl, whisk the confectioners' sugar and enough milk to achieve a drizzling consistency. Tint with food coloring if desired. Place icing in a small heavy-duty resealable plastic bag; cut a small hole in a corner of bag. Carefully pipe icing into indentations. **YIELD:** 6 dozen.

FRUITY PASTEL COOKIES

Prep: 20 min. **Bake:** 10 min./batch

> 3/4 cup butter, softened
> 1/2 cup sugar
> 1 package (3 ounces) lime gelatin *or* flavor of your choice
> 1 egg
> 1/2 teaspoon vanilla extract
> 1-3/4 cups all-purpose flour
> 1/2 teaspoon baking powder
> Red and green colored sugar *and/or* sprinkles

1 In a large bowl, cream the butter, sugar and gelatin powder until light and fluffy. Beat in egg and vanilla. Combine flour and baking powder; gradually add to creamed mixture and mix well. Using a cookie press fitted with the disk of your choice, press dough 2 in. apart onto ungreased baking sheets.

2 Decorate as desired with colored sugar and/or sprinkles. Bake at 400° for 6-8 minutes or until set (do not brown). Remove to a wire rack to cool. **YIELD:** 6 dozen.

LEMON-LIME CRACKLE COOKIES

Prep: 20 min. **Bake:** 10 min./batch + cooling

You can taste the spirit of Christmas' past in these chewy old-time cookies with their crackle tops and lemony flavor. They're a luscious addition to cookie exchanges.

Ada Merwin // Waterford, Michigan

> 1/2 cup flaked coconut
> 2 teaspoons grated lemon peel
> 2 teaspoons grated lime peel
> 2 cups whipped topping
> 2 eggs
> 2 tablespoons whipped topping mix
> 1 teaspoon lemon juice
> 1 package (18-1/4 ounces) lemon cake mix
> Confectioners' sugar

1 In a blender or food processor, combine the coconut, lemon peel and lime peel. Cover and process until finely chopped, about 30 seconds; set aside.

2 In a large bowl, combine whipped topping, eggs, dry whipped topping mix and lemon juice. Add dry cake mix and coconut mixture and mix well.

3 Drop by tablespoonfuls into a bowl of confectioner's sugar. Shape into balls. Place 2 in. apart on greased baking sheets. Bake at 350° for 10-12 minutes or until edges are golden brown. Remove to wire racks to cool. **YIELD:** about 3 dozen.

As rosy pink as Santa's cheeks, these merry meringue cookies are drizzled with dark chocolate and are almost too pretty to eat. Pecans add a nice crunch to these chewy treats. They lend a "berry" festive touch to my Christmas cookie tray.

Iola Egle // Bella Vista, Arkansas

RASPBERRY MERINGUES

Prep: 20 min. + standing **Bake:** 25 min./batch

- 3 **egg whites**
- 1 **teaspoon white vinegar**
- 1/8 **teaspoon salt**
- 3 **tablespoons plus 1 teaspoon raspberry gelatin powder**
- 3/4 **cup sugar**
- 2 **cups (12 ounces) semisweet chocolate chips**
- 1/2 **cup finely chopped pecans**

TOPPING:

- 1/4 **cup semisweet chocolate chips**
- 1 **teaspoon shortening**

1 Place egg whites in a large bowl; let stand at room temperature for 30 minutes. Add vinegar and salt to egg whites; beat eggs until soft peaks form. Combine gelatin powder with sugar. Gradually add sugar mixture, 1 tablespoon at a time, beating until stiff peaks form. Fold in chocolate chips and nuts.

2 Drop by rounded teaspoonfuls onto parchment-lined baking sheets. Bake at 250° for 20-25 minutes or until firm to the touch. Turn oven off; leave cookies in the oven with door ajar for about 1-1/2 hours or until cool.

3 In a microwave, melt chocolate chips and shortening; stir until smooth. Drizzle over cookies. **YIELD:** 7-1/2 dozen.

CHOCOLATE CARAMEL BARS

Prep: 15 min. **Bake:** 25 min.

Taking dessert or another treat to a church or school potluck is never a problem for me. I jump at the chance to offer these rich, chocolaty bars.

Steve Mirro // Cape Coral, Florida

- 1 **package (14 ounces) caramels**
- 1 **can (5 ounces) evaporated milk,** *divided*
- 3/4 **cup butter, softened**
- 1 **package (18-1/4 ounces) German chocolate cake mix**
- 2 **cups (12 ounces) semisweet chocolate chips**

1 In a small saucepan over low heat, melt caramels with 1/3 cup milk; stir until smooth. Meanwhile, in a large bowl, cream butter until light and fluffy. Beat in dry cake mix and remaining milk.

2 Spread half of the dough into a greased 13-in. x 9-in. baking pan. Bake at 350° for 6 minutes; sprinkle with chocolate chips.

3 Gently spread caramel mixture over chips. Drop remaining dough by tablespoonfuls over caramel layer. Return to the oven for 15 minutes or until a toothpick inserted in the bar comes out clean. Cool on a wire rack. Cut into bars. **YIELD:** 3 dozen.

I think that it's impossible to resist this scrumptious dessert. With nuts, chocolate and a creamy cheesecake-like layer, these treats taste like homemade candy bars. I keep the ingredients on hand so I can whip up a batch anytime.
Carolyn Kyzer // Alexander, Arkansas

CHOCOLATE COCONUT BARS

Prep/Total Time: 30 min.

- 1 tube (8 ounces) refrigerated crescent rolls
- 1 package (8 ounces) cream cheese, softened
- 1/3 cup confectioners' sugar
- 1 egg
- 3/4 cup flaked coconut
- 1 cup (6 ounces) semisweet chocolate chips
- 1/4 cup chopped nuts

1 Unroll crescent roll dough into one long rectangle on an ungreased baking sheet; seal seams and perforations. Roll out into a 13-in. x 9-in. rectangle, building up dough around edges.

2 In a small bowl, beat the cream cheese, confectioners' sugar and egg until smooth; stir in coconut. Spread over the crust.

3 Bake at 375° for 10-15 minutes or until cream cheese mixture is set. Immediately sprinkle with chips. Let stand for 5 minutes; spread the melted chips over the top. Sprinkle with the nuts. Cool completely before cutting. **YIELD:** 2-1/2 dozen.

BUTTERSCOTCH RAISIN COOKIES

Prep: 15 min. **Bake:** 10 min./batch

I bake these chewy oatmeal cookies that are full of butterscotch chips and raisins. Every so often I add a half cup of chopped pecans to a batch for something different.
Victoria Zmarzley-Hahn // Northhampton, Pennsylvania

- 1 cup butter, softened
- 3/4 cup packed brown sugar
- 1/4 cup sugar
- 2 eggs
- 3 cups quick-cooking oats
- 1-1/2 cups all-purpose flour
- 1 package (3.4 ounces) instant butterscotch pudding mix
- 1 teaspoon baking soda
- 1 cup raisins
- 1/2 cup butterscotch chips

1 In a large bowl, cream butter and sugars until light and fluffy. Beat in the eggs. Combine the oats, flour, dry pudding mix and baking soda; gradually add to the creamed mixture and mix well. Stir in the raisins and butterscotch chips (dough will be stiff).

2 Drop by tablespoonfuls 2 in. apart onto ungreased baking sheets. Bake at 375° for 9-11 minutes or until lightly browned. Remove to wire racks to cool. **YIELD:** 3-1/2 dozen.

LEMON CRUMB BARS

Prep: 15 min. **Bake:** 40 min. + cooling

- 1 package (18-1/4 ounces) lemon cake mix
- 1/2 cup cold butter
- 1 egg
- 2 cups crushed saltines (about 60 crackers)
- 3 egg yolks
- 1 can (14 ounces) sweetened condensed milk
- 1/2 cup lemon juice

1 In a large bowl, beat the dry cake mix, butter and egg until crumbly. Stir in the cracker crumbs; set aside 2 cups for topping.

2 Press remaining crumb mixture into a 13-in. x 9-in. baking dish coated with cooking spray. Bake at 350° for 18-20 minutes or until edges are lightly browned.

3 In a small bowl, beat the egg yolks, milk and lemon juice. Pour over crust; sprinkle with reserved crumb mixture. Bake 20-25 minutes longer or until edges are lightly browned. Cool on a wire rack. Cut into bars. Store in the refrigerator. **YIELD:** 2 dozen.

PECAN CREAM CHEESE SQUARES

Prep: 15 min. **Bake:** 45 min. + cooling

This rich, easy dessert is perfect after a light meal.
Dorothy Pritchett // Wills Point, Texas

- 1 package (18-1/4 ounces) yellow cake mix
- 3 eggs
- 1/2 cup butter, softened
- 2 cups chopped pecans
- 1 package (8 ounces) cream cheese, softened
- 3-2/3 cups confectioners' sugar

1 In a large bowl, beat the dry cake mix, 1 egg and butter until blended. Stir in pecans. Press into a greased 13-in. x 9-in. baking pan; set aside.

2 In a small bowl, beat the cream cheese, sugar and the remaining eggs until smooth. Pour over pecan mixture.

3 Bake at 350° for 45-55 minutes or until golden brown. Cool on a wire rack; cut into squares. Store in the refrigerator. **YIELD:** 3 dozen.

I make these every time I have to take cookies to a potluck supper or another event. We have plenty to take along...plus enough to fill the cookie jar, too. They're also good using white cake mix, but chocolate is my favorite.

Elaine Fortner // Princeton, Indiana

CHIPPY CHOCOLATE COOKIES

Prep: 10 min. **Bake:** 10 min./batch

    2 packages (18-1/4 ounces *each*) chocolate cake mix
    5 eggs
  2/3 cup canola oil
    1 package (10 to 12 ounces) vanilla *or* white chips
    1 cup chopped pecans *or* walnuts

1 In a large bowl, beat the cake mixes, eggs and oil. Stir in chips and nuts.

2 Drop by rounded tablespoonfuls 2 in. apart onto the ungreased baking sheets. Bake at 350° for 10-13 minutes or until set and tops are slightly cracked. Cool for 2 minutes before removing to wire racks to cool. **YIELD:** about 6 dozen.

PUDDING SUGAR COOKIES

Prep: 15 min. **Bake:** 15 min./per batch

This recipe, which was passed on by a friend, has become a year-round favorite at our house. For fun, substitute other flavors of pudding.

Sharon Reed // Catlin, Illinois

    1 cup butter, softened
    1 cup canola oil
    1 cup sugar
    1 cup confectioners' sugar
    2 eggs
    1 teaspoon vanilla extract
    1 package (3.4 ounces) instant lemon pudding mix *or* instant pudding mix of your choice
    4 cups all-purpose flour
    1 teaspoon cream of tartar
    1 teaspoon baking soda

1 In a large bowl, beat the butter, the oil and sugars until blended. Beat in the eggs, vanilla and dry pudding mix. Combine the flour, cream of tartar and baking soda; gradually add to creamed mixture and mix well.

2 Drop by tablespoonfuls 2 in. apart onto ungreased baking sheets. Flatten with a glass dipped in sugar.

3 Bake at 350° for 12-15 minutes or until lightly browned. Remove to wire racks. **YIELD:** 7 dozen.

If you like peach pie, you'll love these easy-to-make bars with a crunchy almond topping.

Hubert Scott // Cockeysville, Maryland

PEACHES 'N' CREAM BARS

Prep: 15 min. **Bake:** 30 min. + cooling

- 1 tube (8 ounces) refrigerated crescent rolls
- 1 package (8 ounces) cream cheese, softened
- 1/2 cup sugar
- 1/4 teaspoon almond extract
- 1 can (21 ounces) peach pie filling
- 1/2 cup all-purpose flour
- 1/4 cup packed brown sugar
- 3 tablespoons cold butter
- 1/2 cup sliced almonds

1 Unroll crescent dough into one long rectangle. Press onto the bottom and slightly up the sides of a greased 13-in. x 9-in. baking pan; seal perforations. Bake at 375° for 5 minutes. Cool completely on a wire rack.

2 In a large bowl, beat the cream cheese, sugar and extract until smooth. Spread over crust. Spoon pie filling over cream cheese layer.

3 In a small bowl, combine flour and brown sugar. Cut in butter until mixture resembles coarse crumbs. Stir in nuts; sprinkle over peach filling.

4 Bake at 375° for 25-28 minutes or until edges are golden brown. Cool for 1 hour on a wire rack. Store in the refrigerator. **YIELD:** about 2 dozen.

BLACK FOREST BROWNIES

Prep: 10 min. **Bake:** 30 min. + chilling

A brownie mix and canned pie filling help me fix these layered bars fast. Everyone loves the combination of chocolate and cherries.

Heidi Stouffer // Bradford, Ontario

- 1 package fudge brownie mix (13-inch x 9-inch pan size)
- 1 package (8 ounces) cream cheese, softened
- 1/3 cup sugar
- 1/2 teaspoon vanilla extract
- 1/3 cup heavy whipping cream
- 1 can (21 ounces) cherry pie filling
- 2 squares (1 ounce *each*) semisweet chocolate

1 Prepare and bake brownies according to package directions. Cool on a wire rack. Meanwhile, in a large bowl, beat the cream cheese, sugar and vanilla until smooth. In a small bowl, beat cream until stiff peaks form; fold into cream cheese mixture.

2 Spread over brownies. Top with the pie filling. In a microwave, melt the chocolate; stir until smooth. Drizzle over brownies. Refrigerate for 10 minutes or until the chocolate is set. **YIELD:** 2 dozen.

FROSTED PEANUT BUTTER COOKIES

Prep/Total Time: 30 min.

Are you looking for a quick way to dress up an ordinary cookie mix? Try this trick. The frosting can be used on a variety of cookies, including sugar and chocolate chip.

Taste of Home Test Kitchen

    1 **package (17-1/2 ounces) peanut butter cookie mix**
    2 **cups confectioners' sugar**
 1/4 **cup baking cocoa**
 1/4 **cup hot water**
    1 **teaspoon vanilla extract**
Sliced almonds *or* pecan halves

1 In a large bowl, prepare cookie dough according to package directions. Shape into 1-in. balls. Place 2 in. apart on ungreased baking sheets.

2 Bake at 375° for 8-10 minutes or until edges are golden brown. Cool for 1 minute before removing to wire racks.

3 For frosting, in a bowl, combine the confectioners' sugar, cocoa, water and vanilla. Spread over cookies; top with nuts. **YIELD:** about 2 dozen.

TIP

To cut your kitchen time, use two ungreased baking sheets. Arrange a dozen dough balls on each sheet. Stagger the two sheets in the oven and switch positions after 5 minutes of baking.

CHOCOLATE CHIP OATMEAL COOKIES

Prep: 20 min. **Bake:** 10 min./batch

Crazy about chocolate chips? This chewy cookie has plenty, not to mention lots of heart-healthy oatmeal. The gang'll come back for more and more...so this big batch is perfect.

Diane Neth // Menno, South Dakota

- 1 cup butter, softened
- 3/4 cup sugar
- 3/4 cup packed brown sugar
- 2 eggs
- 1 teaspoon vanilla extract
- 3 cups quick-cooking oats
- 1-1/2 cups all-purpose flour
- 1 package (3.4 ounces) instant vanilla pudding mix
- 1 teaspoon baking soda
- 1 teaspoon salt
- 2 cups (12 ounces) semisweet chocolate chips
- 1 cup chopped nuts

1 In a large bowl, cream butter and sugars until light and fluffy. Beat in eggs and vanilla. Combine the oats, flour, pudding mix, baking soda and salt; gradually add to creamed mixture and mix well. Stir in chocolate chips and nuts.

2 Drop by rounded teaspoonfuls 2 in. apart onto ungreased baking sheets. Bake at 375° for 10-12 minutes or until lightly browned. Remove to wire racks. **YIELD:** about 7 dozen.

These chewy coconut cookies start with a boxed angel food cake mix, and can be made up in minutes.
Renee Schwebach // Dumont, Minnesota

ANGEL MACAROONS

Prep: 5 min. **Bake:** 10 min./batch + cooling

- 1 package (16 ounces) angel food cake mix
- 1/2 cup water
- 1-1/2 teaspoons almond extract
- 2 cups flaked coconut

1 In a large bowl, beat the cake mix, water and extract on low speed for 30 seconds. Scrape bowl; beat on medium speed for 1 minute. Fold in the coconut.

2 Drop by rounded teaspoonfuls 2 in. apart onto a parchment paper-lined baking sheet. Bake at 350° for 10-12 minutes or until lightly browned. Remove paper with cookies to wire racks to cool. **YIELD:** 5 dozen.

MOCHA-PECAN BUTTER BALLS

Prep: 15 min. + chilling **Bake:** 15 min./batch

When I was a little girl, one of my mother's co-workers would bring tins of assorted Christmas cookies for my sister and me. These were the ones I reached for first.
Kathleen Pruitt // Hoopeston, Illinois

- 2/3 cup butter, softened
- 1 package (3 ounces) cream cheese, softened
- 1/3 cup confectioners' sugar
- 2 teaspoons vanilla extract
- 1-3/4 cups all-purpose flour
- 2/3 cup instant chocolate drink mix
- 1 teaspoon instant coffee granules
- 1/4 teaspoon salt
- 1 cup finely chopped pecans
Additional confectioners' sugar

1 In a large bowl, cream the butter, cream cheese and sugar until light and fluffy. Beat in vanilla. Combine the flour, drink mix, coffee granules and salt; gradually add to creamed mixture and mix well. Stir in pecans. Cover and refrigerate for 1 hour or until easy to handle.

2 Roll into 1-in. balls. Place 1 in. apart on ungreased baking sheets. Bake at 350° for 15-18 minutes or until firm. Cool on pan for 1-2 minutes. Roll the warm cookies in confectioners' sugar; cool on wire racks. **YIELD:** 4 dozen.

BUTTER PECAN COOKIES

Prep/Total Time: 30 min.

3/4 cup butter, softened
1 package (3.4 ounces) instant butterscotch pudding mix
1-1/4 cups all-purpose flour
1/2 cup chopped pecans

1 In a small bowl, beat butter and pudding mix until smooth. Gradually beat in flour. Fold in pecans. Roll into 1-1/2-in. balls.

2 Place 2 in. apart on greased baking sheets; flatten to 1/2 in. with the bottom of a glass coated with cooking spray.

3 Bake at 375° for 10-13 minutes or until light golden brown. Remove from the pans to wire racks. **YIELD:** about 2 dozen.

MALTED MILK BALL BROWNIES

Prep: 15 min. **Bake:** 30 min. + cooling

You don't have to be a kid to love these scrumptious brownies! Malted milk balls in the batter and sprinkled on top make them extra special. Everyone loves them.
Mitzi Sentiff // Annapolis, Maryland

1 package fudge brownie mix (13-inch x 9-inch pan size)
1-1/3 cups chopped malted milk balls, *divided*
1 cup (6 ounces) semisweet chocolate chips
2 tablespoons butter
2 tablespoons milk
1/4 teaspoon vanilla extract

1 Prepare brownie batter according to package directions; stir in 1 cup malted milk balls. Spread into a greased 13-in. x 9-in. baking pan.

2 Bake at 350° for 28-30 minutes or until a toothpick inserted 2 in. from an edge comes out with moist crumbs. Cool completely on a wire rack.

3 In a microwave, melt the chocolate chips and butter; stir until smooth. Cool slightly. Stir in milk and vanilla. Spread over brownies. Sprinkle with the remaining malted milk balls. Refrigerate for 10-15 minutes or until set. Cut into bars. **YIELD:** 2 dozen.

RASPBERRY BROWNIE DESSERT

Prep: 20 min. **Bake:** 25 min. + chilling

- 1 package fudge brownie mix (13-inch x 9-inch pan size)
- 2 cups heavy whipping cream, *divided*
- 1 package (3.3 ounces) instant white chocolate pudding mix
- 1 can (21 ounces) raspberry pie filling

1 Prepare and bake the brownies according to package directions, using a greased 13-in. x 9-in. baking pan. Cool completely on a wire rack.

2 In a small bowl, combine 1 cup cream and pudding mix; stir for 2 minutes or until very thick. In a small mixing bowl, beat remaining cream until stiff peaks form; fold into pudding. Carefully spread over brownies; top with pie filling. Cover and refrigerate for at least 2 hours before cutting. **YIELD:** 15-18 servings.

ORANGE CRISPY COOKIES

Prep/Total Time: 30 min.

- 1 package (18-1/4 ounces) white cake mix
- 1/2 cup butter, melted
- 1 egg, lightly beaten
- 2 teaspoons grated orange peel
- 2 teaspoons orange extract
- 1 cup crisp rice cereal
- 1 cup chopped walnuts, optional

1 In a large bowl, combine the dry cake mix, butter, egg, orange peel and extract. Stir in cereal and walnuts if desired.

2 Roll into 1-in. balls. Place 2 in. apart on ungreased baking sheets. Bake at 350° for 12-14 minutes or until lightly browned. Cool for 1 minute before removing to wire racks to cool. **YIELD:** about 4 dozen.

Brownie mix makes these biscotti cookies easy to stir up, and a white chocolate and almond topping adds a special touch.
Jeanie Williams // Minnetonka, Minnesota

BROWNIE ALPINE BISCOTTI

Prep: 25 min. **Bake:** 40 min. + cooling

- 1 package fudge brownie mix (13-inch x 9-inch size)
- 3/4 cup ground almonds
- 1/2 cup all-purpose flour
- 3/4 teaspoon baking powder
- 1 egg
- 3 egg whites
- 1 teaspoon almond extract
- 1/4 cup sliced almonds, optional
- 3 squares (1 ounce *each*) white baking chocolate, optional

1 In a large bowl, combine the brownie mix, ground almonds, flour and baking powder. In a small bowl, whisk egg, egg whites and extract. Add to brownie mixture; stir until combined.

2 Divide dough into thirds. On a greased baking sheet, shape each portion into a 7-in. x 3-1/2-in. rectangle. Bake at 350° for 24 minutes. Remove from the oven; cool on baking sheet for 5 minutes.

3 Transfer to a cutting board; cut diagonally with a serrated knife into 3/4-in. slices. Place cut side down on greased baking sheets. Bake 12-14 minutes longer or until firm.

4 Cool on wire racks. If desired, sprinkle with the sliced almonds and drizzle with chocolate. Let stand until the chocolate is completely set. Store in an airtight container. **YIELD:** 2-1/2 dozen.

CHEWY WALNUT BARS

Prep: 10 min. **Bake:** 30 min. + cooling

Since they need just four ingredients and one bowl to dirty, I often whip up a batch of these family-favorite bars. I'm thanked many times over!
Nancy Tuschak // Vacaville, California

- 2-1/3 cups packed brown sugar
- 2 cups biscuit/baking mix
- 4 eggs
- 2 cups chopped walnuts

1 In a large bowl, combine brown sugar and biscuit mix. Beat in eggs until well blended. Fold in walnuts.

2 Pour into a greased 13-in. x 9-in. baking pan. Bake at 350° for 30-35 minutes or until golden brown. Cool on wire rack. Cut into bars. **YIELD:** about 3 dozen.

desserts

CHERRY-CREAM CRUMBLE PIE

Prep: 20 min. **Bake:** 45 min. + cooling

- 1/2 cup sugar
- 3 tablespoons all-purpose flour
- 2 cans (15 ounces *each*) pitted tart cherries, drained
- 1 cup (8 ounces) sour cream
- 1 egg, lightly beaten
- 1/4 teaspoon almond extract
- 1 unbaked pastry shell (9 inches)

TOPPING:

- 1/2 cup quick-cooking oats
- 1/3 cup all-purpose flour
- 1/3 cup packed brown sugar
- 1/4 teaspoon ground cinnamon
- 1/4 cup cold butter
- 1/2 cup chopped pecans

1 In a large bowl, combine the sugar, flour, cherries, sour cream, egg and extract. Spoon into the pastry shell. Bake at 400° for 20 minutes.

2 For topping, combine the oats, flour, brown sugar and cinnamon in a bowl; cut in butter until mixture resembles coarse crumbs. Stir in pecans. Sprinkle over filling. Cover edges of crust to prevent overbrowning.

3 Bake for 25-30 minutes or until the topping is lightly browned. Cool on a wire rack for 1 hour. Store in the refrigerator. **YIELD:** 8 servings.

DESSERT CUSTARD SAUCE

Prep: 10 min. + chilling

No need to stand over the stove to make a custard sauce. I created this streamlined version, and it goes great over fresh fruit or cake.

Bunny Richardson // Russellville, Alabama

- 2 cups cold milk, *divided*
- 1/4 cup plus 2 teaspoons instant vanilla pudding mix
- 1/2 cup heavy whipping cream
- 1/4 cup sugar
- 1/2 teaspoon vanilla extract

1 In a small bowl, beat 1 cup milk and pudding on medium speed for 2 minutes. Add the cream, sugar, vanilla and remaining milk; beat on low speed for 2 minutes.

2 Transfer to a pitcher; refrigerate for 1-2 hours before serving. **YIELD:** 3 cups.

STRAWBERRY PUFF PASTRY DESSERT

Prep: 30 min. **Bake:** 15 min. + cooling

My failed attempt to make a triple-layer strawberry malt mousse resulted in this scrumptious dessert. I don't use puff pastry often, but it was simple to work with. My husband declared it one of the best desserts ever.

Anna Ginsberg // Austin, Texas

- 1 package (17.3 ounces) frozen puff pastry
- 5 cups sliced fresh strawberries, *divided*
- 6 squares (1 ounce *each*) white baking chocolate, chopped
- 1 package (8 ounces) cream cheese, softened
- 1 teaspoon vanilla extract
- 1 cup confectioners' sugar
- 1/3 cup malted milk powder
- 2 cups heavy whipping cream, whipped

Strawberry syrup, optional

1 Thaw one puff pastry sheet (save remaining sheet for another use). Unfold the pastry and cut lengthwise into three 3-in.-wide strips. Cut each strip into thirds, making nine squares.

2 Place 1 in. apart on ungreased baking sheets. Bake at 400° for 11-13 minutes or until golden brown. Remove to wire racks to cool.

3 Place 2-1/2 cups strawberries in a blender; cover and puree; set aside. In a large microwave-safe bowl, melt the white chocolate at 70% power for 1 minute; stir. Microwave at additional 10- to 20-second intervals, stirring until smooth; cool slightly. Add cream cheese and vanilla; beat until smooth. Beat in the confectioners' sugar and malted milk powder until smooth. Stir in the puree. Fold in whipped cream.

4 Split the pastry squares in half horizontally. Line an ungreased 13-in. x 9-in. dish with bottom pastry halves, cut side up; spread with 3-1/2 cups strawberry cream. Top with 1 cup of sliced berries. Cover with pastry tops, cut side down.

5 Spread with remaining strawberry cream. Sprinkle with remaining berries. Drizzle with strawberry syrup if desired. Refrigerate leftovers. **YIELD:** 12 servings.

Wherever I take this delicious coffee cake, everyone loves it. I've been making it for about 30 years. I work as a cook at a county jail and enjoy preparing food for a lot of people.

Carol Roth // Uhrichsville, Ohio

STREUSEL NUT COFFEE CAKE

Prep: 15 min. **Bake:** 1 hour + cooling

- 1 cup butter, softened
- 2-1/2 cups sugar, *divided*
- 4 eggs
- 2 teaspoons vanilla extract
- 2 teaspoons almond extract
- 4 cups all-purpose flour
- 1 teaspoon baking soda
- 2 cups (16 ounces) sour cream
- 1/2 cup chopped walnuts
- 3 teaspoons instant chocolate drink mix
- 2 teaspoons ground cinnamon

1 In a large bowl, cream butter and 2 cups sugar until light and fluffy. Add eggs, one at a time, beating well after each addition. Beat in extracts. Combine flour and baking soda. Gradually add to the creamed mixture alternately with sour cream, mixing well after each addition. Spoon half into a greased 10-in. tube pan.

2 Combine walnuts, drink mix, cinnamon and remaining sugar. Sprinkle half over batter. Top with remaining batter and nut mixture.

3 Bake at 350° for 60-70 minutes or until a toothpick inserted near the center comes out clean. Cool for 10 minutes before removing from pan to a wire rack to cool completely. **YIELD:** 12-14 servings.

PRETZEL DESSERT

Prep: 30 min. + chilling

This is one of my mom's favorite desserts. The salty crust tastes so good with the sweet cream cheese filling.

Erin Frakes// Moline, Illinois

- 2 cups crushed pretzels
- 3/4 cup butter, melted
- 2 tablespoons sugar

FILLING:
- 1 package (8 ounces) cream cheese, softened
- 1 cup sugar
- 1 carton (8 ounces) frozen whipped topping, thawed

TOPPING:
- 1 package (6 ounces) strawberry gelatin
- 2 cups boiling water
- 1/2 cup cold water

1 In a large bowl, combine the pretzels, butter and sugar. Press into the bottom of an ungreased 13-in. x 9-in. baking pan. Bake at 350° for 10 minutes. Cool completely.

2 In a large bowl, beat cream cheese and sugar until smooth. Stir in whipped topping. Spread over pretzel crust. Cover and refrigerate until chilled.

3 For topping, in a small bowl, dissolve gelatin in boiling water. Add cold water; chill until partially set. Carefully pour over filling. Cover and refrigerate for 4-6 hours or until firm. Cut into squares. **YIELD:** 12-16 servings.

Try this tempting take on store-bought ice cream sandwiches that relies on convenient brownie and pudding mixes. The frosty, handheld treats have a sweet filling tucked between fudgy brownie layers.
Taste of Home Test Kitchen

FROZEN MOUSSE BROWNIE SANDWICHES

Prep: 30 min. **Bake:** 15 min. + freezing

- 1 package reduced-fat brownie mix (13-inch x 9-inch pan size)
- 2 cups cold fat-free milk
- 2 packages (1 ounce *each*) sugar-free instant vanilla pudding mix
- 3 tablespoons vanilla *or* white chips, melted and cooled
- 1/2 cup reduced-fat whipped topping

1 Line the bottom and sides of two 13-in. x 9-in. baking pans with parchment paper. Coat the paper with cooking spray. Prepare brownie mix according to package directions; divide the batter evenly between the pans.

2 Bake at 350° for 15-18 minutes or until edges just begin to pull away from sides of pan and a toothpick inserted near the center comes out with moist crumbs. Cool on wire racks.

3 For mousse, in a bowl, whisk together the milk and pudding mixes for 2 minutes. Stir a small amount of the pudding into the melted chips, then return all to the pudding. Fold in whipped topping.

4 Cover two large cutting boards or inverted 15-in. x 10-in. x 1-in. baking pans with plastic wrap. Invert one pan of brownies onto prepared board or pan. Gently peel off the parchment paper. Spread the mousse to within 1/2 in. of edges. Carefully invert second brownie layer onto second board or pan. Gently peel off parchment paper, then place right side up over mousse filling.

5 Cover and freeze for about 4 hours or until the filling is firm. Remove from the freezer 10 minutes before cutting into sandwiches. Individually wrap leftover sandwiches; store in the freezer. **YIELD:** 15 servings.

> # TIP
>
> *To add a little flavor pizzazz to the mousse filling, whisk the vanilla pudding mix with 2 cups of your favorite flavor of refrigerated nondairy coffee creamer.*

CHIP LOVER'S CUPCAKES

Prep: 30 min. **Bake:** 20 min. + cooling

Making chocolate chip cookies is a challenge with three teenagers who are always grabbing the dough to sample. Their love of cookie dough inspired the recipe for these cupcakes that adults will enjoy, too.

Donna Scully // Middletown, Delaware

- 1 package (18-1/4 ounces) white cake mix
- 1/4 cup butter, softened
- 1/4 cup packed brown sugar
- 2 tablespoons sugar
- 1/3 cup all-purpose flour
- 1/4 cup confectioners' sugar
- 1/4 cup miniature semisweet chocolate chips

BUTTERCREAM FROSTING:

- 1/2 cup butter, softened
- 1/2 cup shortening
- 4-1/2 cups confectioners' sugar
- 4 tablespoons milk, *divided*
- 1-1/2 teaspoons vanilla extract
- 1/4 cup baking cocoa
- 18 miniature chocolate chip cookies

1 Prepare cake batter according to package directions; set aside. For filling, in a small bowl, cream the butter and sugars until light and fluffy. Gradually beat in flour and confectioners' sugar until blended. Fold in chocolate chips.

2 Fill paper-lined muffin cups half full with cake batter. Drop filling by tablespoonfuls into the center of each; cover with remaining batter.

3 Bake at 350° for 20-22 minutes or until a toothpick inserted in cake comes out clean. Cool for 10 minutes; remove from pans to wire racks to cool completely.

4 For the frosting, in a large bowl, cream the butter, shortening and confectioners' sugar until smooth. Beat in 3 tablespoons milk and vanilla until creamy. Set aside 1 cup frosting; frost cupcakes with remaining frosting.

5 Stir baking cocoa and remaining milk into reserved frosting. Cut a small hole in a corner of a pastry or plastic bag; insert star tip. Fill bag with chocolate frosting. Pipe a rosette on top of each cupcake; garnish with a cookie. **YIELD:** 1-1/2 dozen.

FLUTED LEMON CAKE

Prep: 15 min. **Bake:** 40 min. + cooling

- 1 package (18-1/4 ounces) yellow cake mix
- 1 package (3 ounces) lemon gelatin
- 4 eggs
- 2/3 cup water
- 2/3 cup canola oil

GLAZE:
- 1 cup confectioners' sugar
- 3 tablespoons lemon juice
- 1 teaspoon grated lemon peel

1 In a large bowl, combine the cake mix, gelatin, eggs, water and oil. Beat on low speed for 1 minute. Beat on medium for 2 minutes.

2 Pour into a greased and floured 10-in. fluted tube pan. Bake at 350° for 38-42 minutes or until a toothpick inserted near the center comes out clean. Cool for 10 minutes before removing from pan to a wire rack.

3 Combine glaze ingredients; drizzle over warm cake. Cool completely before cutting. **YIELD:** 12-16 servings.

SPICE PUFFS

Prep: 20 min. **Bake:** 20 min.

Four ingredients are all you need to bake up a batch of these lovely light-as-air muffins that make a sweet breakfast treat. They're my son's favorite and so simple to make.

Sally Geipel // Franklin, Wisconsin

- 1 package (18-1/4 ounces) spice cake mix
- 1/2 cup butter, melted
- 1/2 cup sugar
- 1 teaspoon ground cinnamon

1 Prepare cake batter according to package directions. Fill 24 greased or paper-lined muffin cups two-thirds full. Bake at 350° for 20-25 minutes or until a toothpick inserted near the center comes out clean. Remove to wire racks. Cool for 5 minutes.

2 Place butter in a shallow bowl. In another shallow bowl, combine sugar and cinnamon. Dip top of the warm puffs in butter, then in the cinnamon-sugar. Serve warm. **YIELD:** 2 dozen.

BERRY-PATCH BROWNIE PIZZA

Prep: 20 min. **Bake:** 15 min. + chilling

I just love the combination of fruit, almonds and chocolate that makes this brownie so unique. The fruit lightens the chocolate a bit and makes it feel like you are eating something sinfully healthy.

Sue Kauffman // Columbia City, Indiana

- 1 package fudge brownie mix (13-inch x 9-inch pan size)
- 1/3 cup chopped unblanched almonds
- 1 teaspoon almond extract
- 1 package (8 ounces) cream cheese, softened
- 1 tablespoon sugar
- 1 teaspoon vanilla extract
- 1/2 teaspoon grated lemon peel
- 2 cups whipped topping

Mixed fresh berries

1 Prepare brownie batter according to package directions for fudge-like brownies, adding almonds and extract. Spread into a greased 14-in. pizza pan.

2 Bake at 375° for 15-18 minutes or until a toothpick inserted near the center comes out clean. Cool in pan on a wire rack.

3 In a large bowl, beat the cream cheese, sugar, vanilla and lemon peel until smooth. Fold in whipped topping. Spread over crust to within 1/2 in. of edges. Top with berries. Refrigerate for 2-3 hours before serving. **YIELD:** 12-14 servings.

If a banana split is on your no-no list, treat yourself to this lower-in-fat option. Each smooth and creamy scoop is generously sprinkled with semisweet chocolate chips.

Taste of Home Test Kitchen

CHUNKY BANANA CHIP ICE CREAM

Prep: 15 min. + chilling **Process:** 20 min. + freezing

- 2 cups 2% milk
- 1 can (14 ounces) fat-free sweetened condensed milk
- 1 envelope whipped topping mix
- 2 tablespoons sugar
- 2 teaspoons lemon juice
- 1 teaspoon vanilla extract
- 3 medium firm bananas, cut into 1-inch pieces
- 1/2 cup miniature semisweet chocolate chips

1 In a large bowl, beat the milks, the whipped topping mix, sugar, lemon juice and vanilla on high speed for 3 minutes. Cover and refrigerate overnight.

2 Stir the bananas into milk mixture. Fill cylinder of ice cream freezer; freeze according to the manufacturer's directions. Stir in the chocolate chips. Transfer to a freezer container; freeze for 2-4 hours before serving. **YIELD:** 8 servings.

CHERRY CAKE

Prep: 10 min. **Bake:** 25 min. + cooling

This pretty pink cake is great for holidays or a little girl's birthday party. It turns out moist and tender with a nice flavor surprise from the cherries.

Amy Kraemer // Hutchinson, Minnesota

- 1 package (18-1/4 ounces) yellow cake mix
- 1 can (21 ounces) cherry pie filling
- 3 eggs, lightly beaten
- 1/2 cup packed brown sugar
- 2 teaspoons all-purpose flour
- 1 teaspoon ground cinnamon
- 2 teaspoons butter, softened
- 1/2 cup chopped pecans

1 In a large bowl, beat the dry cake mix, pie filling and eggs until blended. Pour into a greased 13-in. x 9-in. baking pan. Combine the brown sugar, flour, cinnamon and butter; sprinkle over batter. Top with nuts.

2 Bake at 350° for 25-30 minutes or until a toothpick inserted near the center comes out clean. Cool on a wire rack. **YIELD:** 15 servings.

desserts   223

RASPBERRY COCONUT CAKE

Prep: 20 min. **Bake:** 25 min. + cooling

- 1 package (18-1/4 ounces) white cake mix
- 3 cups flaked coconut, *divided*
- 6 squares (1 ounce *each*) white baking chocolate, chopped
- 1/4 cup heavy whipping cream
- 3/4 cup seedless raspberry jam
- 1 cup butter, softened
- 1 cup confectioners' sugar

1 Prepare cake batter according to package directions; fold in 2/3 cup coconut. Pour into two greased and floured 9-in. round baking pans. Bake at 350° for 25-30 minutes or until a toothpick inserted near the center comes out clean. Cool for 10 minutes before removing from pans to wire racks to cool completely.

2 In a microwave, melt white chocolate and cream at 70% power for 1 minute; stir. Microwave at additional 10- to 20-second intervals, stirring until smooth. Cool to room temperature.

3 In a small bowl, combine jam and 1 cup coconut. Spread over one cake layer; top with second layer.

4 In a small bowl, beat the butter until fluffy. Add the confectioners' sugar; beat until smooth. Gradually beat in white chocolate mixture. Spread over top and sides of cake. Toast remaining coconut; sprinkle over cake. **YIELD:** 12 servings.

APPLE CRUMBLE

Prep: 30 min. **Bake:** 40 min. + cooling

While visiting friends in New Zealand, I watched this dessert being made. Back at home, I came up with my own version. It's great with vanilla ice cream or fresh whipped cream.

Carol Simpkins // Santa Cruz, California

8 sheets phyllo dough (14 inches x 9 inches)
Butter-flavored cooking spray
1/2 cup packed brown sugar
2 tablespoons all-purpose flour
1/2 teaspoon ground ginger
1/2 teaspoon ground cinnamon
4 medium tart apples, peeled and sliced

TOPPING:
1/2 cup all-purpose flour
1/2 cup packed brown sugar
1/2 cup soft whole wheat bread crumbs
1/4 teaspoon ground ginger
1/4 teaspoon ground cinnamon
1/2 cup cold butter
1/4 cup slivered almonds

1 Cut phyllo sheets in half; spritz with butter-flavored spray. Layer phyllo, sprayed side up, in a greased 8-in. square baking dish.

2 In a large bowl, combine the brown sugar, flour, ginger and cinnamon; add apples and toss to coat. Spoon over phyllo dough.

3 In another large bowl, combine the flour, brown sugar, bread crumbs, ginger and cinnamon; cut in butter until mixture resembles coarse crumbs. Add the almonds; sprinkle over apple mixture.

4 Bake at 350° for 40-45 minutes or until filling is bubbly and topping is golden. Cool for 10 minutes before serving. **YIELD:** 9 servings.

With just a few simple ingredients, you can create this fun cake for a kid's or even adult's party. Change the color scheme by using different flavored Fruit Roll-Ups.

Flo Burtnett // Gage, Oklahoma

POLKA DOT CAKE

Prep: 20 min. **Bake:** 20 min.

  1 package (18-1/4 ounces) chocolate cake mix
  1 can (16 ounces) vanilla frosting
  1 package (5 ounces) Fruit Roll-Ups
Round cookie cutters, 1 inch, 1-1/2 inch, 2 inch and
    2-3/4 inch

1 Prepare and bake the cake according to package directions, using two greased and floured 9-in. round baking pans. Cool for 10 minutes before removing from pans to wire racks to cool completely.

2 Spread the frosting between layers and over top and sides of cake. Unroll Fruit Roll-Ups. Using the cookie cutters and a variety of Fruit Roll-Up colors, cut out circles. Arrange the circles on the top and sides of cake.
YIELD: 12 servings.

DELUXE STRAWBERRY SHORTCAKE

Prep: 25 min. **Bake:** 20 min. + cooling

This tasty shortcake is perfect for the Fourth of July. I love the moist, from-scratch flavor of this simple cake. It's foolproof and always brings lots of compliments.

Janet Fant // Denair, California

  1 package (18-1/4 ounces) yellow cake mix
  1 cup water
1/2 cup sour cream
1/3 cup canola oil
  3 eggs
  1 teaspoon vanilla extract
FILLING:
  1 package (8 ounces) cream cheese, softened
1/3 cup sugar
  1 carton (8 ounces) frozen whipped topping, thawed
  3 cups chopped fresh strawberries

1 In a large bowl, combine the dry cake mix, water, sour cream, oil, eggs and extract; beat on low speed for 30 seconds. Beat on medium for 2 minutes. Pour into two greased and floured 9-in. round baking pans.

2 Bake at 350° for 20-25 minutes or until a toothpick inserted near the center comes out clean. Cool for 10 minutes; remove from pans to wire racks to cool completely.

3 In a small bowl, beat the cream cheese and sugar until smooth. Fold in whipped topping. Place one cake on a serving plate; top with half of the cream cheese mixture and strawberries. Repeat layers. Store in the refrigerator.
YIELD: 12 servings.

When my mom was told to avoid sugar and fats, I whipped up this light, delectable dessert. Mom loves indulging her sweet tooth while following doctor's orders.

Annette Abbott
Charlotte, North Carolina

PEANUT BUTTER CHOCOLATE CAKE

Prep: 25 min. **Bake:** 20 min. + cooling

> 1 package (18-1/4 ounces) devil's food cake mix
> 1 cup water
> 3 eggs
> 1/3 cup unsweetened applesauce
> 1/4 cup reduced-fat creamy peanut butter

FROSTING:

> 1/2 cup cold fat-free milk
> 1 package (1.4 ounces) sugar-free instant chocolate pudding mix
> 1 package (8 ounces) reduced-fat cream cheese
> 1/2 cup reduced-fat creamy peanut butter
> 1 carton (8 ounces) frozen reduced-fat whipped topping, thawed

1 In a large bowl, combine the dry cake mix, water, eggs and applesauce. Beat on low speed for 30 seconds. Beat on medium speed for 2 minutes. Transfer to a 13-in. x 9-in. baking dish coated with cooking spray.

2 Bake at 350° for 30-35 minutes or until a toothpick inserted near the center comes out clean.

3 Immediately drop small amounts of peanut butter over hot cake; return to the oven for 1 minute. Carefully spread peanut butter over cake. Cool on a wire rack.

4 For frosting, in a small bowl, whisk milk and pudding mix for 1 minute. In a small bowl, beat cream cheese and peanut butter until smooth. Gradually beat in pudding. Beat in half of the whipped topping; fold in remaining whipped topping. Frost cake. Store in the refrigerator. **YIELD:** 18 servings.

BLUEBERRY UPSIDE-DOWN CAKE

Prep: 10 min. **Bake:** 40 min. + cooling

Turn a simple yellow cake into a terrific dessert with blueberries and a handful of other ingredients. It's great for company, too.

Nancy Kramer // Newmanstown, Pennsylvania

> 1/4 cup butter, melted
> 1/2 cup sugar
> 2 cups fresh *or* frozen blueberries
> 1 package (18-1/4 ounces) yellow cake mix

Whipped cream

1 Coat the bottom of a 13-in. x 9-in. baking dish with butter; sprinkle with sugar and blueberries. Prepare cake batter according to the package directions; spread over the blueberries.

2 Bake at 350° for 40-45 minutes or until a toothpick inserted near the center comes out clean. Cool for 10 minutes on a wire rack. Invert onto a serving plate. Serve warm with whipped cream. **YIELD:** 12-15 servings.

EDITOR'S NOTE: If using frozen blueberries, do not thaw before adding to batter.

JELLIED CRANBERRY NUT CANDIES

Prep: 25 min. + chilling

- 1 teaspoon butter
- 1 can (16 ounces) jellied cranberry sauce
- 1-3/4 cups sugar, *divided*
- 2 packages (3 ounces *each*) lemon gelatin
- 1 package (3 ounces) orange gelatin
- 1-1/2 cups chopped walnuts

1 Line an 8-in. square pan with foil and grease the foil with 1 teaspoon butter; set aside. In a large saucepan, combine cranberry sauce, 1 cup sugar and lemon and orange gelatin. Bring to a boil over medium heat; stir constantly. Remove from the heat; stir in walnuts. Pour into prepared pan. Cover; chill overnight.

2 Using foil, lift candy out of pan. Discard foil; cut into 1-in. squares. Roll in the remaining sugar. Store at room temperature between layers of waxed paper in an airtight container. Best when stored at least three days before serving. **YIELD:** 2-1/2 pounds.

CHOCOLATE HAZELNUT PARFAITS

Prep: 10 min. + chilling

Hazelnut coffee creamer adds great flavor to the chocolate pudding in these special parfaits. Shortbread cookie crumbs and fresh strawberry slices complete the lovely layered desserts.

Christy Hinrichs // Parkville, Missouri

- 3 cups cold milk
- 1 cup refrigerated hazelnut nondairy creamer
- 2 packages (3.9 ounces *each*) instant chocolate pudding mix
- 1 cup crushed shortbread cookies
- 2 cups sliced fresh strawberries
- Whipped cream, optional

1 In a large bowl, whisk the milk, creamer and pudding mixes for 2 minutes. Let stand for 2 minutes or until soft-set.

2 Spoon 1/4 cup pudding into each of eight parfait glasses; sprinkle each with 1 tablespoon cookie crumbs. Top with strawberries and remaining pudding and crumbs. Refrigerate for 1 hour before serving. Garnish with whipped cream if desired. **YIELD:** 8 servings.

FRUITY COCONUT CAKE ROLL

Prep: 30 min. **Bake:** 20 min. + chilling

Kiwi and coconut add tropical flair to this moist, fruity and simply delicious dessert. It makes a light, refreshing and stunning finale to even the fanciest meal!

Nancy Granaman // Burlington, Iowa

- 1 package (16 ounces) angel food cake mix
- 1/2 teaspoon plus 3 tablespoons confectioners' sugar, *divided*
- 3/4 cup cold fat-free milk
- 1 package (1 ounce) sugar-free instant white chocolate pudding mix
- 1 carton (8 ounces) frozen fat-free whipped topping, thawed
- 1/2 teaspoon coconut extract
- 2 medium kiwifruit, peeled and thinly sliced
- 2 cups fresh strawberries, sliced
- 1/3 cup plus 2 tablespoons flaked coconut, *divided*
- 2 tablespoons apricot spreadable fruit
- 1/2 teaspoon hot water

1 Line a 15-in. x 10-in. x 1-in. baking pan with waxed paper; coat the paper with cooking spray and set aside. Prepare cake batter according to package directions. Spread evenly in prepared pan.

2 Bake at 350° for 16-20 minutes or until golden brown. Turn cake onto a kitchen towel dusted with 1/2 teaspoon confectioners' sugar. Gently peel off the waxed paper. Dust with remaining confectioners' sugar. Roll up cake in the towel jelly-roll style, starting with a short side. Cool completely on a wire rack.

3 For filling, in a large bowl, whisk milk and pudding mix for 2 minutes. Let stand for 2 minutes or until soft-set. Stir in 1 cup whipped topping. Fold in the remaining whipped topping; stir in extract.

4 Unroll cake; spread with filling to within 1 in. of edges. Arrange kiwi and strawberries over filling. Sprinkle with 1/3 cup coconut. Roll up again. Refrigerate for 1-2 hours.

5 Toast the remaining coconut. In a small bowl, whisk the spreadable fruit and water until smooth. Drizzle over cake. Sprinkle with toasted coconut. Cut into slices. Refrigerate leftovers. **YIELD:** 12 servings.

There's no pitting cherries and peeling peaches when you're throwing together this quick cobbler. It uses convenient canned fruit and purchased pie filling.

Sandra Pierce
North Bonneville, Washington

CHERRY PEACH COBBLER

Prep: 15 min. **Bake:** 20 min.

  1 can (21 ounces) cherry pie filling
  1 can (8-1/2 ounces) sliced peaches, drained
    and halved
  2 teaspoons lemon juice
1/2 teaspoon ground cinnamon
BISCUIT TOPPING:
  1 cup biscuit/baking mix
  4 teaspoons sugar, *divided*
  3 tablespoons milk
  2 tablespoons butter, melted
  1 teaspoon grated lemon peel
1/8 teaspoon ground cinnamon
  3 cups vanilla ice cream

1 In a greased microwave-safe 8-in. square baking dish, combine pie filling, peaches, lemon juice and cinnamon. Microwave, uncovered, on high for 3-4 minutes or until heated through, stirring once.

2 In a small bowl, combine the biscuit mix, 3 teaspoons sugar, milk, butter and lemon peel. Drop by rounded tablespoonfuls onto filling. Combine cinnamon and remaining sugar; sprinkle over topping. Bake at 400° for 17-19 minutes or until golden brown. Serve warm with ice cream. **YIELD:** 6 servings.

EDITOR'S NOTE: This recipe was tested in a 1,100-watt microwave.

TIP

Mix up this delightful cobbler using a variety of pie fillings. Peaches will be great paired with apple or blueberry pie filling. To change up the topping, try brown sugar for the sugar, orange peel for the lemon peel and a dash of ground nutmeg for the cinnamon.

Looking for the perfect ending to any summertime meal? Here's a swift-to-fix, creamy tart that boasts a crunchy chocolate layer tucked next to the crust. You could also make individual tartlets instead of one big one.

Dawn Tringali
Hamilton Square, New Jersey

STRAWBERRY TART
Prep: 20 min. **Bake:** 10 min. + chilling

 1 sheet refrigerated pie pastry
 3 ounces German sweet chocolate, melted
 2 packages (8 ounces _each_) cream cheese, softened
 3 tablespoons heavy whipping cream
 2 teaspoons vanilla extract
1-3/4 cups confectioners' sugar
2-1/2 cups sliced fresh strawberries
 1/4 cup red currant jelly

1 Press pastry onto the bottom and up the sides of an ungreased 9-in. fluted tart pan with a removable bottom. Place on a baking sheet. Bake at 450° for 10-12 minutes or until golden brown. Cool on a wire rack.

2 Spread melted chocolate over bottom of crust. Cover and refrigerate for 5-10 minutes or until almost set. Meanwhile, in a large bowl, beat the cream cheese, cream and vanilla until smooth. Gradually beat in confectioners' sugar. Spread over chocolate layer.

3 Arrange strawberries over filling; brush with jelly. Cover and refrigerate for at least 2 hours. Remove sides of pan before serving. **YIELD:** 6-8 servings.

ALMOND EGGNOG POUND CAKE
Prep: 15 min. **Bake:** 40 min. + cooling

I love to bake pies, cookies, cakes and anything else I can think of. This pound cake recipe is one of my family's favorites, especially around the holidays.

Rick Aynes // Oklahoma City, Oklahoma

 6 tablespoons butter, softened, _divided_
2/3 cup sliced almonds
 1 package (18-1/4 ounces) yellow cake mix
1-1/2 cups eggnog
 2 eggs
 1 teaspoon rum extract
 1/8 teaspoon ground nutmeg

1 Grease a 10-in. fluted tube pan with 2 tablespoons butter. Press almonds onto the bottom and sides of pan; set aside.

2 Melt remaining butter. In a large bowl, beat the cake mix, eggnog, eggs, rum extract, nutmeg and melted butter on low speed for 30 seconds or just until moistened. Beat on medium for 2 minutes or until smooth. Pour into prepared pan.

3 Bake at 350° for 40-50 minutes or until a toothpick inserted near the center comes out clean. Cool for 15 minutes before removing from pan to a wire rack. **YIELD:** 12-14 servings.

EDITOR'S NOTE: This recipe was tested with commercially prepared eggnog.

CHOCOLATE WALNUT TART

Prep: 20 min. **Bake:** 25 min.

You'll have no hassle, no fuss and no leftovers with this dessert. It looks impressive, but it's actually so simple. It can be prepared in a 9- or 11-inch pan and tastes wonderful served warm with ice cream or whipped topping.

Sue Shank // Harrisonburg, Virginia

- 1 sheet refrigerated pie pastry
- 1 cup (6 ounces) semisweet chocolate chips
- 1 cup coarsely chopped walnuts
- 3 eggs, lightly beaten
- 3/4 cup dark corn syrup
- 1/2 cup packed brown sugar
- 1/4 cup butter, melted
- 1 teaspoon vanilla extract

Whipped cream, optional

1 On a lightly floured surface, roll out pastry to fit an 11-in. fluted tart pan with removable bottom. Transfer pastry to pan; trim edges. Sprinkle with chocolate chips and walnuts. In a small bowl, whisk the eggs, corn syrup, brown sugar, butter and vanilla. Pour over the chips and nuts.

2 Bake at 350° for 25-30 minutes or until a knife inserted near the center comes out clean. Cool on a wire rack. Serve with whipped cream if desired. **YIELD:** 8-10 servings.

TIP

If you have a favorite pie crust recipe, feel free to use it instead of the refrigerated pie pastry called for in this recipe. If your recipe makes a double crust, cut out the extra dough with small cookie cutters, sprinkle with cinnamon-sugar and bake. Enjoy the mini-pastries as a special treat.

I got the recipe for this wonderful no-bake treat from my mother-in-law because it's my husband's favorite. I'm frequently asked to bring it to get-togethers where it's always a hit.

Linda Winter // Enid, Oklahoma

BUTTERFINGER DELIGHT
Prep: 30 min. + chilling

- 1 cup crushed butter-flavored crackers (about 30 crackers)
- 1 cup graham cracker crumbs
- 4 Butterfinger candy bars (2.1 ounces *each*), crushed
- 3/4 cup butter, melted
- 1-1/2 cups cold milk
- 2 packages (3.4 ounces *each*) instant vanilla pudding mix
- 1 quart reduced-fat chocolate frozen yogurt, softened
- 1 carton (12 ounces) frozen whipped topping, thawed, *divided*

1 In a large bowl, combine the first four ingredients; set aside 1/2 cup for topping. Press remaining crumb mixture into an ungreased 13-in. x 9-in. dish. Chill for 5 minutes.

2 Meanwhile, in a large bowl, whisk milk and pudding mixes for 2 minutes. Let stand for 2 minutes or until set (mixture will be thick). Stir in frozen yogurt and 1 cup whipped topping until smooth. Spread over crust.

3 Top with remaining whipped topping. Sprinkle with reserved crumb mixture. Refrigerate for 8 hours or overnight. **YIELD:** 12-15 servings.

LEMON DREAM PIE
Prep: 10 min. + chilling

A lovely lemon filling flavors this light pie. Served atop a raspberry jam drizzle, it's refreshing on a warm day.

Taste of Home Test Kitchen

- 1 tablespoon water
- 1 envelope unsweetened lemonade soft drink mix
- 1 tablespoon lemonade concentrate
- 2 packages (3 ounces *each*) cream cheese, softened
- 1 cup confectioners' sugar
- 1 teaspoon vanilla extract
- 1-1/2 cups heavy whipping cream, whipped
- 1 graham cracker crust (9 inches)
- 2 tablespoons seedless raspberry jam, warmed

1 In a small bowl, combine the water and soft drink mix until dissolved. Stir in lemonade concentrate.

2 In a large bowl, beat the cream cheese, confectioners' sugar, vanilla and lemonade mixture until fluffy. Fold in whipped cream. Spread into crust. Chill for at least 1 hour or until set.

3 Drizzle jam onto dessert plates; top with a piece of pie. Refrigerate leftovers. **YIELD:** 6-8 servings.

Mouthwatering fresh raspberries star in this luscious pie. There's nothing to distract from the tangy berry flavor and gorgeous ruby color. A big slice is an excellent way to enjoy the taste of summer.

Patricia Staudt // Marble Rock, Iowa

FRESH RASPBERRY PIE

Prep: 15 min. + chilling **Cook:** 5 min. + cooling

- 1/4 cup sugar
- 1 tablespoon cornstarch
- 1 cup water
- 1 package (3 ounces) raspberry gelatin
- 4 cups fresh raspberries
- 1 graham cracker crust (9 inches)

PEANUT GOODY CANDIES

Prep: 30 min. + chilling

A small piece of this rich, sweet candy is all you need so one batch goes a long way.

Bonnie Frahm // Prior Lake, Minnesota

- 1-1/2 teaspoons plus 1/2 cup butter, softened, *divided*
- 1 cup semisweet chocolate chips
- 1 cup butterscotch chips
- 1 cup peanut butter
- 1 cup dry roasted peanuts
- 1/4 cup milk
- 2 tablespoons cook-and-serve vanilla pudding mix
- 3-1/4 cups confectioners' sugar
- 1/2 teaspoon maple flavoring

1 Line a 13-in. x 9-in. pan with foil and grease the foil with 1-1/2 teaspoons butter; set aside.

1 In a small saucepan, combine sugar, cornstarch and water until smooth. Bring to a boil, stirring constantly. Cook and stir for 2 minutes or until thickened. Remove from the heat; stir in gelatin until dissolved. Cool for 15 minutes.

2 Place raspberries in the crust; slowly pour gelatin mixture over the berries. Refrigerate until set, about 3 hours. **YIELD:** 6-8 servings.

2 In a microwave-safe bowl, combine the chips and peanut butter. Microwave, uncovered, on high for 1-2 minutes or until melted; stir until smooth. Spread half of the chocolate mixture into prepared pan; refrigerate. Stir peanuts into remaining chocolate mixture; set aside.

3 In another microwave-safe bowl, combine the milk, pudding mix and the remaining butter. Microwave, uncovered, on high for 1-2 minutes or until the mixture comes to a boil, stirring once. Gradually stir in the confectioners' sugar and maple flavoring.

4 Spread over chocolate layer. Carefully spread with the reserved peanut mixture (may need to reheat in the microwave to spread easily). Refrigerate for 4 hours or until firm.

5 Using foil, lift candy out of pan. Discard foil; cut into 1-in. squares. Store in an airtight container in the refrigerator. Remove from the refrigerator just before serving. **YIELD:** 2-3/4 pounds.

EDITOR'S NOTE: This recipe was tested in a 1,100-watt microwave.

CINNAMON APPLE TART

Prep: 15 min. **Bake:** 20 min. + cooling

I got the idea for this delicious fall dessert from a lovely Italian woman who's also a fabulous cook. It's so simple to make—and cleanup is just as easy! I often make two and freeze one. It's great at brunch alongside eggs and bacon.

Stacie Blemings // Heath, Texas

- 1 large apple, peeled and chopped
- 1 teaspoon lemon juice
- 1 sheet refrigerated pie pastry
- 2 tablespoons apple jelly
- 2 tablespoons sugar
- 1/4 cup cinnamon baking chips
- 1/3 cup sliced almonds
- 1 teaspoon milk

ICING:
- 1 cup confectioners' sugar
- 1/4 teaspoon almond extract
- 1 to 2 tablespoons milk

1 In a small bowl, toss apple with lemon juice; set aside. On a lightly floured surface, roll pastry into a 14-in. circle. Transfer to a parchment paper-lined baking sheet. Spread jelly to within 2 in. of edges. Sprinkle with apple mixture, sugar, baking chips and almonds. Fold up edges of pastry over filling, leaving center uncovered. Brush folded pastry with milk.

2 Bake at 400° for 20-25 minutes or until golden brown. Use parchment paper to slide tart onto a wire rack to cool. In a small bowl, combine the confectioners' sugar, extract and enough milk to achieve desired consistency. Drizzle over tart. **YIELD:** 6 servings.

TIP

The apples are tossed with lemon juice to help prevent them from browning. If you're out of lemon juice, you can use orange juice, pineapple juice or lemon-lime soda instead.

PINA COLADA PUDDING CUPS
Prep: 15 min. + chilling

- 3 cups fat-free milk
- 2 envelopes whipped topping mix
- 2 packages (1 ounce *each*) sugar-free instant vanilla pudding mix
- 2 cans (8 ounces *each*) unsweetened crushed pineapple, undrained
- 1/2 teaspoon coconut extract
- 1/4 cup flaked coconut, toasted
- 8 maraschino cherries

1 In a large bowl, whisk the milk, whipped topping and pudding mixes for 2 minutes. Let stand for 2 minutes or until soft-set. Stir in the pineapple and extract.

2 Spoon into eight dessert dishes, 3/4 cup in each. Cover and refrigerate for 30 minutes or until chilled. Sprinkle each serving with 1-1/2 teaspoons coconut and top each with a cherry. **YIELD:** 8 servings.

CHOCOLATE BANANA CREAM PIE
Prep: 15 min. + chilling

I have three daughters, and this is their favorite pie to help make and to eat. Most of the time, we make two pies so there's enough for seconds.
Lynn McAllister // Mt. Ulla, North Carolina

- 1-1/4 cups sugar
- 1/3 cup cornstarch
- 1/3 cup baking cocoa
- 1/4 teaspoon salt
- 3 cups milk
- 3 tablespoons butter
- 1-1/2 teaspoons vanilla extract
- 1 pastry shell (9 inches), baked
- 2 medium firm bananas, sliced
- 1 cup whipped topping
- Chocolate curls and additional sliced bananas, optional

1 In a large saucepan, combine the sugar, cornstarch, cocoa, salt and milk until smooth. Bring to a boil; cook and stir for 2 minutes or until thickened. Remove from the heat; stir in butter and vanilla.

2 Pour half of the filling into pastry shell. Top with sliced bananas and remaining filling. Refrigerate for 3-4 hours.

3 Garnish with whipped topping. Decorate with chocolate curls and additional bananas if desired. **YIELD:** 6-8 servings.

CARAMEL CHOCOLATE TRIFLE

Prep: 20 min. **Bake:** 20 min. + cooling

- 1 package (9 ounces) devil's food cake mix
- 2 packages (3.9 ounces *each*) instant chocolate pudding mix
- 1 carton (12 ounces) frozen whipped topping, thawed
- 1 jar (12-1/4 ounces) caramel ice cream topping
- 1 package (7-1/2 *or* 8 ounces) English toffee bits *or* almond brickle chips

1 Prepare and bake cake according to package directions for an 8-in. square baking pan. Cool on a wire rack. Prepare pudding according to package directions.

2 Cut cake into 1-1/2-in. cubes; place half of the cubes in a 3-qt. trifle bowl or large glass serving bowl; lightly press down to fill in gaps. Top with half of the whipped topping, pudding, caramel topping and toffee bits; repeat layers. Cover and refrigerate until serving. **YIELD:** 16 servings.

TIP

This is such a fun recipe to experiment with. If you're not a chocoholic and would like to cut back a little on the chocolate theme of this rich trifle, use butterscotch or vanilla pudding mix and chopped pecans for the English toffee bits.

BLACK 'N' BLUE BERRY CRUMB PIE

Prep: 15 min. **Bake:** 55 min. + cooling

Here's a very easy recipe for a mouthwatering, fresh pie that features two kinds of berries and is simply delicious! The brown-sugar crumb topping adds buttery old-time crunchiness and flavor to this summery dessert classic.

Linda Palmer // Greenville, Ohio

- 1 sheet refrigerated pie pastry
- 3 cups fresh blackberries
- 2 cups fresh blueberries
- 3/4 cup sugar
- 1/4 cup cornstarch
- 1/8 teaspoon ground nutmeg

TOPPING:
- 1/2 cup all-purpose flour
- 1/4 cup packed brown sugar
- 1/4 cup cold butter

1 Unroll pastry into a 9-in. pie plate. Trim pastry to 1/2 in. beyond edge of plate; flute edges.

2 In a large bowl, combine blackberries and blueberries. Combine the sugar, cornstarch and nutmeg; sprinkle over berries and toss gently. Pour into crust.

3 In a small bowl, combine flour and brown sugar; cut in butter until crumbly. Sprinkle over filling.

4 Bake at 375° for 55-60 minutes or until set (cover the edges with foil during the last 15 minutes to prevent overbrowning if necessary). Cool on a wire rack. **YIELD:** 6-8 servings.

This scrumptious recipe eases event preparations because it makes two pies that chill overnight. My family loves the smooth texture of these silky pies. The combination of chocolate and peanut butter satisfies even the strongest sweet-tooth craving.

Maryann Thomas // Clay City, Kentucky

TWO-LAYER SILK PIE

Prep: 30 min. + chilling

 2 **unbaked pastry shells (9 inches)**
2-1/2 **cups cold milk**
 1 **package (5.9 ounces) instant chocolate pudding mix**
 1 **can (14 ounces) sweetened condensed milk**
1/2 **cup creamy peanut butter**
 1 **carton (12 ounces) frozen whipped topping, thawed**
Chocolate curls and chopped peanuts, optional

 1 Line unpricked pastry shells with a double thickness of heavy-duty foil. Bake at 450° for 8 minutes. Remove foil; bake 5 minutes longer. Cool on wire racks.

PUMPKIN PIE DESSERT

Prep: 20 min. + chilling

This tasty dessert is an easy alternative to traditional pumpkin pie. It's particularly quick when you need a special dessert and is good any time of the year. It doesn't require baking, which frees up the oven for the rest of your meal.

Tina Lust // Nevada, Ohio

2-1/4 **cups crushed butter-flavored crackers (about 50 crackers)**
1/2 **cup sugar**
3/4 **cup butter, melted**
 2 **cups cold milk**
 2 **packages (3.4 ounces** *each***) instant vanilla pudding mix**
 1 **can (15 ounces) solid-pack pumpkin**

 2 In a large bowl, whisk the milk and pudding mix for 2 minutes. Let stand for 2 minutes or until soft-set. Pour into crusts.

 3 In another large bowl, beat condensed milk and peanut butter until smooth. Set aside 2 cups whipped topping for garnish; cover and refrigerate.

 4 Fold remaining whipped topping into peanut butter mixture. Spread over the pudding layer. Refrigerate for 6 hours or until set.

 5 Garnish with the reserved whipped topping; top with the chocolate curls and peanuts if desired. **YIELD:** 2 pies (6-8 servings each).

 1 **teaspoon pumpkin pie spice**
1/2 **teaspoon ground cinnamon**
1/4 **teaspoon ground ginger**
1/4 **teaspoon ground nutmeg**
Whipped topping and chopped pecans

 1 In a small bowl, combine the cracker crumbs, sugar and butter. Press into a greased 13-in. x 9-in. dish; set aside.

 2 In a large bowl, whisk the milk and the pudding mix for 2 minutes. Let stand for 2 minutes or until soft-set. Stir in the pumpkin and spices. Spread over the crust. Refrigerate for 3 hours or until set. Garnish with whipped topping and nuts. **YIELD:** 12-15 servings.

CAPPUCCINO CHEESECAKE PIE

Prep: 20 min. + standing **Bake:** 40 min. + chilling

With a rich mocha filling and cute chocolate garnish, this yummy pie is delightful on special occasions or any time at all.

Elisa Pellegriti // Florida, New York

- 2 packages (8 ounces *each*) cream cheese, softened
- 1/2 cup sugar
- 1 envelope mocha cappuccino mix (1/4 cup)
- 2 eggs, lightly beaten
- 1/4 cup milk
- 1 extra-servings-size graham cracker crust (9 ounces)

GARNISH:
- 1/4 cup semisweet chocolate chips
- 1/2 teaspoon shortening

1 In a large bowl, beat the cream cheese, the sugar and cappuccino mix until smooth. Add eggs and milk; beat just until combined. Pour into the crust.

2 Bake at 325° for 40-45 minutes or until the center is almost set. Cool on a wire rack for 1 hour. Refrigerate for 3 hours or overnight.

3 In a small microwave-safe bowl, melt the chocolate chips and shortening; stir until smooth. Spread into a 4-in. square on a sheet of waxed paper. Let stand at room temperature until firm, about 1 hour.

4 Using a small heart-shaped cookie cutter, cut out eight chocolate hearts. Top each serving with a heart. Refrigerate leftovers. **YIELD:** 8 servings.

This impressive-looking dessert is at the top of my list of speedy standbys. It's simple to make because it starts with a boxed brownie mix. Then the nutty brownie layers are dressed up with a fluffy frosting that has a rich, creamy texture and irresistible maple taste.

Amy Flory // Cleveland, Georgia

MAPLE-MOCHA BROWNIE TORTE

Prep: 30 min. **Bake:** 20 min. + cooling

- 1 package brownie mix (13-in. x 9-in. pan size)
- 1/2 cup chopped walnuts
- 2 cups heavy whipping cream
- 2 teaspoons instant coffee granules
- 1/2 cup packed brown sugar
- 1-1/2 teaspoons maple flavoring
- 1 teaspoon vanilla extract

Chocolate curls *or* additional walnuts, optional

1 Prepare batter for brownie mix according to package directions for cake-like brownies. Stir in walnuts. Pour into two greased 9-in. round baking pans.

2 Bake at 350° for 20-22 minutes or until a toothpick inserted 2 in. from the edge comes out clean. Cool for 10 minutes before removing from pans to wire racks to cool completely.

3 In a large bowl, beat cream and coffee granules until stiff peaks form. Gradually beat in the brown sugar, maple flavoring and vanilla.

4 Spread 1-1/2 cups over one brownie layer; top with the second layer. Spread the remaining cream mixture over top and sides of torte. Garnish with the chocolate curls or walnuts if desired. Store in the refrigerator. **YIELD:** 12 servings.

CHERRY GELATIN SUPREME

Prep: 20 min. + chilling

2 cups water, *divided*
1 package (3 ounces) cherry gelatin
1 can (21 ounces) cherry pie filling
1 package (3 ounces) lemon gelatin
1 package (3 ounces) cream cheese, softened
1/3 cup mayonnaise
1 can (8 ounces) crushed pineapple, undrained
1 cup miniature marshmallows
1/2 cup heavy whipping cream, whipped
2 tablespoons chopped pecans

1 In a large saucepan, bring 1 cup water to a boil. Stir in cherry gelatin until dissolved. Stir in pie filling. Pour into an 11-in. x 7-in. dish. Cover and refrigerate for 2 hours or until set.

2 In a small saucepan, bring remaining water to a boil. Stir in lemon gelatin until dissolved. In a small bowl, beat the cream cheese and mayonnaise until smooth. Beat in lemon gelatin and pineapple. Cover and refrigerate for 45 minutes.

3 Fold in the marshmallows and whipped cream. Spoon over the cherry layer; sprinkle with pecans. Cover and refrigerate for 2 hours or until set. **YIELD:** 12 servings.

TIP

This makes a great dessert for a potluck affair. It makes a lot, is easy on the grocery budget and its great flavor—cherry, pineapple and cream cheese—will appeal to a broad group...kids and adults!

Add apples and a crumb topping to a packaged gingerbread cake mix for a speedy treat.

Taste of Home Test Kitchen

APPLE GINGERBREAD CAKE
Prep: 5 min. **Bake:** 25 min. + cooling

    1 package (14-1/2 ounces) gingerbread
      cake/cookie mix
1-1/4 cups water
    1 egg
    1 cup chopped peeled apple
1/2 cup chopped pecans
    2 tablespoons brown sugar

1 In a large bowl, beat the cake mix, water and egg until combined. Add apple; stir to combine. Pour into a greased 11-in. x 7-in. baking dish. Combine the pecans and brown sugar; sprinkle over the top.

2 Bake at 350° for 23-25 minutes or until a toothpick inserted near the center comes out clean. Cool on a wire rack. **YIELD:** 9 servings.

LIGHT TOFFEE CRUNCH DESSERT
Prep: 20 min. + chilling

This is one of my favorite desserts. But the original recipe had too much fat and too many calories, so I trimmed it down by using fat-free and sugar-free ingredients. Guests will never suspect this fluffy, layered treat is on the lighter side.
Kim Belcher // Kingston Mines, Illinois

1-1/2 cups cold fat-free milk
    1 package (1 ounce) sugar-free instant vanilla
      pudding mix
    2 cartons (8 ounces *each*) frozen fat-free whipped
      topping, thawed
    1 prepared angel food cake (16 ounces), cubed
    4 Butterfinger candy bars (2.1 ounces *each*), crushed

1 In a large bowl, whisk the milk and pudding mix for 2 minutes. Let stand for 2 minutes or until soft-set. Stir in the 2 cups of whipped topping. Fold in the remaining whipped topping.

2 In a 13-in. x 9-in. dish coated with cooking spray, layer half of the cake cubes, pudding mixture and crushed candy bars. Repeat layers. Cover and refrigerate for at least 2 hours before serving. **YIELD:** 15 servings.

BANANA CREAM CHEESECAKE

Prep: 25 min. + chilling

This lovely and delicious banana dessert can be made a day or two in advance.

Margie Snodgrass // Wilmore, Kentucky

1-3/4 cups graham cracker crumbs
  1/4 cup sugar
  1/2 cup butter, melted
FILLING:
    1 package (8 ounces) cream cheese, softened
  1/2 cup sugar
    1 carton (8 ounces) frozen whipped topping, thawed, *divided*
    3 to 4 medium firm bananas, sliced
1-3/4 cups cold milk
    1 package (3.4 ounces) instant banana cream pudding mix

1 In a small bowl, combine cracker crumbs and sugar; stir in butter. Set aside 1/2 cup for topping. Press remaining crumb mixture onto the bottom and up the sides of a greased 9-in. springform pan or 9-in. square baking pan. Bake at 350° for 5-7 minutes. Cool on wire rack.

2 In a large bowl, beat cream cheese and sugar until smooth. Fold in 2 cups whipped topping. Arrange half of the banana slices in crust; top with half of the cream cheese mixture. Repeat layers.

3 In a small bowl, whisk the milk and pudding mix for 2 minutes. Let stand for 2 minutes or until soft-set; fold in remaining whipped topping. Pour over the cream cheese layer. Sprinkle with reserved crumb mixture. Refrigerate for 1-2 hours or until set. **YIELD:** 10 servings.

Instead of making individual cream puffs, make this rich dessert with a cream puff base and sweet toppings.
Lisa Nash // Blaine, Minnesota

CREAM PUFF DESSERT

Prep: 20 min. + chilling **Bake:** 30 min. + cooling

- 1 cup water
- 1/2 cup butter
- 1 cup all-purpose flour
- 4 eggs

FILLING:
- 1 package (8 ounces) cream cheese, softened
- 3-1/2 cups cold milk
- 2 packages (3.9 ounces *each*) instant chocolate pudding mix

TOPPING:
- 1 carton (8 ounces) frozen whipped topping, thawed
- 1/4 cup chocolate ice cream topping
- 1/4 cup caramel ice cream topping
- 1/3 cup chopped almonds

1 In a large saucepan, bring the water and butter to a boil over medium heat. Add flour all at once; stir until a smooth ball forms. Remove from the heat; let stand for 5 minutes. Add the eggs, one at a time, beating well after each addition. Continue beating until mixture is smooth and shiny.

2 Spread into a greased 13-in. x 9-in. baking dish. Bake at 400° for 30-35 minutes or until puffed and golden brown. Remove to a wire rack to cool completely.

3 For filling, beat the cream cheese, milk and pudding mix in a large bowl until smooth. Spread over the puff; refrigerate for 20 minutes.

4 Spread with whipped topping; refrigerate until serving. Drizzle with the chocolate and caramel toppings; sprinkle with the almonds. Refrigerate leftovers. **YIELD:** 12 servings.

PALMIERS

Prep: 20 min. **Bake:** 20 min.

It takes just two ingredients to make these impressive but easy-to-do French pastries, which are often called palm leaves.
Taste of Home Test Kitchen

- 1 cup sugar, *divided*
- 1 sheet frozen puff pastry, thawed

1 Sprinkle a surface with 1/4 cup sugar; open puff pastry sheet on surface. Sprinkle with 2 tablespoons sugar. Roll into a 14-in. x 10-in. rectangle. Sprinkle with 1/2 cup sugar to within 1/2 in. of edges. Lightly press into pastry.

2 With a knife, very lightly score a line widthwise across the middle of the pastry. Starting at one short side, roll up jelly-roll style, stopping at the score mark in the middle. Starting at the other side, roll up pastry jelly-roll style to score mark. Cut into 3/8-in. slices.

3 Place cut side up 2 in. apart on parchment paper-lined baking sheets. Sprinkle lightly with 1 tablespoon sugar.

4 Bake at 425° for 12 minutes. Turn the pastries over and sprinkle with remaining sugar. Bake 5 minutes longer or until golden brown and glazed. Remove to wire racks to cool completely. Store in airtight containers. **YIELD:** About 2 dozen.

indexes

ALPHABETICAL INDEX

Refer to this index for a complete alphabetical listing of all the recipes in this book.

GENERAL RECIPE INDEX

This index lists each recipe by major ingredients and mixes or convenience items used.

ICE CREAM/FROZEN YOGURT
Butterfinger Delight, 233
Cherry Peach Cobbler, 230
Ice Cream Sticky Buns, 185

LEEKS
Chicken with Leek Sauce, 119
Potato Leek Soup, 171

LEMON & LIME
Crab Cakes with Lime Sauce, 129
Fluted Lemon Cake, 221
Lemon Crumb Bars, 206
Lemon Dream Pie, 233
Lemon Garlic Shrimp, 124
Lemon-Lime Crackle Cookies, 203
Lemon Poppy Seed Muffins, 182
Lemon Poppy Seed Waffles, 43
Lemon Pull-Apart Coffee Cake, 195

MINT
Mint Mocha Shakes, 27

MUSHROOMS
Beef Stroganoff, 60
Cheesy Mushroom Appetizers, 11
Ginger Plum Stir-Fry, 137
Green Beans with a Twist, 144
Hot Cheddar-Mushroom Spread, 20
Loaded Pizza, 57
Marinated Mushrooms, 18
Mushroom Chicken Alfredo, 110
Mushroom Rib Eyes, 53
Pork Tenderloin with Gravy, 89
Spinach-Mushroom Beef Patties, 68
Stuffed Mushroom Caps, 12
Tenderloin in Puff Pastry, 73

NUTS & PEANUT BUTTER
Almond Eggnog Pound Cake, 231
Berry-Patch Brownie Pizza, 222
Broccoli-Hazelnut Bake, 156
Butter Pecan Cookies, 212
Butterfinger Delight, 233
Cherry Pistachio Bread, 180
Chewy Walnut Bars, 214
Chicken Satay Wraps, 108
Chippy Chocolate Cookies, 207
Chocolate Hazelnut Parfaits, 228
Chocolate Walnut Tart, 232
Cinnamon-Nut Coffee Cake, 198
Coconut Pecan Rolls, 35
Cranberry Pecan Sandies, 200
Frosted Peanut Butter Cookies, 209
Jellied Cranberry Nut Candies, 228
Light Toffee Crunch Dessert, 243

Macadamia Coconut Bars, 200
Mocha-Pecan Butter Balls, 211
Peanut Butter Brownie Bars, 201
Peanut Butter Chocolate Cake, 227
Peanut Goody Candies, 234
Pecan Chocolate Waffles, 41
Pecan Cream Cheese Squares, 206
Pecan Sweet Roll Rings, 196
Pecan Tossed Salad, 155
Quick Coconut Muffins, 187
Streusel Nut Coffee Cake, 218
Surprise Banana Muffins, 198
Two-Layer Silk Pie, 239
Walnut Bacon Bread, 182

OATS & OATMEAL MIX
Blueberry Oatmeal Pancakes, 44
Butterscotch Raisin Cookies, 205
Chocolate Chip Oatmeal Cookies, 210
Cherry-Cream Crumble Pie, 216

ONIONS
Bacon-Onion Pan Rolls, 194
Barbecued Onion Meat Loaves, 51
Flavorful Oniony Asparagus, 148
Onion-Basil Grilled Vegetables, 149
Onion-Beef Muffin Cups, 66
Onion Potato Rolls, 183
Onion-Stuffed Acorn Squash, 145
Red Onion Focaccia, 183
Swiss-Onion Bread Ring, 190
Swiss Onion Loaf, 180

ORANGES
Citrus Rice Pilaf, 149
Mandarin Pork and Wild Rice, 81
Marmalade-Glazed Ham Loaf, 90
Orange Crispy Cookies, 213
Orange-Mascarpone Breakfast Rolls, 186
Tropical Smoothies, 14

PANCAKE MIX
Apple Ham Bake, 86
Baked Apple Pancake, 34
Pecan Chocolate Waffles, 41
Perch Fillets, 131
Weeknight Catfish Wraps, 123

PASTA
(also see Pasta Dinner Mix)
Alfredo Seafood Fettuccine, 131
Broccoli Tortellini Alfredo, 139
Cheese-Topped Beef Bake, 56
Chicken Fajita Spaghetti, 114
Chili Cheddar Penne, 147
Chili-ghetti, 48

Garlic Chicken Penne, 99
Ham and Swiss Casserole, 80
Hearty Tortellini Soup, 162
Italian Bow Tie Bake, 135
Italian Wedding Soup, 163
Mexican Lasagna, 58
Picnic Pasta Salad, 150
Potluck Pasta Soup, 167
Sloppy Joe Pasta, 54
Southwest Lasagna Rolls, 140
Spinach-Stuffed Shells, 139
Taco Noodle Dish, 116
Turkey Noodle Soup, 165
Veggie Spiral Salad, 143
Wagon Wheel Supper, 69

PASTA DINNER MIX
Angel Hair Tuna, 122
Cajun Macaroni, 59
Chicken and Shells Dinner, 103
Creamy Corn, 156
Fancy Mac 'n' Cheese, 93
Golden Tuna Casserole, 126
Mac 'n' Cheese Soup, 164
Mushroom Chicken Alfredo, 110
Pizza Macaroni Bake, 65
Pork Lo Mein, 92
Sausage 'n' Black Bean Pasta, 93
Simple Seafood Alfredo, 130

PEACHES & PEARS
Cherry Peach Cobbler, 230
Peaches 'n' Cream Bars, 208
Peachy Chicken, 118
Pear-Cranberry Coffee Cake, 187
Tropical Smoothies, 14

PEAS
Chicken and Shells Dinner, 103
Citrus Rice Pilaf, 149
Garlic Chicken Penne, 99
Pork Lo Mein, 92
Turkey Noodle Soup, 165